Praise for *Stephen Crane*

"Berryman has put [Crane's life] together w̄   ̄ue sense of relevance."

"The curious facts of Crane   ry-man examines thoroughly, cr   ̄uspicion of bias, moralistic or other. But   ̄ordinary con-tribution to our knowledge com   ̄u his diligent search for a clue to Crane's mystery—which involves, among other things, Crane's peculiar unconcern with the length of his own life."

—*Yale Review*

"Berryman's writing has a density that compresses much matter, and there is always thought behind it."

—EDMUND WILSON, *New Yorker*

"A critical biography in the full sense of the term: it is thorough, it is vivid as well as factual."

—*Commonweal*

"A compelling and high calibered piece of literary criticism. . . . A real addition to modern critical writing."

—*Kirkus Reviews*

"Recommended for serious readers, as a fresh and emphatic judgment on a neglected subject."

—*Library Journal*

"The choice of [Berryman] to write a critical biography of the master has produced a sensitive, enthusiastic and much needed reappraisal. . . . [His] probing of the art and soul of Crane is thorough and must be reckoned with."

—*Saturday Review of Literature*

Frances Cabané Scovel Saportas

Stephen Crane on the *Three Friends* off Cuba, 1898

STEPHEN CRANE

A Critical Biography
(Revised Edition)

JOHN BERRYMAN

Cooper Square Press

This Cooper Square Press paperback edition of *Stephen Crane* (originally published in 1950) is an unabridged republication of the revised edition published in New York in 1962. It is reprinted by arrangement with Farrar, Straus and Giroux, LLC.

Published by Cooper Square Press
An Imprint of the Rowman & Littlefield Publishing Group
150 Fifth Avenue, Suite 817
New York, New York 10011

Distributed by National Book Network

Library of Congress Cataloging-in-Publication Data

Berryman, John, 1914–1972.
    Stephen Crane : a critical biography / John Berryman.—Rev. ed.,
1st Cooper Square Press ed.
        p. cm.
    Includes bibliogrpahical references and index.
    ISBN 0-8154-1115-4 (pbk. : alk. paper)
    1.   Crane, Stephen, 1871–1900. 2. Authors, American—19th
century—Biography.   I. Title.

PS1449.C85 Z56 2001
813' .4—dc21

2001028324

♾™ The paper used in this publication meets the minimum requirements of
American National Standard for Information Sciences—Permanence of
Paper for Printed Library Materials, ANSI/NISO Z39.48–1992.
Manufactured in the United States of America.

To EILEEN

Contents

Preface to the Revised Edition

Circumstances have dictated the reissue of the book more or less unchanged and the reader of 1962 may need to be reminded that when I was writing in 1950 Crane's position in our literature was far from being the settled matter that it probably now is. It is true that I spoke of his seeming "now to be accepted as standard," but this was only propaganda, gentle reader; I felt some surprise at his inclusion in the American Men of Letters Series at all. His work being very uncurrent, then, I quoted from it more extensively than I should now do, simply to display it. Little had been written about him, also, and it was uncertain whether much more would be. I did not succeed, for instance, in getting his friend Corwin Linson's memoir published, though I tried (Syracuse have now done it). I had read this in manuscript for the Princeton University Press, but Mr. Linson did not know that I had, and I did not like making an aging unpublished man nervous about the possibility of my lifting something, so I accepted with delight his unconscious help in controlling the damnable early chronology, which I felt sure he would not object to, and borrowed nothing, I believe. The position with respect to Crane's letters to Nellie Crouse was similar. A New York bookdealer kindly let me see them, forbidding quotation, and I summarized them on page 129.

These were two of the three "sources which I am not permitted to cite" — an innocent allusion that seems to have bothered some scholars, though it intended only to protect Mr. Linson's sensibility and the dealer's confidence. The third was of course Cora Crane's collection of papers, which had disappeared; I knew a good deal about this, from various sources, but nothing with certainty except many dates and quotations, and so could not rely on it. It is now at Columbia and has been explored in Daniel G. Hoffman's very interesting book *The Poetry of Stephen Crane* (1957), the collected *Letters* of 1960 (edited by R. W. Stallman and Lillian Gilkes), and Miss Gilkes's biography of Cora Crane. These correct some of my errors. "Dan Emmonds," for instance, was not an earlier title for *George's Mother*, but a separate work if *Letters*, p. 122, is correct in locating the manuscript in the Butler Library at Columbia; James gave five pounds, not fifty, to the fund for Frederic's orphans, and Hall Caine seems to have sent something (my p. 246, *Letters* p. 190); it may be Crane went down into Virginia only in 1896, not 1893 as on Frederick Lawrence's evidence I said, though my opinion is that he went twice — as an unknown writer looking around for help as of *The Red Badge*, and as a celebrity years later to study the Fredericksburg battlefield for an historical article; and so on. Without complacency I may whisper that I am surprised that after so much research since, there appear to be so few of them, and anyway Professor Stallman, who has been savaging my book for ten years when not propped on it, and even when, will sooner or later find them all, real and fancied. The question is how far the new materials change the picture I tried to draw.

I think: not substantially. Willis Hawkins was a closer friend of Crane's during 1896 and 1897 than I knew, much closer, as the correspondence in *Letters* makes clear; to no one else, perhaps, did he write so relyingly, to no one else did he apologize so often and vividly. Whether he was Crane's "best" friend, as *Letters* baldly asserts, I do not know, not having been there; Crane had at different times friends of different kinds — his brother Ed, Linson, Marshall, Vosburgh and Senger and the rest, Garland, Scovel, Frederic, Conrad, Sanford Bennett, others; who has a thermometer? This seems to me the main alteration needed, and though the letters are in themselves uninteresting except to a biographer, it is a considerable one. That more that is significant has not emerged about Cora Crane I confess disappoints me, though Miss Gilkes's job of work done was thorough. Amy Leslie turns out to have been mentally ill, as I suspected. On the whole, I think the curious reader is still stuck with either my picture or Thomas Beer's, to the degree that those pictures differ. From Stallman, who considers Stephen Crane an "irresponsible heel" (*Letters*, p. x), will no doubt crawl forth in due time one more satisfying. Crane's will is given by Miss Gilkes, who also quotes a frightening letter from Cora about the man dying: " My husband's brain is never at rest. He lives over everything in dreams and talks aloud constantly. It is too awful to hear him try to change places in the *Open Boat!*"

A word about two misconceptions, as I believe they are. I admire Beer's book and always have done. It was maddening to work with in a scholarly way, but it is brilliant. I consider it to be in certain basic respects *wrong*, for reasons that I have tried in this study to suggest; but who agrees with everyone he admires? Who — often — agrees with Robert Graves?

The other error I risked reluctantly but deliberately, in agreeing with myself to throw into the book some results of my psychological findings. These have been treated with more good-nature, and even acceptance, than I expected, by some critics — Edmund Wilson, Daniel Hoffman, Maxwell Geismar, among others. But I knew that they would, in putting some critics off, provide a basis for discrediting the book as a whole, and of course this has happened. Critics unable to judge such matters for themselves are naturally unable to see a work containing them as a biography (that is, a history of a life) *also*, and a critical work as well. We readily note parallels to this simple-minded provincialism in academic life: a man familiar with what happened in 1590 must not also be familiar with what happened in 1890; or — does he really know either? since most of the judging persons do not know either. The general point of view can be put with simplicity: *I* know nothing of Freud, so neither do you, and moreover in pretending to do so you confess your documentary incompetence and critical ineptitude.

The most serious omission in the book, I think, is an absence of consecutive detailed critical investigation of the major works. The scope of the volume did not allow for anything of the sort; nevertheless I have been frequently reproached for the omission, and felt it myself — the more so, since part of my biographical as well as my psychological knowledge could not get into the book either. The galleys, for instance, were chopped up by the publisher's lawyer. No studies comparable to Mr. Hoffman's of the poetry exist, so far as I am aware, of the important stories and novels. There is no hurry about this, I believe. Crane will doubtless be here for a long time, and literature is not a hunting-preserve for advancement-hungry professors. I tried, however, to repair some of the omission with an account of "The Open Boat" several years ago (in *The Arts of Reading*, by Ralph Ross, the present writer, and Allen Tate, New York, 1960, pp. 279-87) and hope some time to say something of "The Blue Hotel." Miss Joan Griscom I understand objects to all published studies of *The Red Badge of Courage* and I hope will publish one superior.

Some additions to the original "Bibliographical Note" will be found at the end of this volume.

17 December 1961   J. B.

Preface

This is a biography, though it did not begin as one, and a critical study. After Crane's death at twenty-eight in 1900 his reputation disintegrated rapidly. For twenty years he was forgotten except by friends, authors whom he influenced, and a few other writers like A. E. Housman and T. E. Lawrence, so that in 1921 Edward Garnett was complaining that "If America has forgotten or neglects Crane's achievements, above all in 'Maggie' and 'The Open Boat', she does not yet deserve to produce artists of rank." Very likely; and when did countries or men get what they deserve? That same year, at any rate, appeared here Vincent Starrett's little pioneering collection *Men, Women and Boats*, followed then by Thomas Beer's *Stephen Crane: A Study in American Letters* (1923) and a costly twelve-volume assemblage of his *Work* (1925–1927), majesty and trash scrambled together. Through the 'twenties Crane's fame rose, it dropped during the sociological 'thirties and rose again during the latest war, depending always mostly upon *The Red Badge of Courage*. For some reason he seems now to be accepted as standard, though few read his best tales and no critical study has ever appeared. Until *Twenty Stories* (1940) his fiction apart from the war novel was hard indeed to come by and this is no doubt one reason why scarcely any critic of consequence has thought it necessary to reckon with him. Through fifteen years of intensive criticism of everything in our serious magazines I remember three or four pages on Stephen Crane in 1935 (by a friend of his), 1947, 1949 (by a friend of the friend). Our view of his fiction, so far as we have one, is still that of the 'twenties, which I have been at pains to damage. His poetry too is accepted as important, and has not been studied; but it is read. The *Collected Poems* of 1930, without assistance from criticism, has gone steadily through five printings, the last in 1948. In the circumstances some criticism of Crane's work seemed to be desirable, however awkwardly it would have to run against the grain of this curious record; by luck my impression that Crane is demonstrably a great writer strengthened with study; and when invited to write a book about him I designed it as more substantially an essay in literary criticism than I should have done if I had known I would have to construct a full-scale biography as well.

For the ability displayed in Beer's book—read first twenty years ago with delight—I keep a high regard. It is perhaps, as Edmund Wilson remarks, only a sort of memoir by one who did not know Crane, but it is a brilliantly adroit, colorful, knowledgeable one. It is not quite a biography but rather "a study of the times, in strong light, and across that light moves an inconspicuous figure called Stephen Crane." This was the estimate (to which Beer assented) of its admirer Mr. Starrett. Its incompleteness, where it does embody a narrative of Crane's life, has long been recognized; so has, in a lesser degree, its unreliability; and these defects, together with its casualness and Beer's neglect of Crane's writings as a biographical source, have formed a basis of frequent calls for a careful biography. I am the last person to feel surprise that no biography has appeared. When the other materials have begun to reveal their difficulties, and, as one's investigation proceeds, Beer's frank iconoclastic tone ceases to hypnotize, one may well be dismayed; for what one has then to face in Beer is grand inaccuracy, expurgation, and distortion. Beer, by discrediting en masse the scandals surrounding Crane, did us a service in restoring him to decent life, where he belongs. But most of the scandals had some basis and he left Crane incomprehensible. Only the truth really will serve us long.

So the present biography tries to tell the truth. It is formal and critical. I suppose it is also a psychological biography and I am sorry about this. The results literary men have usually gotten in biography with the findings of depth psychology hardly encourage one to join their ranks. On the other hand, the view which seems to have gained ground in reaction to thirty years of careless and vague exploitation—namely, that the reader ought to be left to draw his own conclusions—affects one as the subject for a humorous cartoon (unless the author really has little more psychoanalytic knowledge than his readers, in which event—a very common one—that view deserves profound consideration). It has never been suggested that the reader ought to be left to draw his own conclusions in geology or physics. Our familiarity in America with psychoanalysis as a technique of therapy is much greater than our familiarity with it as a science—a system, that is, of description and explanation of reality. This latter is the role with which the biographer is concerned, and the role, in fact, wherein its greatest advances have been made of recent years, as recorded in the technical journals and certain comprehensive syntheses. The studies of artists in these journals, by now very numerous, are much more illuminating than the studies by literary men of which I was speaking; they seldom, however, handle enough material to justify confidence, and they incline to be numb in certain respects. Psychological inquiry is certainly not literary criticism, and can reasonably begin only after full account has been taken of literary questions. My impression, moreover, is that of many artists psychoanalytic study will have little to tell us. Why this should be so is a subject very difficult indeed, upon which I had better not attempt to say anything at present. Stephen Crane, at least, is not one of them. Without at all intending any psychological investigation, I found myself as the work went forward able to understand things in his life and art of which I had had no idea previously—nor had any one else—that understanding was possible. Little pieces of understanding are scattered through the biographical chapters; the general inquiry occupies the final chapter. My conclusions are tentative but definite. I am afraid some of them will appear extremely fantastic to most readers; and I have been much encouraged, since I abandoned this book, by coming on Ernest Jones's study of *The Nightmare* (1931) where most of what I was forced to say about the symbol of the Horse seems to be abundantly and independently confirmed.

My debt to Thomas Beer's work is very considerable. Halfway between Crane's death and the present he talked with many persons now dead, and he made (his sister tells me) no notes, working from memory. Most of the bulk of letters upon which he relied too have disappeared, or are not to be found among his papers, which the kindness of Miss Alice Beer has let me examine. For a number of letters and incidents, therefore, he is my only authority. I never differ with him unless, for any reason, he appears to be wrong. The notion of a full documentation, which I once entertained, I dismissed partly because it would have involved a continual argument with him, which seemed undesirable, and partly because my conclusions rest heavily upon unpublished materials, including three extensive, important sources which I am not permitted to cite. No one will ever be able to work casually at Crane and be certain of anything. So many people have been wrong about him so often that in documentation it might have proved difficult to avoid wholly a graceless tone of irritable triumph. "I spent ten years planning a study of Crane," Henry McBride told Beer, "and ended by deciding there was no such animal, although I knew him for eleven years." Book after book on the man has been announced, labored at, and laid by in despair. I am alive to the violent deficiencies of mine, which was a matter of "pain, despair almost." I feel some confidence, only, that the materials not yet available will fail to alter essentially the portrait here drawn—one substantially new, and drawn at any rate with candor and upon reflection. I shall continue to be grateful for the communication of material relating to Crane.

For information and permissions and kindnesses I am indebted to: Frances Cabané Scovel Saportas, Frederick B. and Mrs. Smillie, Dr. Walter A. Dunckel, Corwin Knapp Linson, Alice Baldwin Beer, Ames W. Williams, George D. Max, Charles L. Morgan, Professor A. J. Hanna, Benjamin Swann, David A. Randall, H. B. Collamore, Josiah K. Lilly, Jr., Clifton Waller Barrett, Louise T. Thompson and James D. Thompson, Rupert Croft-Cooke; the officials of the Newark Public Library, the Princeton University Library (especially, and in particular Malcolm O. Young), the New York Public Library, the Library of Congress, the Free Library of Philadelphia, the libraries of Columbia University, Dartmouth College (particularly Robert Swanton), the University of Illinois; several personal friends who will not wish to be named, and the Editors of the Series, among whom however I must thank Mark Van Doren who once taught me a good deal and whose extraordinary gift of the Knopf edition of Crane's *Work* eased a thankless labor. One other debt is mentioned on another page.

J. B.

One ‒ BEGINNING

Very Young

When Stephen Crane was a freshman at Syracuse, at nineteen, a fraternity brother who happened to see the manuscript of an essay he had read to the chapter one night was astonished by its exquisite legibility,—knowing that Crane had already been a newspaper reporter,—and asked him about it. Crane explained. When he had begun writing, several years before, he had known that compositors' earnings depended on how fast they could set copy, and so on how fast they could read it, and he had kept this in mind. He had kept this in mind. The trait, like most expressions of grave consideration, entire commitment, seems all but affected. What it warns us toward is a recognition, however, without which Crane's life will be unintelligible, of an altitude and tenacity of purpose altogether extraordinary. He sometimes failed; but in this life's marriage of ideal and awkward fact, in the heroic character of its effort, in purposiveness, it seems often less like an author's than like the profound, marvelous lives of the most interesting and effective persons the country has till now produced, Washington, Jefferson, and Lincoln. If Crane struck many of his contemporaries as a typically irresponsible "genius," his will strikes us—his patience and generalship and will. The lives

3

of modern authors run invisible and eventless. What author, famous and young, is headlined repeatedly in the press of New York for personal heroism? or for a magnanimity is persecuted by the police of New York through years? Crane was a writer and nothing else: a man alone in a room with the English language, trying to get human feelings right. He was even a very pure writer. Americans seem sometimes—until the transforming waves of immigration in the last two decades of the 19th century—to be all descended from Franklin and Jefferson, multifarious, inquisitive, factual. The documentary burden is nearly as full in *Moby Dick* and *Leaves of Grass* as it is in *Walden* and *Life on the Mississippi*. Stephen Crane has nothing of this anxiety; his work is wrung as clear as Poe's or Hawthorne's; and unlike theirs his revolt did not drive him at his best into fantasy and allegory. His eyes remained wide open on his world. He was almost illusionless, whether about his subjects or himself. Perhaps his sole illusion was the heroic one; and not even this, especially if he was concerned in it himself as a man, escaped his irony.

A celebrated statement of Crane's for once brings to bear upon his work a third moral quality, which ranked for him with kindness and courage. "I understand" (he wrote to a friend) "that a man is born into the world with his own pair of eyes and he is not at all responsible for his vision—he is merely responsible for his quality of personal honesty. To keep close to this personal honesty is my supreme ambition." The rest of the passage is never quoted. "There is a sublime egotism" (he continues) "in talking about honesty. I, however, do not say that I am honest. I merely say that I am as nearly honest as a weak mental machinery will allow." First he was limiting the will to the administration of vision, and now he limits it further; in each case the material is "given," determinant; responsibility can operate only outside the realm of the necessary. A little surprising, this, because it seems to leave no role for the Chance whose exponent the 1920's took

4

Crane to be. We hear of Liberty, we hear of Necessity, but of Chance we do not hear. Now it is one of Crane's claims to permanent interest as a writer that in certain works, among which "The Open Boat" stands highest, he handled an art intensely singular with a balance so confident as to produce an effect of inevitability, a classical effect. It is also true that his life, for all its velocity and color, impresses one as profoundly, if mysteriously, schematic—not perhaps in the pages of Thomas Beer, where it is agreeably incomprehensible, but in the materials now available, carefully looked at. Few other lives, since occasional individual human lives began to be recorded in detail about two centuries ago, can be so hard upon the view—apparently the current biographical view—that human existence is governed by habit and chance.

It seems, on credible contemporary witness, that Cromwell was in the habit of smearing filth over ladies' gowns at dinner, howling meanwhile with laughter—a fact that has dropped out of his biographies. Trying to write an honest biography of Cromwell, how would one treat this lapse of consideration? An automatic impression of self-indulgence is unavoidable, but it would be a naive biographer who rested in the impression; the whims of a man of powerful character do not take this form casually, and the whim moreover was recurrent. A habit, we called it. "Habit" we use for the quotidian, the neither strongly resisted nor strongly willed pattern of usual life, not for the extraordinary, the willful. Willful is the mildest word our ancestors would have applied to such activity. To us, though, it looks much more obviously will-*less*. If no conscious action perhaps is quite will-less, at least in this action of Cromwell's his will has suffered a defeat (after what struggle, we know not) as it is clear that in the instance cited of Crane's unusual consideration his will has enjoyed a triumph. Or is it? What have their wills been struggling with?

Compulsion, call it, the representative of Necessity in the human character. Now the wills have not been struggling unaided. They also have on their side compulsion—other compulsions. But it is solely in the will's role in the battle that we can locate responsibility, and praise or blame it. The way in which we find out what this role was is partly direct, in the analysis of will, and partly indirect, in the description of Necessity as it works in the life. Without some such attempt made, a biography may have charm, aplomb, a hundred virtues, while leaving the life it deals with utterly meaningless. A matter of "habit and chance," in fact—instead of the war that perhaps it is, brilliant and dark, of Liberty against Necessity. We must say "perhaps," because it is by no means certain, and does not even appear probable, that all human lives are governed by the same forces. More honest biographies would tell us more about this considerable question. It may be that in lives where the will is huge, it forces itself outwards in many directions and thus comes more constantly or wrathfully into contact with Necessity than do the wills of most men; so that little space is left in the middle ground for the indifferent operation of chance and habit. Crane's appears to be such a life. His work, as the chief outcome of the life, has the same character, and he recognized this character in the activity that produced it. He was replying to a younger writer towards the end, when years of thought condensed: "An artist, I think, is nothing but a powerful memory that can move itself at will.through certain experiences sideways and every artist must be in some things powerless as a dead snake." The sentence would repay a long analysis, but it will have to suffice that the liberty of "move itself at will" is gravely conditioned. Everything was related in this man, will and living and work and fate, but the context was Necessity.

Why did the child born belatedly into a peaceful Newark parsonage on November 1, 1871, spend his life imaging, chasing, reporting, remembering War? And it will be long before Crane's preference in his fiction for characters degraded or uprooted, ancestorless, relates itself to the coat-

of-arms whose gloomy colors adorned the wheels of his trap
in England, never explained by him—relates itself to the
pride of race in this decided democrat which Beer remarks
was one of his secrets. These colors had been seen on the
saddlebag of a Stephen Crane prominent in Colonial and
Revolutionary affairs. "We have named him Stephen," wrote
the Reverend Dr. Crane, "for his ancestor who signed the
Declaration." This ancestor didn't, having left Philadelphia
a few months too early—in order to enter (at nearly seventy)
the State Senate of New Jersey, where he had been Speaker of
the Assembly before his two terms in the First Continental
Congress. Two sons were killed, Stephen and Jonathan. But
the family was twice as old as this in the state, tracing itself from another Stephen Crane who was settled at Elizabeth-
town by 1665, perhaps a son of Jasper Crane who helped
settle New Haven (1639) before he went south. A Crane
had come over long before that, with Drake; another was of
the first company that landed at Massachusetts Bay. Montclair,
New Jersey, was Cranetown once. The pride of race is an open
secret in Stephen Crane's reply to a Newark newspaper in
1896: "My great-great-great-grandfather was one of the seven
men who solemnly founded Newark. He was Jasper Crane.
. . . During the Revolution the Cranes were pretty hot people. The old man Stephen served in the Continental Congress
(for New Jersey) while all four sons were in the army. William Crane was Colonel of the Sixth Regiment of New Jersey
infantry. The Essex Militia also contained one of the sons. I
am not much on this sort of thing or I could write more, but
. . . I am about as much of a Jerseyman as you can find."
And he was one of the new race of displaced Americans; he
had not been in his state for years when he wrote this and he
never returned alive.

The Reverend Jonathan Townley Crane, acting now in
1871 as presiding elder for the Newark district of Methodism,
was widely respected, but his life had been and would be still
a grinding one. The youngest of six children, left an orphan,

he attended a Newark trunk factory in order to enter the College of New Jersey (now Princeton University); and since graduation except for a decade as principal of the Methodist Seminary at Pennington, he had moved as pastor every year or so to some new village in New Jersey or New York, with small pay, heavy duties, and a mushrooming, far from robust family. Neither cares nor the routine of preaching, baptizing, marrying, burying, conferring, visiting the faithful and faithless, from which he salvaged hours for study and writing, nor those hours, affected Dr. Crane's innocence of mind. This found quiet expression in earnest mild books reproving intemperance, card-playing, and theater-going, and it was worthy of an earlier condition of our society. "The Scriptures tell us," he mused, "that Noah planted a vineyard and on one occasion drank of the wine until he was drunken. Very possibly the process of fermentation had not before been noticed, the results were not known, and the consequences in this case were wholly unexpected." He was indeed "so simple and good" (his youngest son told an interviewer) "that I often think he didn't know much of anything about humanity. Will, one of my brothers, gave me a toy gun and I tried to shoot a cow with it over at Middletown when father was preaching there and that upset him wonderfully. He liked all kinds of animals and never drove a horse faster than two yards an hour even if some Christian was dying elsewhere." This sensibility his son inherited, and much of his forbearance, and some of his nobility—though little unworldliness except in regard to money.

His force the boy got from his mother. She had been Mary Helen Peck, daughter of a line of Methodist clergymen in Pennsylvania, sister of others—herself educated, ambitious, dogmatic, influential in women's affairs as speaker and journalist. Her religion was evidently much narrower and more insistent than her husband's. Quite the strongest expression in a late, surviving diary of his concerns a difference of opinion: and yet how little zealous: "We did not so much argue," he recorded after a ministerial meeting, "as simply state our positions, with all good humor. I confess that I was surprised to find the most repulsive features of old style Calvinism advanced with scarce an apology for their deformities. Mr. Clark declared that he does not believe in the doctrine of free agency. . . ." Perhaps Dr. Crane had been always thus gentle, though his conversion at eighteen from the Presbyterian faith, upon the question of infant damnation, attests an independence. As for Mrs. Crane, "You could argue just as well with a wave"—and this is her favorite son speaking, adored because unexpected and frail and final. Five of thirteen much older children she had lost already. She alone when home combed Stephen's fair hair and nursed him through recurrent colds. Pampered him? No. The summer he was introduced to waves at Ocean Grove, a new Methodist settlement where she had carried him, he had a dream he never forgot—of black riders on black horses charging at him from the surf up the shore— and woke again and again screaming, to be rebuked. He was either two or three. Even before this she simply told him not to be afraid when he was held one day on the back of a white horse that he remembered long after as a savage beast. She had courage herself, a combative nonparochial charity. "My mother was a very religious woman," he recalled carefully, "but . . . my brothers tell me that she got herself into trouble before I was old enough to follow proceedings by taking care of a girl who had an accidental baby. . . . Mother was always more of a Christian than a Methodist and she kept this girl at our house in Asbury until she found a home."

The world was smaller then. When he was about two, a young fellow named Gilder whom we shall meet again called at the red-brick parsonage at 14 Mulberry Place, Newark, with a young lady, whose red skirt Stephen followed unnoticed out of the front door, down steep steps and to the corner. Delighted, gift-bearing next day, but not in red, she was ignored; red again, he loved her. One handkerchief used for his colds was a great red silk affair he loved, howling when it dropped into the aisle—his stories glow with affectionate childhood reds, red-topped boots, a mother's scarlet cloak. His first known inquiry, however, was practical and professional. Sitting up scrawling in imitation of his brother Townley, who as a reporter sometimes asked Mrs. Crane a spelling, "Ma," said the baby, "how do you spell *O?*"

After a second laborious period as presiding elder, this time for the Elizabeth district, Dr. Crane moved his family from Bound Brook to Paterson, where he had been appointed to the Cross Street Church at a salary of $2,000, in the spring of 1876. Aside from listening at the Catholic church to a "brief Sermon on the dignity and powers of the Priest," looking thoughtfully at pictures in New York and at the Centennial Exhibition in Philadelphia, reading Herbert Spencer (who he suspected was "better at collecting facts, than reasoning on them"), illness, writing, and fatigue, he devoted himself to his congregation so strenuously that by October he had visited six hundred at their own homes, and on February 3rd, during a revival, he felt "Much encouragement in my work. . . . Still, thus far, no wave of power has come sweeping all before it, as we sometimes see. Perhaps it will, if we hold on our way, doing our duty. . . ." This spring his salary was fixed at $1,800 "and a determination was expressed to make up $200, to add to the $1,600 paid last year." Of the new salary $1,250 was paid. In March 1878 he noted without a word of resentment that though they promised him $150 more, "The brethren talked despondingly, and seemed to take it for granted that they can not give me what they know I need." That week therefore, close on sixty, he was appointed pastor at Port Jervis, an attractive, fairer town in the New York hills near the junction of New Jersey and Pennyslvania.

"Our people seem to be good listeners," he smiled on Easter. The whole family were happier and Stephen's health improved. On September 2nd his father recorded: "Stevie began his public school education today." Kept out the year before, he was nearly seven now and could read and write, humiliated among tots. "They tell me that I got through two grades in six weeks which sounds like the lie of a fond mother at a teaparty but I do remember that I got ahead very fast and that father was pleased with me. He used to take me driving to little places near Port Jervis where he was going to preach or bury somebody." No explanation is wanted for anyone's moving rapidly, if not feeble-minded, through an American grammar school, and here are two— preparation and motive; but so little has been known of the Crane family that we might see here whether an analogy will not make one son's later, spectacular precocity seem less surprising. The precocity of Coleridge, also the last of a clergyman's fourteen children, has been accounted for as a response to the others' resentment and hostility towards him as his parents' darling. This suggestion as transferred to Crane will be interesting particularly because it sees genius not in the light of will but of *stimulus* to will—few writers having displayed ever less will than Coleridge or more than Crane. Beer's picture of the family is uniformly affable, but one of the most intelligent children called it (Agnes): "such an oyster-like family." Its warmest heart was probably the father's un-demonstrative heart. "Held the Love Feast: many present, and an unusually melting time," says a rare note of September 21st, 1879.

Dr. Crane next month "Began to try my ideas down on paper, in regard to a very interesting, but difficult subject, the original state of man, his fall, &c." Stephen had been very ill in the summer at Hartwood, a hamlet fifty miles north in Sullivan County where part of the family vacationed. Mrs. Crane rushed down for medicine and flew back. But he missed school this second autumn only a few days at the end of October, going down with her to Jersey City where the health of Townley's wife was failing, and getting home on his eighth birthday. Dr. Crane voted, wrought at a sermon on "Atheism triumphant, & what it led to," and was in New York collecting signatures for a petition to get his eldest son George placed in the Jersey City Post Office. Some of the children home for the holiday from Hackettstown Seminary gave a literary and musical entertainment. All his children but the two senior sat down at home for Christmas dinner: Nellie and William and Agnes, Edmund and Wilbur and Luther, and Stephen. He continued very busy, though he enjoyed taking Stevie one Tuesday evening to "a little neighborhood festival, for my benefit, as a sort of return for my preaching at the Clove. Dreadful roads, & yet a house full of people." As February set in, "Cold & fierce winds, from the North, froze up everything." But on the 8th he preached from John 1:47 ("a Christian indeed") in the morning and then in the evening preached against the "Liberals"—"so long that we omitted the Prayer meeting." Thursday his wife was "tortured all day by nervous headache." Townley came to visit a day or two on Saturday, the 14th, and so was there in Port Jervis when Dr. Crane died on Monday. Coming back from seeing Aggie to Newark, where also he had hunted new work for a boy who had written asking help, he had just caught cold and it was enough. A saintlike life.

Then the house was full of people. The whispering, the hymns, the heavy odors, the darkness, his tall brothers in black, were ghastly to a thin small boy, and he was terrified when one of his hands brushed a handle of the coffin, cold and silvern. Twenty years later to Stephen Crane this day was vivid. "We tell kids that heaven is just across the gaping grave and all that bosh and then we scare them to glue with flowers and white sheets and hymns. We ought to be crucified for it! . . . I have forgotten nothing about this, not a damned iota, not a shred."

For the rest of childhood Stephen had his mother. She moved for a few months to a boardinghouse in Roseville, near Newark, but he had scarlet fever here and they went back to Port Jervis. "After my father died, mother lived in and for religion. We had very little money. Mother wrote articles for Methodist papers and reported for the [New York] *Tribune* and the [Philadelphia] *Press*. Every August she went down to Ocean Grove and reported proceedings at the Methodist holy show. . . . She was always starting off when she felt well enough to some big prayer meeting and she spoke very well. Her voice was something like Ellen Terry's but deeper. She spoke as slowly as a big clock ticks and her effects were impromptu." Cherishing his long curls as she watched his health, she encouraged the boy's reading with worthy narratives like the Rev. James Dixon's tour of America, while Agnes gave him the comparatively rakish *Sir Wilfred's Seven Flights*, which he liked.

With his plain, fifteen-year-older schoolteacher sister Stephen was close; they were sometimes rebels together in the family. Desiring to be a "Christian lady," Agnes desired also to "*write*," and from his dissertation at eight on Little Goodie Brighteyes she followed his stories and verses with pride for four years, which were all she had. Meanwhile the boy had been devouring Western paper-backs, becoming ingenious—as his health improved—in gang games based on them. Mrs. Crane saw no objection to his brooding on rainy days over Harper's vast illustrated history of the Rebellion, and Edmund (besides donating a quarter for the death of the curls) was giving him year by year Harry Castlemon's beloved "Frank" series—Frank here, Frank there during the War, like the Tom Swift and Don Sturdy of a later day. He marched his mother's buttons up and down in little regiments, absorbedly, into inscrutable battles. He must have hung on veterans' talk too. Aged eleven, on the Jersey shore, he was digging a corpse out of the sand when the corpse's aunt loomed: Stephen explained that Johnny had just been buried, carelessly, with a canteen of whiskey still on him. A civilian tragedy the following May was real, like the death of Agnes. Mrs. Crane had moved again, to Asbury Park, and riding his aged pony past a roadmakers' camp outside town, Stephen saw a white girl stabbed by her Negro lover. He galloped home drenched with fear and said nothing.

The corpse's aunt had spanked him but there was no question of that, now, from his mother. Perhaps the boy's reticence or consideration was growing in him, as Beer says, or he was silent for another reason. Mrs. Crane at fifty-seven was less active, though active enough still for some years, and more anxious. When in the surf one Methodist Sunday he had to save Wallis McHarg, he promised to punch the older boy if he told her about it. "Don't understand that mother was bitter or mean," Stephen Crane said slowly to a young admirer (Willis Clarke, who came to see him in England toward the end and took down in shorthand the memories to which we have been repeatedly indebted), "but it hurt her that any of us should be slipping from Grace and giving up eternal damnation or salvation or those things. . . . I used to like church and prayer meetings when I was a kid but that cooled off and when I was thirteen or about that, my brother Will told me not to believe in Hell after my uncle had been boring me about the lake of fire and the rest of the sideshows. . . ." This imagery is from the itinerant carnivals along the shore, bristling with characters who charmed the boy with tales and gestures: wiseacres, roustabouts, hearts of steel and gilt. When he was fourteen, "an organ grinder on the beach at Asbury gave me a nice long drink out of a nice red bottle for picking up his hat for him. I felt ecstatic walking home and then I was an Emperor and some Rajahs and Baron de Blowitz all at the same time. I had been sulky all morning and now I was perfectly willing to go to a prayer meeting and Mother was tickled to death. And, mind you, all because this nefarious Florentine gave me a red drink out of a bottle." Whether the boy's separation from the army of the faithful was so offhand as he recalled it will not appear for years.

School fooled along. He had high marks except in algebra, never forgot a word, and was absorbed in baseball, deciding at fifteen to be a professional ball-player. "But ma says it's not a serious occupation," he admitted to McHarg, "and Will says I have to go to college first." He was master already of outlandish words like "pyrotechnic" and "irascible," which he had used right in an essay written hastily one day the summer before—between games—for a prize of a quarter. Beer was told he made one up, *higgle*—to behave in the manner of a schoolteacher. It is not recorded that any teacher ever much liked this indifferent boy with steady blue ironical eyes. "Stevie" (his mother worried to friends) "is like the wind in Scripture. He bloweth where he listeth." Military training in a decent Methodist school was what was wanted, so off at sixteen went a lean fair boy who could catch barehanded any baseball thrown in Asbury Park.

But Claverack College, absorbed by then into the Hudson River Institute, had entered a carefree era under the founder's son. Stephen Crane found the coeducational school in its tiny Dutch village across from the Catskills near Hudson, New York, "simply pie" and he stayed two and a half years. "I never learned anything there," of course. "American private schools are not as bad as our public schools, perhaps, but there is no great difference." He can't have treated it seriously, because after so long, in the "academic" department to be sure —three years in the "classical" let one enroll as a junior at a major university—he would still enter Lafayette as freshman in the fall of 1890. He arrived bristling with pipes and signed the school register first on January 4, 1888. Beer places in this spring the fight, costing him part of a tooth, which started when he called Tennyson "swill." This was less a critical estimate, presumably, than residue of an agony earlier in having to memorize and recite "The Charge of the Light Brigade"— an experience so acute that he devoted long afterward a whole small story to it ("Makin' an Orator"). What a "league" was, who the mystic six hundred were, the schoolboy had no idea, but he learned the lines with dreadful distinctness and feared so the ordeal of recitation that "If he could have engaged the services of a real pain, he would have been glad. . . ." This summer, sixteen, he began helping his mother and Townley with newspaper items, cycling dusty miles for a piece of resort news.

At Claverack "it was his pose," says Harvey Wickham, who entered in the fall, when Crane was already a first lieutenant, "to take little interest in anything save poker and baseball, and even in speaking of these great matters there was in his manner a suggestion of *noblesse oblige*." He drilled Wickham hard, however, and sang hard as leading tenor for the younger boy, who was proxy-choirmaster. There were a number of Cuban pupils and "as they qualified very well as social outcasts, Crane was much among them, acquiring that liking for things Spanish and that smattering of their language which afterward stood him in good stead." Smattering, say, not stead, for Crane acknowledged: "I tried to learn French because my mother thought it important but no foreign language will ever be my friend." On the other hand his roommate and chum Earl Reeves was the richest boy in school, Wickham says. "In the slums or among aristocrats he could breathe. With the middle class he was always a little David throwing stones at the collective Goliath. . . . He held aloof, too, when an indignant undergraduate mob hanged a certain unpopular student in effigy. He was rather given to holding aloof, especially if the human animal was manifesting its capacity for collective action." When one Cuban, named by his mother Antonio but by Crane "Chick," one night tried to cut Wickham's throat with his own razor and then fled shouting murder, Crane paid no attention: it was just one little boy after another. But when after challenging another boy Chick kicked him in the shin, Crane "insisted upon a formal Queensbury affair. He had, poor genius, the insane idea that the world might be regulated by justice."

Just before his interest in a redheaded Miss Mattison with an adorable Irish nose, "our best pianist," we hear of his membership briefly in a secret society of six, misogynist. "S. S. T.

Girlum" this was called, formed by the boys after a walk with their girls all together one bright fall afternoon, blue-and-gold uniforms and fluffy ruffles. The girls had refused to dally in a byway when the boys insisted, and must be punished. Sic semper tyrannis! for several weeks. Harriet Mattison drew him away—so markedly that the school *Vidette* printed a comment: "Stephen was the first martyr. He seems also to be the last. Anyway, these red sunsets must be very Harrying. Why, oh why, did the S. S. T. Girlum have to be, just now when Indian Summer is coming on?" It cannot be said that Crane, during the strange life he would have, in some part of his mind ever forgot this; in the last of the *Whilomville Stories* he wrote dying, the little boy who had had to recite Tennyson is undergoing now an ordeal in a new Sunday school, where, casually—not casually when we shall get there —"Behind the superintendent's chair hung a lithograph of the martyrdom of St. Stephen." The *Vidette* also created the first of a procession of epithets: "the Stephen cranium." Then Miss Mattison died. There was friendship, some recalled, with a tall dark girl from Sioux City, later with another redhead. Jennie Pierce he loved "madly" (his word years later) at seventeen, and she tortured him. Into the students' wicked city, Hudson, he never went; nor often to one pie shop relished because of its dark stairway. "I hear you're bad—I hear you're damn bad," somebody heard him declare to a young Don Juan.

"But heaven was sunny blue," Stephen Crane remembered, "and no rain fell on the diamond when I was playing baseball. I was very happy, there." At a battalion drill, colored ribbons were seen tied—startlingly—to the officers' swords when the first company marched onto the field; in companies following, the ribbons grew to bows; then Crane came on at the head of his men with a whole blue silk sash. There was a poolroom swirling with smoke and beer-fume; his drawled ejaculation was "Ho hell." We see him collecting tobacco with Reeves through the dormitory, one dressed in the height of collegiate fashion, the other in a dirty aged sweater under a "whimsical, wistful" expression. He was always a listener and he probably listened to a white-haired old elocution teacher when chance put Crane at his table in dining hall. The very popular Reverend General John B. Van Petten liked to reminisce during meals, he got excited, and he had something to reminisce about. He had been chaplain of the 34th New York Volunteers from the beginning through the rout with Sedgwick's brigade at Antietam on September 16, 1862, when it got separated on the extreme left of the Union line under terrific fire, losing nearly half its men in the flight (150, and four officers)—though most of them found their way finally back to the command. One who did not was the color-sergeant. Struck five times and compelled to drop his colors, he called upon his comrades to seize them, and fell dead. A few days later Van Petten had been commissioned lieutenant-colonel of the 160th New York and gone through the war with it, commanding a brigade once in 1863, being severely wounded the next year at Opequon and complimented in general orders for conspicuous gallantry. He was a sort of hero.

When the boy wrote, it was not about war. A two-column sketch by "S. Crane" of the explorer Stanley appeared in the *Vidette* for February 1890, probably his first signed work. But if he had a slightly sheepish air on the parade ground—which Wickham attributed to his fear of ridicule, especially his own—he was a serious, severe drillmaster, with "enough of the true officer in him to have a perfectly hen-like attitude toward the rank and file." Wickham, who never became his friend, he exasperated with rebukes. But the unspeakably important prize-drill on Washington's Birthday this year was won by his company, and in the evening there was a reception. He reported baseball for the May *Vidette*, after playing it. "The village dominie, who ordinarily is looked upon with awe and reverence, sinks gloomily behind the pall of favoritism on these occasions, and may be seen to complacently stand for more than an hour beside the worst boy of boarding school fame, and look admiringly upon his sin stained brow, as he explains a new feature in the game. . . . Crane, catcher, was tendered the office of captain, but declining, Jones, 1st base, was elected Captain." He may have shunned the honor, but probably he declined because he knew he was not coming back. The school didn't: in June the *Vidette* recorded his promotion to Captain (military)—so that if he had returned, the British reviewers of a book later on who made him "Captain Crane" would have been more nearly right.

These summers he spent on the Jersey shore chasing news, more and more helpful to his brother Townley who was building up a news agency at Asbury Park. Townley helped in turn with his stamp collection. Crane later wrote that he did his first fiction this last year ("at eighteen"), for the New York Sunday *Tribune*—sketches; but nothing is known of these, and no doubt the stories of two years later are meant, for he was as careless always about dates as about money. When a circus broke up one summer, he borrowed five dollars from his mother to start a lost cowboy back to Wyoming, and the man endowed him with a real revolver alleged to have slain six Indians. A Canadian lady he adored, with seven children, gave him a paper-bound *Sevastopol*.

Then Stephen Crane sat out a year of our higher education. He registered at Lafayette College in Easton, Pennsylvania, on September 12, 1890, and was initiated on the 18th into Delta Upsilon. A week later he had a bad fright in 170 East Hall where he roomed alone. Hazing was atrocious. "Steve tried to play possum by not answering a loud summons"—a contemporary describes it—"and the usual practice followed by battering in the door. The sophomores crowded in, lighted a lamp. . . . Steve was petrified with fear and stood in a grotesque nightgown in one corner of the room with a revolver in his hand. His usual sallow complexion seemed to me a ghastly green. Whether he ever pointed the revolver or not, I do not know, but when I saw him, both arms were limp and the revolver was pointed to the floor." They left him alone. As a "technical" freshman—preparing for mining-engineering —he took algebra, chemistry, French, and lesser doses of drafting, Bible, elocution, theme-writing; or rather he didn't take them. At term's end in December three grades were not returned at all and he had zero in theme-writing. He played intramural baseball, boxed, seemed to smoke incessantly (few boys smoked at this period), and was "very reticent"—except apparently to a young civil engineer convalescing in Easton, with whom Beer reports his playing bad pool and pronouncing on authors. Count Tolstoy was the world's foremost writer. There was also one Flaubert who had written *Salammbô*, too long, but better than anything the English were capable of. Stevenson he didn't like; Henry James he didn't know. He now tried *The Reverberator*, unluckily, and was bored; odd chance, that sent him to one of James's dullest stories and one of his few studies of journalism. Crane seldom went to class, was advised by the faculty to leave, and early in January quietly did. He treated schools very much as he did, all his life, cigarettes: he would light one after another, hold them, watch them burn, but would scarcely ever puff on them. Perhaps just lighting them was rebellion enough against his father— as not studying was rebellion against his mother, whom he loved.

But Syracuse University, where Townley got him a job as city correspondent for the New York *Tribune*, was the last try. He registered for the winter term on January 9, 1891, attended the first meeting of Delta Upsilon that night, and after staying for a little with the widow of his mother's uncle, Bishop Jesse Peck, a founder of Syracuse, he moved "in a cab and a cloud of tobacco smoke" to the D.U. house at the top of Marshall Street hill. His favorite subject is said to have been history, but the one grade recorded this term was an A in English Literature under Dr. Sims, the Chancellor. He "devoted himself to athletics," as the Latin professor put it later on, and he haunted the Central Railroad Station and the police court, watching, listening. After lunch he usually retired to the cupola of the D.U. house to read, smoking his water-pipe, and write sketches for the *Detroit Free Press* or the Syracuse dailies. He was writing stories also and posting them about in vain. But one about a dog named Jack, though *St. Nicholas* returned it, was praised by the editor; and a fraternity brother, Frank Noxon, got the impression that "Stephen regarded this as friendly not only to him but to the dog; and his gratitude in literary defeat had a note of affectionate pride." He coasted and played poker and expressed angular opinions. "Tut tut, what does Saint Paul say, Mr. Crane?" observed the psychology professor. "I know what Saint Paul says, but I disagree with Saint Paul." This created an impression at the Syracuse of 1891 which was painfully augmented by his declining to meet the celebrated reformer Miss Willard on the ground that he thought her a fool. He was reading constantly, late into the night, and thinking. "I cannot see," he wrote, "why people hate ugliness in art. Ugliness is just a matter of treatment. The scene of Hamlet and his mother and old Polonius behind the curtain is ugly, if you heard it in a police court. Hamlet treats his mother like a drunken carter and his words when he has killed Polonius are disgusting. But who cares?"

He was ill for a week in February. Seldom so unhealthy as he looked, Crane had exceptional stamina as well as physical strength unusual in a man so slight—he was about five feet six and weighed one hundred twenty pounds or less. Child of age, nevertheless, feeble in childhood, he certainly bore into the years of privation and neglect to come an unenviable constitution; and tuberculosis killed him, worn out, at twenty-eight. He ate and slept irregularly from now on. His teeth are mentioned by men who knew him a little later as among the worst they ever saw; of course he refused to do anything about them. Crane's stoicism prevents our having a clear image of what he endured and overcame in order to do his work—or to do, for that matter, any of the things he required of himself. But squatting in his crimson sweater, catching, he was "so light that he seemed to bound back with every catch." The pitcher for whom he caught, Mansfield French, noticed: "His throwing arm was weak . . . the strain upon the ligaments of his shoulder would, at times, cause him to double up with pain." When Crane in a rare, open moment wrote of *The Red Badge of Courage* that it was "an effort born of pain, of despair almost," one burden of the words is physical.

With spring, in the intervals of baseball, he captained the fraternity cricket club, but what he did academically during this second term—if anything—is unknown. A story "The King's Favor" is signed "S.C." in the *University Herald* for May: the experience of a New York tenor who when performing before King Cetewayo in British South Africa sings a war-song so brilliantly that he is acclaimed a great warrior. He can have the six-foot-two Mursala, one of Cetewayo's wives. Alarmed and wishing to decline, he has to offer the Zulu as propitiation a red-and-white sun-umbrella and a toy pistol, a pair of suspenders and an opera glass, a jackknife and a bottle of red ink, a pack of cards and a silk handkerchief, a dozen clay pipes and a banjo—but we shall return to this far from meaningless story. Mainly Crane played baseball that became legendary: at short stop, sometimes as catcher, in one game at first base and in left field. He played with "fiendish glee . . . a good batman, although not a hard hitter . . . a fast base-runner," French remembered, and found him free in speech on the ball field, sarcastic but generous and companionable. His roommate too calls him "volatile, entertaining, and giftedly profane . . . his countenance usually displayed an amused, satirical, but kindly grin."

But this man notes as well a "very gentle and diffident way of speaking," and there can be no doubt that Crane struck his friends generally, hereafter, as mild, taciturn except now and then, deliberate in speech and movement. Of course testimony varies and his conduct did. Thus he seems to have united from the beginning an iron self-assurance with a deep shyness, and the first did not always govern the second. So with his irreverence and carelessness, which were interrupted by a spasmodic, extreme attention to "form." Crane was already a Bohemian in regard to dress; but we are told that on the night of the big Delta Upsilon party in the winter, after getting into his own evening dress, he went about the house with a box of shirt-studs and a punch, attending carefully to brethren whose starched bosoms had neither stud nor hole. So with his supernatural consideration for other people, in some matters, was combined a distinct absence of respect for human beings wholesale, and a certain coldness: Crane had perhaps never any *intimate* friends.

As often with such men (Chekhov, as his character is illuminated by recent studies, was another), affection inspired bore small relation to affection given. Certain traits based deep in character, like Crane's passionate tenderness for children and dogs and horses, made him beloved—this is the word that is used—by most of the people who knew him at all well, now or later. Others were impressed by him, liking him with an eagerness for which they could not account. There were his abrupt vivacity of speech, his sublime air of independence, his short-circuiting thought; but these weren't it. He "wasn't like anybody else." Very early he seemed to many who met him a genius. To others he seemed disagreeably indifferent, arrogant, shocking. Opinions of his character, from now on, vary wildly, and even impressions of his appearance do, though neither character nor appearance changed much for years and he is described as "boyish" almost to the end. Crane was sallow-complexioned, with a pointed face, weak probably about the mouth, and a thin nose. His light brown hair—it photographed dark—was as untidy usually as his dress and posture. Most women were to think him handsome. Nearly everyone mentions his eyes, even to such refinements as (this is a man, French again) that "his eyeballs were of the same deep cream tint but the iris was of a cold, bluish gray color." They were intense and prominent—bulging even, in one account, shortsighted in another. He was to see much with them, and in June of 1891 he was through with American education. Beer says that he was made captain of the baseball team, after a vehement argument. If so, the title was most of what he had to show for his official year in two colleges.

"Not that I disliked books," he wrote later on, "but the cut-and-dried curriculum of the college did not appeal to me. Humanity was a more interesting study. . . . So, you see, I had first of all to recover from college; I had to build up. . . ." The extent of Crane's reading has always been understated, as with other very original authors. For short, scattered periods Crane read curiously, and instinct or luck or fate led him early to what mattered for him. But it is true that it is not easy to think of another important prose-writer or poet so ignorant of traditional literature in English as Stephen Crane was and remained. Besides Tolstoy and Flaubert in his mind, the unavoidable master Shakespeare, and a crowd of authors English and American whom he disliked, there was the English Bible heard through childhood, there were Emerson, Whitman, Mark Twain and Kipling. Poe's rhythmical prose he is said to have liked as a boy. The sole influence besides Emerson that we might trace to his college year is also critical, not narrative. He told Noxon that a passage in Goethe "analyzed the effect which the several colors have upon the human mind. Upon Crane this had made a profound impression and he had utilized the idea to produce his effects." Conceivably he came on this passage in his psychology course; but Noxon dates the conversation years later and the report is uncertain—as uncertain as any profit from Crane's thirteen years of schooling. No doubt his time for reading would be limited; he wrote an immense amount in the nine years to come. He is said too to have refused to read on principle, for fear of imitating; but other writers have confessed to this qualm, including poets as polar to each other

and as idiosyncratic as James Whitcomb Riley and Wallace
Stevens. It was the persistent indifferent failure to read which
mattered, and for which his education must bear the blame.
What an artist requires to know it is not indeed easy to de-
te-mine. A useful indolence seems to be an equipment. "Art
comes only when there is *abandon*," said John Butler Yeats,
"and a world of dreaming and waiting and passionate medi-
tation." Probably no education would have affected this character in Crane. Less than any other American writer of the
century had he a sense of tradition or continuity in letters,
whether English or American; the sense grew in him intermittently only toward the end of his life. And certainly the image
of a lean boy lounging on the beach at Asbury, studying the
late afternoon bathers, dreaming, is more agreeable than the
image of our novelists and poets clamped in universities about
the country now or preparing themselves to be. "My complaint is—" wrote further from New York the elder Yeats,
and long ago, "My complaint is that all literature has gone
over to the side of the schoolmaster and that it used to be
carried on by the boys themselves." Stephen Crane scooped
up a handful of sand and tossed it to the sea breeze, watching
it. "Treat your notions like that," he said sideways to Arthur
Oliver lazily. "Forget what you think about it and tell how
you feel about it. . . ."

> Small glowing pebbles
> Thrown on the dark plane of evening
> Sing good ballads of God. . . .

Though a better training might have soothed his grammar,
it could hardly have helped him toward the style he was now
to develop with bizarre velocity. As Goethe informed young
Eckermann, the art of putting things shortly is not assisted
by education; and this was one of Crane's arts. There was
very little, after all, to "recover from." He was left free to
move in the direction of what H. G. Wells profoundly terms
his "enormous repudiations."

He had decided to become a writer. "I could never do what I didn't feel like doing—not even writing," an acquaintance quotes him, "but as I felt more often and more intensely like writing than like anything else, I thought I'd better try newspaper work." How Mrs. Crane accepted his failure in college we can guess, but she is said to have been willing for him to be a writer. With this son's character, if she knew it, she might have felt a satisfaction few parents ever can. Let us name the three fronts upon which this character seems to be advancing—or had advanced, for perhaps Stephen Crane was never, as this chapter has been pretending, very young. His mind was acrid. Irony, says one of Jouhandeau's characters, is "a form of reserve, of prudence, of experience; a premature old age. Not to be ironical . . . is the only real youth." "He was old at twenty," said a friend of Crane's. But if false values were being burnt up in this mind, values were burning in another sense. He was independent. Emerson's "Self-Reliance" never had a tougher exponent. He was preparing himself for courage—unsparing of himself, illusionless, rigorous.

And he was the master now at nineteen of an idea of consideration, a practice of consideration, so little common in human beings that one alludes to it with diffidence. But Crane, who made a point of impatience with ideals, himself once mentioned that he thought human kindness paramount among the virtues towards which our nature lets us struggle. Of the strength of the boy's purpose actually thus engaged, and of his commitment by the way to his profession, we learn from Frank Noxon the singular instance with which we began.

Losses, Momentum

One of the things impossible to understand about Stephen Crane has always been where he got the experience of life and of art condensed in *Maggie*. In Thomas Beer's sparkling pages Crane now loses a first, irreplaceable love, prints "tales of the Wyoming Valley," "dismisses himself" from a job, and finishes *Maggie* some six months—in fact—before he began the final, slow, severe revision (in the fall of 1892) that produced the book as we have it. A careful scrutiny of Beer reveals knowledge not only of two but of three versions of *Maggie*, despite his dictum that Crane "would not rewrite"; but nothing could be less conspicuous than this peaceful fact, and his picture will hardly do for this preparatory period of Crane's delay and pain. We must put over till the next chapter all notion of *Maggie* as it came to be, contenting ourselves in this one with its author's crowded approach to it. Crane was precocious for reasons. While his contemporaries were enjoying their sophomore year and two summer vacations, he crashed into life: began a career in journalism, suffered two unhappy romances (both intense on his side), lost his mother, studied a city, began to test himself against hunger and cold, created with some blunt paragraphs a political sensation (losing thus the second of two jobs and intermitting his career in journalism), emerged full in his theme, began to find his style, and wrote two books, both very crude, one of which he printed half of (and later repudiated), the other of which—early, as it were, in his junior year—he rewrote into *Maggie*. False starts mostly, this year and a half, but all experience, and some true starts.

Back from Syracuse, he was a beachcomber of summer news again for Townley in 1891. Between a baby parade, a tennis tournament, and meetings of the Seaside Assembly (an educational summer session at Avon) he played baseball, went camping with friends north in Sullivan County, and began to get into New York City when he had fare. In mid-August he met his first real authors: an enthusiastic young novelist from the West by way of Boston, Hamlin Garland, who lectured on Ibsen, Poe and others, and William Dean Howells. Howells was "by all odds the most American and vital of our literary men today," Crane reported Garland in the *Tribune*. "*A Modern Instance* is the greatest, most rigidly artistic novel ever written by an American, and ranks with the great novels of the world. *A Hazard of New Fortunes* is the greatest, sanest, truest study of a city in fiction." Brave opinions— Stephen Crane is said to have been pleased by Howells's informal manner; but Garland liked the accuracy of the report, and the two talked and practised pitching ball together till the Assembly closed.

The young man fell in love, hard, at the summer's end, through a fortnight admirably recounted by Beer. She had his mother's name,* a tall dark pretty girl older than he, trained in Europe as a contralto, Helen Trent. Though she'd hardly noticed him at Avon, he wired after her his sorrow at not seeing her to say goodbye. She and her guardian, an invalid Mrs. Potter, were domiciled briefly on 12th Street in New York preparing to go to Switzerland. The house loomed spectacular around the flag of Ireland done in colored

---

* He gave his mother's name at Claverack as "M. Helen Crane," and later as "Mrs. M. H. Crane," never as "Mary."

tiles over the fireplace,—one reason for Crane's shyness on the evening of September 10th, when he called and sat to stare at her. Conversation was infrequent. Once he asked whether she had seen Hamlin Garland at Avon. No; what did he look like? "Oh, like a nice Jesus Christ." Next morning, however, arrived a long letter written at the old Fifth Avenue Hotel. What was her favorite color? Did she like flowers? Dogs? He was a reporter, and his brother Wilbur had a baby named Helen.* He came again, and again, now pleasing, now upsetting her with his slow talk. A Negro might be handsome, and if American religion was mildewed, Buddhism was interesting. A tired man named Melville dying this week a few blocks north, author of some forgotten books, would not have been startled by these ideas, but Miss Trent was, and she was shocked when he turned up with a wrecked eye, caught by an ill-hurled bottle while Crane was sitting in a saloon in the Bowery. She forbade him to go near there again. It was not nice. It—— until Crane exploded: "Hully gee!" The Bowery was the most interesting place in New York. Nobody had written anything sincere about it. He was going to write a book himself some time soon about the Bowery, a sincere one, and he had to see how these people lived and what they thought. She protested again, and they quarreled under the colossal chandelier. He left, but then mailed a note from the ferry: "I shall come back tomorrow night and we can start all over again." They differed later on the subject of Stevenson, but mostly in the florid house she sang or played Chopin for him, while the tenor lounged on the piano and hummed. He lit her cigarettes, disapproving.

---

* Or he may have said: his brother Will(iam) had a daughter named Helen; she was now nine or ten, and Crane was very fond of her. This was the niece who visited him abroad later. Beer scrambled his account ("Will had a baby named Helen") and in the absence of the letters the evidence is awkwardly balanced. Wilbur, always called Burt, did now have a baby named Helen, and Crane was very fond of babies, though since Wilbur had married a servant in Will's house named Mattie whom Crane is said to have disliked, he had seldom seen this brother.

She sewed a button on his coat. She showed him Mrs. Potter's boudoir, velvet and enamel, and "When will the stage hands take it away?" he drawled. He escorted her to a play at Wallack's. On September 18th he found out somehow—had he been making inquiries?—that the house belonged to an infamous Italian who had fitted it out for an Irish dancer, and wrote and came excitedly to see her: she and her guardian must move at once. Then she knew she had to do with a lover. The next night she was not at home, and found a note in the morning mail: "Your window was lighted all last night but they said you were not in. I stood and looked at your window until a policeman came and made me go away. But I came back and looked until my head was just a sponge of lights. Please do not treat me like this. Nothing else counts but that." He came that evening while she was dressing to dine with friends uptown, and rode beside her in a hansom up Fifth Avenue after rain, under the gleaming lamps, silent. When she went home there was another note: "You have the most beautiful arms I ever saw. You should never have to wear dresses with sleeves. If I could keep your arms nothing else would count. It would not matter if there was nothing else to hope for in the world or if there was no more world. In dreams, don't you ever fall and fall but not be afraid of anything because somebody safe is with you? I shall be here tomorrow. I must get back to Ed's house, now." He stood in the drawing-room the next night, September 21st, and she had to tell him she was to be married, soon, to a young surgeon in London. He gasped, putting his hands to his face, and left.* But in *The Black Riders*—so Beer ends the episode—

* She saw him once more, and—inasmuch as one of the most powerful unconfessed urges toward achievement is desire for a sort of revenge for early disappointment, a passion to "show" people who have slighted one—the irony of this sequel must not be omitted. A few months before his death, the famous author was pointed out to her across a London theater, and she wondered what Stephen Crane was famous for.

Should the wide world roll away,
Leaving black terror,
Limitless night,
Nor God, nor man, nor place to stand
Would be to me essential,
If thou and thy white arms were there,
And the fall to doom a long way.

A romance of the next summer resembled this, though. Both were utterly tenuous, brief, ineffective. Neither woman appears to have returned his love in any degree—both in fact had other ties—and Stephen Crane was altogether more submissive than from his character as we are coming to know it we might otherwise have expected. Both women were older than he. Both had lived abroad, and were accustomed to move in a society more elaborate than any that Crane had known. "In the slums or among aristocrats. . . ."

It is into the slums that we now follow him, the broad foul busy Bowery and its sordid environs. It was not the picturesque that drew or held him. Besides the bums, whores, clowns, dialect, and drinking for which the region was already celebrated, it was packed thick with the laboring or shiftless immigrant and native poor, and phases of his absorption must be distinguished. "In Chatham Square there were aimless men strewn in front of saloons and lodging-houses, reminding one vaguely of the attitudes of chickens in a storm. He aligned himself with these men," Crane was to write in 1894 of his nameless young man's "Experiment in Misery," "and turned slowly to occupy himself with the flowing life of the great street." In the fall of 1891 he was concerned above all with family life, and he spent long days and evenings listening and watching. He was living with his brother Edmund's family in Lakeview (then a suburb of Paterson, now part of it), writing in the attic at night, organizing the town's first football team—for his passion had shifted from baseball—and coaching it, as its quarterback, in the afternoons. Trying to get a job in Park Row, he began to make acquaintances among the footloose horde of young stragglers who thronged the metropolis hoping for fame. One or another put him up when he stayed in the city overnight. Stephen was twenty, and his mother, who was often in Boston or somewhere speaking, wrote to him to be good and always independent, always honest.

Then she fell ill, and died in hospital in Paterson, on December 7th. In two days before Christmas he drafted a story about a Bowery girl driven by her drunken mother into her seduction by a bartender, then into the streets, and so to her death.

Or so he told Wallis McHarg when his friend turned up in New York in January 1892, secured Crane's address from the *Herald*, and went to see him over far east on 23rd Street where he shared a bedroom with a young actor. But he may have been working at a short novel on this subject even at Syracuse. "Two days" (especially as transmitted through Mc-Harg's sister and Beer) need not be taken literally for the composition of the small "book" which Crane, after conducting McHarg down through the glories of the Bowery, abruptly gave him to read. McHarg, no reader, seems to have been appalled and bewildered. Nobody would print such a thing, so realistic, he said, but at least the characters ought to have names. Crane's lawyer brother William had been similarly troubled: it was confusing. And after a little (late in February, according to Beer) McHarg, who had gone to Germany to study medicine, received a dateless note saying Will had named the book: "Maggie: A Girl of the Streets."* There was also a postscript: "The *Herald* fired me last week."

* Crane copyrighted the book a year later as "A Girl of the Streets" and the new *Bibliography* by Williams and Starrett is inclined therefore to date McHarg's note February 1893. But the note (which is not available except in Beer's paraphrase) may not have given the girl's name; also Crane may have changed his mind temporarily about the name (he gives for copyright a

American journalism remained on occasion during the Nineties unfettered as it had been ten years before when the *Chicago Tribune* was brooding over Garfield's assassin: "Guiteau is not insane. He is a lazy, worthless, malignant devil. . . ." The New York press of the period strikes one as more temperamental, more literate perhaps, than the press we have. The *Herald*, for that matter, was a crusading paper, brisk with satire. Late in January of 1892 the social arbiter Ward McAllister, who had dismissed a servant, was quoted thus: "The fact of the matter is just this, don't you know. . . . He attempted to dictate to me, don't you know . . . it gave me a good deal of bother, don't you know." But Stephen Crane was no ordinary satirist, and for years he remained one of the queerest reporters who, growing up more or less in the profession, can ever have tried to make a living at it. Neglecting names, addresses, political affiliations, the amenities of journalism generally, he just said how things struck him. Beer recovers a pleasing instance when, sent to interview a big alderman under charge of corruption, Crane merely observed that he "sat like a rural soup tureen in his chair and said 'Aw!' sadly whenever ash from his cigar bounced on his vest of blood and black." Also there was beginning to be his style, in which a street-cleaner hurt in 23rd Street "flattened his face toward heaven and sent up a jet of violet, fastidious curses." Editors cut these things. One to whom later, at the *Press*, came a piece on "Sixth Avenue" says "there was little left of it after the crossing-out of comments and descriptions that would have caused sorry inroads

subtitle, "A Story of New York," which he then abandoned), or simply have omitted the girl's name when typing the title-page. Such carelessness is by no means incredible of Crane. The note is not (as the *Bibliography* says) "dated February" anyway; this is only Beer. One would be inclined, in fact, to wonder whether the composition of *Maggie* and the whole McHarg episode did not belong a year later if the present dating were not borne out by Crane's statement (to be given shortly) and by the address in East 23rd Street—the next winter he was living at the Pendennis Club. This draft must have been written at Edmund's house where he was staying during his mother's last illness.

on the newspaper's Sixth Avenue advertising receipts, to say nothing of libels. Then the [senior] editor read the remainder, and threw it away, too, as not being exciting enough." Editors also prodded him for facts, and added, and rewrote; so that his early New York news stories are hard to identify. "Youse Want 'Petey,' Youse Do" in the *Herald* of January 4th may be one. "Three small boys with hardened faces stood at the bar of Jefferson Market Police Court. . . . 'Yer see . . . we was doin' notten but playen tag in der street when a blokie wat's called "Petey" come along and says, "Hi, fellers, let's go a swipen." We went wid him—see? Youse wants "Petey," youse do. He did her swipen. . . . "Petey" Larkin, a mug wot lives in Thompson Street.' " The language is nearly *Maggie's,* and even the opening sentence recalls the novel's; if he wrote this, maybe Petey gave him the name for his older tougher boy, later the bartender, on whose lips at sixteen already sat "the chronic sneer of an ideal manhood." What the *Herald* fired him for is not recorded, though there seems no reason to spare vanished sensibilities by imagining with Beer that Crane dismissed himself. But editors were impressed by the pungencies that annoyed them, and Crane began to make a semi-hemi-demi-living by free-lancing, like hundreds of other young men lured to New York by the profession out of which had risen Kipling and Richard Harding Davis. Now and for years to come, that is, he sometimes earned something. His brothers lent him small sums, and friends did—the crowd of aspirants scattered over the city, reporters, illustrators, actors, internes, mostly as poor as he was, among whom he treaded water. A financial independence, real enough, has been exaggerated; Crane was wildly generous himself when he could be, and borrowed freely. But he once ordered Ed never to lend him more than five cents at a time, and for long periods would undergo any hardship in silence, accepting only a place to sleep. Besides the actor in East 23rd (perhaps William Riley Hatch), a friend named Eddie (E. J. Edwards?) in 217th Street put him up, and later others. He wrote on any friend's couch or in Lakeview. And in March a new version of *Maggie* was finished, evidently the third, by no means the last.

What this version was like we have no way of knowing. A legend that Crane never revised his work was propagated by Thomas Beer in relation to several exceptional remarks Crane made much later on, about two books already published, adopting Hamlin Garland's peculiar idea that it was not "honest" to rewrite work that was already before the public. "He would not rewrite," says Beer, and "He restored only a few paragraphs of *The Red Badge* for its final form"—telling us only that Beer had not seen the newspaper version of the war novel. We can assume if we like that the manuscript *Maggie* which people saw in 1892 resembled the book we know in violence of style, in the girl who "blossomed in a mud-puddle," her red mother, her brother Jimmie who "lived some red years" before becoming a truck-driver, in her seducer Pete; but we do not even know this. What seems certain is that it was much cruder.

Crane took it, with a note from Townley, to Richard Watson Gilder of the *Century*. The boy looked "thin and his blue eyes seemed enormous. He sat wrapped in a gray ulster much too big for him, talking very slowly about his family with whom I had lost touch. I saw that his manuscript was not long and gave him an appointment for the next day"—March 23, 1892. Gilder had a poem of his own in his current number:

> How Paderewski plays! . . . all life, grief,
>   wrong,
> Turns at the last to beauty and to song!

What he was obliged to read that night was by the same mind that finally began the book like this:

> A very small boy stood upon a heap of gravel for the honour of Rum Alley. He was throwing stones at howling urchins from Devil's Row, who were circling madly

35

about the heap and pelting him. His infantile countenance was livid with the fury of battle. His small body
was writhing in the delivery of oaths. . . .

and ended its heroine not in beauty and song but in the following paragraph:

> At the feet of the tall buildings appeared the deathly
> hue of the river. Some hidden factory sent up a yellow
> glare, that lit for a moment the waters lapping oilily
> against timbers. The varied sounds of life, made joyous
> by distance and seeming unapproachableness, came
> faintly and died away to a silence.

Then there would be two final scenes, of Pete's sodden fatu-
ousness among the tarts who fleece him, and finally of the
raging self-pity of the mother as neighbors beg her to forgive
the ruin and suicide of her "bad bad chil'." The story would
close on the mourner's "scream of pain: 'Oh, yes, I'll fergive her! I'll fergive her!' " Whatever the version, Gilder did
not enjoy it. Perhaps it dazed him with shock, indeed, except
that Maggie's seduction and brief career soliciting were presumably handled indirectly as now—like her death—without
detail. But what he mainly protested next day was that it
seemed "cruel," and then he pointed out excesses of detail
and errors until the author looked up: "You mean that the
story's too honest?" Gilder, to his honor, nodded. After trying
other magazines for a few weeks, Crane locked the book up
in a box at Edmund's house.

He had chosen Ed, on their mother's death, as his guardian
for the year remaining of his minority, though several other
brothers were older. With Will, who lived with his wife and
daughters in Port Jervis, Stephen's relations would remain
close; and he would spend one more summer working for
Townley, a widower now, in Asbury Park. William Howe
Crane, the only brother who is said to have had much money,
acted as financial adviser to the others. But it was Edmund's
house, now at Lakeview and later at Hartwood, that Stephen

seems to have regarded as his own home, wherever he was actually staying, during the next four or five years. Of the three other surviving members of the family we hear from now on little or nothing. When Crane wrote, not often, it was to Edmund or William.

In May, after a visit to Syracuse, he took off from Will and Cornelia Crane's into Sullivan County again, camping with three old friends (probably Louis Senger and his brother and Frederic Lawrence). They loafed and fished and poked about in the wilderness, drawling curses at each other's cooking, daring each other up rotten trees. Then Crane had to get back to Lakeview and on the 26th he requisitioned by letter five dollars from Acton Davies or Ed's front door and baby would make his next meal. Through warm nights in the attic he wrote a series of queer stories, before going down the coast late in June to help Townley report summer activities. Townley urged him to show them to his *Tribune* boss, an old family friend Willis Fletcher Johnson, who was vacationing on the shore, and when he demurred spoke to Johnson. So Stephen gave some, shyly, to the editor, who accepted them immediately. Five appeared on successive Sundays in July. They are known as the "Sullivan County Sketches," and it will be convenient to consider all ten together.

Taking them frankly as apprentice work, we see a mind at stretch which seems to have no clear idea why it is at stretch; it keeps inventing reasons for being; but these reasons do not satisfy the creating mind at all, and the tales end in deliberate anticlimax. Most of them, that is, have the form of jokes. The jokes are not in the least funny; nearly all the tales have a dark, grotesque air and they depend upon just two emotions, both furiously exaggerated—fear and wrath, especially fear. But the jokes are not intended to be funny: they are intended to rebuke the fear. Sometimes this rebuke occurs early in the fear, *if* it is a reasonably founded fear, and genuine humor occurs then. A little man sitting by a campfire alone hears "the approach of the unknown": "The little

37

man arose slowly to his feet; his clothes refused to fit his back. . . . 'Hah!' he bellowed hoarsely in menace. A growl replied, and a bear paced into the light of the fire. The little man supported himself upon a sapling and regarded his visitor."

If a power here of representing psychological detail physically, succinctness, self-possession, show that we are dealing with the apprentice work of an unusual talent, these qualities must not be supposed continuous. Though so small, the tales are spasmodic and absurdly uneven. Thus the wrath with which they swell is never effective, but always rhetorical, and the fear-inspiring objects are never frightening, but always ludicrous. Sometimes the ludicrous is attractive, as when this bear "started intensely around the campfire," sometimes not. The fear is more real. A rather tedious ghoul may be contrasted with the feelings of the little man whom with a smile he wakes up—"He began to feel his flesh slide to and fro on his bones as he looked into this smile"—and drives through the forest: "The little man's blood turned to salt. His eyes began to decay and refused to do their office. He fell from gloom to gloom." The ghoul takes him to a house where there is a wild gray man, and "They regarded the little man with eyes that made wheels revolve in his soul. . . . The little man wriggled his legs in agony." Upon beholding this ghoul: "The campfire threw up two lurid arms and, quivering, expired." Amid the stories' gaucherie and strain, a natural animism produces moments of pure feeling. "The moon rested for a moment on the top of a tall pine on a hill"—if sculls are mentioned they have been whittled from "docile" pine boards—"A scrawny stone dam, clinging in apparent desperation to its foundation, wandered across a wild valley." Almost the sole sense of tenderness arises from such a passage, when the little man "sat close to his companion, the campfire, and encouraged it with logs."

An absence of companionship is striking. The stories seem to have been intended to describe various adventures of four men camping together in Sullivan County, and the four men are sometimes referred to, but except for the little man only a pudgy man is discriminated, who is regularly the little man's rival or enemy. The little man is chief or sole victim and hero. Crane was conceivably at this time the greatest living egoist, feeling his way towards self-dramatization in art. No doubt it was on this ground, as well as for style, that in 1896 he was "heartily ashamed" of them. In 1895 however, while still willing to collect them in a book (which he never did), he speaks of them as written "when I was clever," and it will be well to say something of what their actual materials seem to be. Crane thought he had simply been experimenting, making things up at will, perhaps. But in the first story, tumbling down into a cave, the little man (with the other three) comes upon a terrifying gray-bearded hermit standing before a great stone "cut squarely like an altar" with "what seemed to be a small volume" clasped in his hand and dreadful eyes that sweep until they find the little man's face. His voice is "cold, solemn, and damp" and what he says is: "It's your ante." Eventually, "The shaking little man took a roll of bills from a pocket and placed three ones upon the altar-like stone. The recluse looked at the little volume with reverence in his eyes. It was a pack of playing cards." He cleans the little man out and howls "Go!" Escaping, they learn from the guide that Tom Gardner was once a family man with a nice little farm who took to gambling, sold everything, his wife died then, and he went crazy. If this casual summary leaves much doubt that we have here a fantasy on Crane's father and the child's sense of abandonment (impoverishment) at his resented death, doubt will be weakened by a glance at the second story, where the abandonment is literal. Wanting to fish for pickerel, the four men hire a "creature with a voice from a tomb," who is said to be "disguised," and from his boat he deposits them on four stumps, where they fish while he perches on a stump-top, smoking "black, eloquent tobacco," and utters loudly "spasmodic philosophy."

At sunset he is discovered also to have been boozing; sodden, he refuses to collect them, even after the little man's oration upon his alleged good qualities and their distress—all he thunders is: "Dern fool, g'home." One may smile at the way in which the Reverend Jonathan Townley Crane's gentle reprobation of gambling, smoking, drinking, has returned as degradation-fantasy upon his image. But at a sentence set by the orphaned author after this second rejection (an identical rejection by the wild gray man ends the third story) one does not smile. A night wind roars, rain threatens, the four men shiver on their stumps and turn up their collars. "Suddenly it struck each that he was alone, separated from humanity by impassable gulfs."

The world, indeed, emerging dimly from the imperfect expression of these sketches is one of perfect aloneness, in which relations are possible only through rage and fear. Sometimes Crane's brooding diction lifts it fully to view, when a slate-colored man moves about in a "small personal atmosphere of gloom" or the men slumber through "the trees' song of loneliness and the lay of isolation of the mountain grass." It is when one realizes that the whole ordinary world of intercourse is unable, for some reason, to make its way into the Sullivan County Sketches that the writer's singularity glares. Of the themes that make their way in instead, we have glanced at several and must be content with one or two others. Fear, first, is by no means given its head. The little man, assaulted in one story, "arrived at the critical stage of degradation. He would resist." His companions, in another, "had reached the cellar of fear. They were now resolved to use weapons on the great destruction." This perception will seem slight perhaps to the reader; not slight in a mind devoted to the occasions of fear. Second, Crane was, if bound still in himself, unlocking his way fast toward the dramatization of *Maggie* and *The Red Badge of Courage*. "Swift pictures of himself in a thousand attitudes under a thousand combinations of circumstances, killing a thousand bears, passed panoramically through him," he writes of the little man.

This last of the *Tribune* Sketches, "Killing His Bear," is with "The Mesmeric Mountain" the most finished of the ten—best sustained, that is, and sharpest in their closing irony. It is pointless, and has not the fabulous character of the mountain story (some of the imagery of which will be permanent in Crane); but it is mature in manner. Only it is not Crane's manner, it is Kipling's, except in details. Some of the other Sketches are more nearly characteristic and, though various influences (Mark Twain, Bierce) have been named and can even be found, Poe is their master. The clouded, the obsessive, the grotesque are his. What is remarkable is that the most interesting parts of the stories are all Crane's. He was really his own master—a fantasist, an ironist, a realist, already half an impressionist: "The swirling mass"—the men are pitching into the cave—went some twenty feet, and lit upon "a level, dry place in a strong yellow light of candles. It dissolved and became eyes." As for style, color is strong— mostly gray, red, black—though not yet muscular; the un- ceremonious, half from Mark Twain, half from Kipling, is hobbledehoy; the flat, from Mark Twain and S. C., is very uncertain. But here is the bear-death. "On the ridge-top a dismal choir of hemlocks crooned over one that had fallen. The dying sun created a dim purple and flame-coloured tumult on the horizon's edge. . . . A hound, as he nears large game, has the griefs of the world on his shoulders and his baying tells of the approach of death. He is sorry he came. . . . The little man, with nerves tingling and blood throbbing, remained in the shadows, like a fantastic bronze figure, with jewelled eyes swaying sharply in its head. . . . A mad froth lay in the animal's open mouth. . . . The little man saw swirling fur over his gun barrel. The earth faded to nothing. Only space and the game, the aim and the hunter. . . . Creation rocked and the bear stumbled. . . . He ran up and kicked the ribs of the bear. Upon his face was the smile of the successful lover." Crane was writing at twenty like a man who has no time to lose. "A Ghoul's Accountant," however presently it clogs, sprang into motion thus: "In a wilderness sunlight is noise. Darkness is a great, tremendous silence, accented by small and distant sounds. The music of the wind in the trees is songs of loneliness, hymns on abandonment, and lays of the absence of things congenial and alive. . . ." Johnson, the editor who handled them, says that they caused excitement on week-ends of July in 1892 and one is not surprised.

Overleaf from "A Ghoul's Accountant" is the sort of reporting Crane was doing, about an Asbury Park fakir: ". . . He, or she, wore a dress which would take a geometrical phenomenon to describe. He, or she, wore orange stockings, with a bunch of muscle in the calf. The rest of his, or her, apparel was a chromatic delirium of red, black, green, pink, blue, yellow, purple, white and other shades and colors not known. . . ." This was well enough, but a few weeks later in mid-August he was describing the vacationers themselves: "The people come to see the people. . . . The average summer guest here is a rather portly man, with a good watch-chain and a business suit of clothes, a wife and about three children. . . . He enjoys himself in a very mild way. . . ." This was resented. Stephen Crane's sense of humor was felt already as odd. Without the "summer girl," he mused, "the men would perish from weariness or fall to fighting . . . the bands would play charges and retreats and the soda-water fountains would run blood." It is hardly to be supposed that everyone smiled at his cadenza later in the article, on a new placard by the sacrosanct "Founder" of Asbury Park, James A. Bradley: "Modesty of apparel is as becoming to a lady in a bathing-suit as to a lady drest in silks and satins." "There are some very sweet thoughts," sang Crane, "in that declaration. It is really a beautiful expression of sentiment. It is modest and delicate. Its author merely insinuates. There is nothing to shake vibratory senses in such gentle phraseology. Supposing he had said: 'Don't go in the water attired merely in a tranquil smile. . . .' "

Townley Crane, whose passion for his press bureau had got him a nickname "The Shore Fiend," valued his dignity as dean of the shore correspondents. Why he let his kid brother run on so is a mystery. But he was away next week—Beer says—at a funeral, when hell broke loose. The Junior Order of United American Mechanics held a state-wide gathering in Asbury Park, and gave an "American Day" parade, which Stephen Crane reported. Somehow the story slid past the editors in New York and appeared in the *Tribune* on August 21st. Accounts of this famous incident have been wonderfully garbled. The parade, Crane wrote, was "a deeply impressive one to some persons. . . . It probably was the most awkward, ungainly, uncut and uncarved procession that ever raised clouds of dust on sun-beaten streets. . . . Asbury Park creates nothing. It does not make; it merely amuses. There is a factory where nightshirts are manufactured, but it is some miles from town. This is a resort of wealth and leisure, of women and considerable wine. The throng along the line of march was composed of summer gowns, lace parasols, tennis trousers, straw hats and indifferent smiles. The procession was composed of men, bronzed, slope-shouldered, uncouth and begrimed with dust. Their clothes fitted them illy, for the most part, and they had no ideas of marching. They merely plodded along, not seeming quite to understand, stolid, unconcerned and, in a certain sense dignified—a pace and bearing emblematic of their lives." An Asbury Park summer crowd "was vaguely amused. The bona fide Asbury Parker is a man to whom a dollar, when held close to his eye, often shuts out any impression he may have had that other people possess rights. . . . Hence the tan-colored, sun-beaten honesty in the faces of the members of the Junior Order of United American Mechanics is expected to have a very staggering effect upon them. The visitors were men who possessed principles."

43

Not to speak of his disinterested account of the march, the contempt for their submissiveness which gleams through Crane's respect for the workers' honesty might have been expected to give offence in an ordinary situation, and the situation was as ordinary as a simoon. Whitelaw Reid, the owner-editor of the *Tribune*, was Republican candidate for the Vice-Presidency of the United States, in a rough campaign. Opposition papers seized on the story, garbling it as contemptuous of labor in general, insulted mechanics wrote in to call it un-American, and for some days there was a great sensation. The *Tribune* hurriedly apologized to the Order and a week later was still lamenting the "random letter," explaining its regret for the publication of "sentiments utterly foreign to the Tribune." Crane even elected Cleveland, according to later fantasy. The consequences in Asbury Park have been less obviously misrepresented. Carefully exculpating Reid, Beer wrote that "Somebody in Park Row sent Townley Crane a heated message and Stephen retired to Port Jervis." The editor concerned, Johnson, then asserted that nothing had happened: he just gave Stephen some fatherly advice, and the reason Crane had nothing further in the *Tribune* was that after the parade on Labor Day the resort season closed. Of course the parade was earlier than this. Crane in fact had two more pieces in the *Tribune*, on the 29th ("The Seaside Assembly's Work at Avon") and September 11th ("Seaside Hotel Hop"). But although plainly his, these are routine, nontopical reports, and we seem bound to suppose—what is plausible enough—that they were filed much earlier and finally used for space, because there seems to be little doubt as to what happened in Asbury Park. Garland, with whom Crane discussed the episode, is one witness to his dismissal, and a reporter who was there at the time has left a full account. Townley was fired by mail, though allowed to stay on till the end of the season, glum as a discrowned king; William Howe Crane told an inquirer many years later that he was a broken man thereafter—his character, so far as it is known, does not suggest that Stephen has much responsibility to bear for this. "Stevie"—Art Oliver wrote—was fired by wire and "greeted me with a saintly smile he always had ready for every disaster. . . ."

This summer the boy had fallen in love again. She was a young matron, Lily Brandon Munroe, who divided her time among London, New York, and Washington, and was then briefly in Asbury Park with her mother-in-law, a suffragist. With her came a sister of fifteen or so, Dottie, whom Stephen Crane was fond of and teased with the special gentleness he was always to show toward young girls; he bet her a necklet Townley would not remarry. The younger Mrs. Munroe's husband was off on a geological survey, but though the marriage had already become unsatisfactory there is no suggestion that his blonde, very handsome wife felt special interest in her unkempt, dry, taciturn junior. She did not even—being exceptional in this—think him handsome. What he felt some surviving letters show.

"Dearest L.B.," he wrote the following spring from 1064 Avenue A, and he must have seen her in New York about December: "I am sure that you have not concluded that I have ceased to remember. The three months which have passed have been months of very hard work to S. Crane. I was trying to see if I was worthy to have you think of me. . . . Well, at least, I've done something. I wrote a book"—of which he gives her some news then. "And I? I have merely thought of you and wondered if you cared that they said these things. Or wether you have forgotten?" Did she answer this? Late in the fall (1893) he wrote again. "Dearest: Although I do not now know what I am to you. . . . Many months— or a thousand years: I hardly know—have passed since we met and were comrades; I can readily see that, in that time, I have, perhaps, become a memory to you, a mere figure in a landscape of the past. And it is well for you if it [is] so, and for it I must be glad. Yet you, to me, are still a daily vision. . . . Your face is a torturing thing. . . . It is beyond me to free myself from the thrall of my love for you; it comes always between me and what I would enjoy in life —always—like an ominous sentence—the words of the parrott on the death-ship: 'We are all damned.'

"And yet, would I escape from it? Not I. It is the better part. . . . I would not give up one small remembrance of your companionship. Yet, with it, I suffer and I wished you to know it because you are a woman and though [you] may value me as a straw, you will comprehend. . . . For, surely, it is a small thing. I ask nothing of you in return. Merely that I may tell you I adore you; that you are the shadow and the light of my life;—the whole of it." And he begged a letter to 143 East 23rd Street before going to Europe as he expected to do shortly: "Even though you can only consistently be cold, do me this grace. . . ."

No other letters of Crane like these are known, and in their painful simplicity they are probably wholly sincere, flatness testifying to prostration. Mrs. Munroe did write to him then, but it is not clear that he answered till the following March with a long letter, which must be quoted later, quite different in tone until the end: ". . . . Don't forget me, dear, never, never, never. For you are to me the only woman in life. I am doomed, I suppose, to a lonely existence of futile dreams. It has made me better. . . . And to it I owe whatever I have achieved and the hope of the future . . . goodbye, beloved." And the hearts of young men forget as well as remember. More than a year later (about July of 1895):

My dear L.B.:

Copeland and Day of Boston which [*for* wish] to reprint those old Sullivan County tales of mine and there is no one in the world has any copies of them but you. Can you not send them to me?

Are you coming north this summer? Let me know, when you send the stories. I should like to see you again.

Yours as ever
S. C.

From the Lanthorne Club this is, undated like the others. The Lanthorne Club was still unfounded, his career in journalism seemed to be at an end, and no publisher was seeking the Sullivan County Sketches or the third *Maggie* in her box, or any other work of Stephen Crane's, in the fall of 1892 when he entered the crucial year of his life.

Two — MIDDLE

New York

After the Asbury Park debacle Stephen Crane was a month or so at Port Jervis with his brother Will before he moved into New York. His old Syracuse and Port Jervis friend Frederic Lawrence, studying medicine occasionally, roomed in a hangout for young people called the Pendennis Club at 1064 Avenue A (East or Eastern Boulevard) and took him in. Crane was here all fall and winter, jobless and hungry, writing. Reporting was out of the question until editors forgot. *Cosmopolitan* accepted "A Tent in Agony" for the December issue but this first magazine luck was his last for a long time. When the Syracuse *University Herald* wanted something for the Christmas number he sent one of the weakest Sullivan sketches, then never printed any more. Twenty-one on November 1, 1892, he repudiated the sketches and resolved upon something different, a definite attempt to create a masterpiece—ambitious, continuous, objective, faithful, and his own. Then he did it.

Maggie when he took it in hand for this purpose seems to have been at least eighteen months old and in its fourth version, so that evidence had better be given for its creation, as we know it, at the Pendennis Club. Lawrence is specific.* Louis Senger wrote: "I read 'Maggie' from chapter to chapter

* Private letter to Beer.

in a house over on the far East Side, where he lived with a crowd of irresponsibles." Neither of these witnesses mentions any previous version at all; Beer testifies that Crane borrowed for it some phrases from the Pendennis chambermaid (though he places her elsewhere, at Crane's residence the year after *Maggie* was published). Everything, also, ineptly foreshadowed in the Sullivan sketches is blazing in *Maggie*. Their author had obviously no conception of the phrase-by-phrase concentration, the steady brilliance, and the large design, of the little novel; on testimony as to the composition later of *The Red Badge*, *Maggie* would have taken some months of labor *after* this conception had been arrived at. And Crane has some remarks. He began it at twenty (too late, this) "and finished it when I was somewhat beyond 21." As was usual with him, he seems never to have mentioned it to Mrs. Munroe during the summer or fall, not in fact until late March of 1893 when he wrote: "The three months which have passed have been months of very hard work to S. Crane. . . . I wrote a book." Various things have already then happened to this book, as we shall see, and three may be too short for the period, but *Maggie* it was.

His alteration of outlook this fall initiated modern American writing, and must engage us. He had been writing about himself, now he was writing about other people; that was one thing. But how did he try to put the alteration himself? "When I left you [in August 1892, apparently]," he wrote to Mrs. Munroe somewhat later, "I renounced the clever school in literature. It seemed to me that there must be something more in life than to sit and cudgel one's brains for clever and witty expedients. So I developed all alone a little creed of art which I thought was a good one. Later I discovered that my creed was identical with the one of Howells and Garland and in this way I became involved in the beautiful war between those who say that art is man's substitute for nature and we are most successful in art when we approach the nearest to nature and truth, and those who say—well I don't know what they say. They don't, they can't say much but they fight villianously. . . ." Not very intelligible, but "identical" is flat enough, especially when we link it with an inscription later still to Howells: a book presented "as a token of the veneration and gratitude of Stephen Crane for many things he has learned of the common man and, above all, for a certain re-adjustment of his point of view victoriously concluded some time in 1892."

Young men cast about for support as they can, and in support of these linkings by Crane of his aesthetic with the "realism" of William Dean Howells and the "veritism" of Hamlin Garland, it is easy to cite passages in Howells's *Criticism and Fiction* (1891) that might have impressed him if he read them. Howells urged a fiction that would deal with plain, working American life, avoiding anything romantic, bizarre, heroic. Of James Barrie's work he observed in *Harper's,* May 1892, that its method was the "American" method, in which the story's interest depended not upon the use of dialect but "upon what the characters had to say, and upon their *exhibition of real human life. . . .* Mr. Barrie never *caricatures* his people and never patronizes them. The humor is their humor, and not the *smartness* of the author; and *the pathos is in the situation, the inevitable sadness of human life limited and at disadvantage,* and not in the sentimentality of the observer. *To put himself in this attitude towards his material requires the finest literary art.*" A blow to the attitudinizing of Crane's sketches, these italics (not Howells's) would have been. Crane would have found something also in Howells's gentle, honest report of "An East-Side Ramble" (*Impressions and Experiences,* 1890). Howells thought the Irish and Jewish poor "tame and peaceful" on the whole in their squalor. His immediate sense of its loathsomeness he found rapidly blunted, so that their conditions "do not seem so dreadful as they are." "Perhaps," he pursues quietly, "this was partly their fault; they were uncomplaining, if not patient, in circumstances where I believe a

53

single week's sojourn, with no more hope of a better lot than they could have, would make anarchists of the best people in the city. Perhaps the poor people themselves are not so thoroughly persuaded that there is anything very unjust in their fate, as the compassionate think. They at least do not know the better fortune of others, and they have the habit of passively enduring their own." Crane's belief, later, that "the root of Bowery life is a sort of cowardice" is essentially—though more explicit—in agreement with this. The belief is entirely implicit, if it exists at all, in *Maggie* where the much more obviously implied social content concerns the determinant power of environment. But this power too is emphasized by Howells, and it was perhaps to this or to some other social view expressed in the critic's voluminous writings, rather than to an aesthetic, that Crane recorded his obligation.

For the difficulties with supposing Stephen Crane's "little creed of art" indebted to the views of Howells or Garland are two: it does not resemble theirs, and he already had Tolstoy before him. Tolstoy was Howells's great master also, but he did not learn from the Russian what Crane did. Crane learnt how an ironic mind takes expression in literary art, or learnt something about this; and since this is the dominant aspect of what is called Crane's "realism," it is not very easy to see how his creed could have been "identical" with Howells's and Garland's, neither of these men being really an ironist at all. Labels are slippery, of course. "I decided," Crane said on another occasion, "that the nearer a writer gets to life the greater he becomes as an artist, and most of my prose writings have been towards the goal partially described by that misunderstood and abused word, realism. Tolstoy is the writer I admire most of all." The term is so heavily qualified that we may hope to learn more from one of the phrases, "the nearer a writer gets to life," especially when we repeat in connection with it his formulation to Mrs. Munroe: "we are most successful in art when we approach the nearest to nature and truth." The question is what he meant by these statements: *how*, that is, one approaches life or nature or truth.

What he seems to have meant is impressionism. Well before any of these statements were made, late in the same year he finished *Maggie* (1893), Crane spoke his faith repeatedly to a friend who has recorded it. "Impressionism was his faith. Impressionism, he said, was truth, and no man could be great who was not an impressionist, for greatness consisted in knowing truth. He said that he did not expect to be great himself, but he hoped to get near the truth." This was to his fellow-lodgers on 23rd Street, and the book he was then writing is identical in method with *Maggie*. Impressionism must be the creed which he developed late in 1892 and in terms of which he rewrote his story of the slums. But literary impressionism had no status, and he could hardly announce "I believe in Irony," so he allied himself as best he could with the few men who seemed to be trying at any rate to get at the truth. If he came in *Crumbling Idols* (1894) on Garland's conviction that art was a question of "one man facing certain facts and telling his individual relations to them," Crane could feel less alone, and it was easy to ignore Garland's insistence that "The realist or veritist is really an optimist"; he knew better. So if he came (probably in 1895) on Henry James's "A novel is in its broadest definition a personal, a direct impression of life: that, to begin with, constitutes its value, which is greater or less according to the intensity of the impression," or the master's view that among the qualifications of the young aspirant in fiction "the first is a capacity for receiving straight impressions," or his dictum that the only condition attaching to the composition of the novel was "that it be sincere"—he could feel reassured and reinforced. These men, with Howells, were "realists," and so was he. Stephen Crane's program, however, was his own.

When he finished his story this time he apparently wasted

no hopes on editors. If anything was due him still from his father's estate, he used this, and the rest he borrowed from William Crane, to invest it in the literary future of Johnston Smith. "I hunted a long time for some perfectly commonplace name," he told Willis Clarke. "I think that I asked [George Post] Wheeler what he thought was the stupidest name in the world. He suggested Johnson or Smith [Crane is quoted also as saying he thought of his friend the *Tribune* editor's name] and Johnston Smith went on the ugly yellow cover of the book by mistake. You see, I was going to wait until all the world was pyrotechnic about Johnston Smith's 'Maggie' and then I was going to flop down like a trapeze performer from the wire and, coming forward with all the modest grace of a consumptive nun, say, I am he, friends! . . . The bill for printing eleven hundred copies was $869 and Appleton's tell me that the printer must have made about $700 out of me. . . . A firm of religious and medical printers did me the dirt. You may take this as proferred evidence of my imbecility. Will made me get the thing copyrighted. I had not even that much sense." The name of this firm, which refused it for the title-page, has resisted inquiry, and the genius neglected to deposit two copies, or even one, in the Library of Congress, so that month of issue is uncertain. But on January 19, 1893, the Librarian received from Stephen Crane at the Pendennis Club one sentence, one typed title-page ("printed" he called it), and one dollar if he enclosed the dollar. It was early in February, perhaps, that *Maggie: A Girl of the Streets* went on sale at fifty cents a copy.*

* Williams and Starrett place the publication "sometime between late February and May," owing to the omission of the name "Maggie" from the title-page Crane typed (if he typed it) and their consequent postdating by a year of the note to McHarg. But the book was causing a stir already in March, and time must be allowed for delay, especially in relation to Howells. Admittedly the matter is confusing and unluckily not all the evidence can be given. No attention, unless something should corroborate it, need be paid to Beer's assertion that Crane had got rid of a hundred copies by the

In these cheap pages Crane established his manner, the powerful, careful, remorseless instrument without the example of which we should have forgone some of our most characteristic achievements in the present century. The material here opened up by it for art seems now less important, except as it gave the instrument a way of getting at life. In its own time it amazed. The story is that of a chaotic, drunken, bellicose family of the slums named Johnson. The small boy, Jimmie, fighting, is come on by his father, cursed, and kicked home. He strikes his ragged little sister Maggie and she curses him quaveringly. The parents booze and battle, uniting the brother and sister at least in mad terror. The baby Tommie, who has stared out from under the table, his face working with excitement, dies, and the father dies. Under the terrifying mother the children grow up, Jimmie to live "some red years" without laboring, during which time his sneer becomes chronic, and then to become a truck-driver, disdainful, brutal, frequently arrested for fighting, with two seductions to his credit. Maggie however "blossomed in a mudpuddle," and he offers her a choice: "See? Yeh've eeder got t'go on d' toif er go t' work!" She goes to work in a stifling room where collars and cuffs are made at machines by twenty girls in "various stages of yellow discontent" under a foreigner who bullies them and pays them five dollars a week. Timid and helpless, she is awed by the superior clothes and contempt and strength of a bartender Jimmie knows, Pete, who dangles his legs one day from the Johnson table and brags. The utmost defiance of fate she can imagine herself is a feeling "that she should love to see somebody entangle their fingers in the oily beard of the fat foreigner." In Pete she perceives the ideal man. She is utterly grateful for his atten-

---

end of January; one is reminded of the hundred signed copies of *Bowery Tales* that a literary clergyman, in Beer's pages, turned up at Brede to demand from Crane and was "peculiarly outraged by the sight of Crane in a gray flannel shirt rolling dice with strange adjurations on the hall's depressed floor." These were adjurations strange indeed, the book having been issued posthumously.

57

tions and will only, to his wonder, not kiss him. One night when he comes to take her out, the mother lies screeching on the floor in the wrecked apartment, beaten in a physical battle with her son; she curses Maggie as a disgrace to the family, who has gone to the devil, and that night Pete seduces the girl. Next day the mother is first astounded at this news, then wildly vindictive. When Jimmie, after a tremendous inconclusive fight with Pete, once suggests nervously that he might look up Maggie and bring her home, the mother weeps with rage at an idea so shameful and insulting to "yer own mudder." Pete shortly deserts the girl for a "woman of brilliance and audacity" named Nell, a former mistress who knows how to cow him—to Maggie's dazed astonishment. Maggie creeps home to be mocked and ejected. On a wet evening several months later, a painted girl wanders across the city accosting men in vain, until she enters the blackness of the final block. In two final chapters, Pete is drunk in a saloon, affectionate toward the universe and the half-dozen women who are fleecing him, weeping with anxiety that it should be recognized that he is a "goo' f'ler," and the mother receives in the middle of a meal the news of her daughter's death, concludes the meal, and then howls with grief. Neighbors gather, especially one in black, Miss Smith, who pleads with her to forgive her "bad, bad chil'," and after the mother's shrieking Jimmie out to get his sister so that they can put on her feet the worsted boots she wore as a baby, the book ends on the mother's "scream of pain": "Oh, yes, I'll fergive her! I'll fergive her!"

Several remarks are to be made of this little book, and first in regard to its *art*, which is an effect of intense pressure and nearly perfect detachment. No American work of its length had driven the reader so hard; in none had the author remained so persistently invisible behind his creation. The incongruity of these qualities forces our attention to the strangeness—the daring and ambition—of Crane's attempt. Everything here was incongruous also. He was describing a modern slum-world, ferocious and sordid, with a fidelity that reached down to Pete's amiable reminiscence: "I met a chump deh odder day way up in deh city. . . . When I was a-crossin' deh street deh chump runned plump inteh me, an' den he turns aroun' an' says, 'Yer insolen' ruffin!' he says, like dat. 'Oh, gee!' I says, 'Oh, gee! git off d' eart'!' I says, like dat. See? 'Git off d' eart'!' like dat. Den deh blokie he got wild. He says I was a contempt'ble scoun'el, er somethin' like dat, an' he says I was doom' teh everlastin' pe'dition, er somethin' like dat. 'Gee!' I says, 'gee! Yer joshin' me,' I says. 'Yer joshin' me.' An' den I slugged 'im. See?" But dialogue aside (in Pete's jawing, for that matter, we hear a rhythm of the artist), Crane was to describe this world with an Alexandrian stylization; with imagery ranging from the jungle up through war to medieval and hieratic imagery; with the last possible color, force, succinctness—without destroying the illusion of fidelity. The banal story, that is, had to be given heroic and pathetic stature and yet not falsified. At the same time, its melodramatic character called for disguise under an air of flatness and casualness. Furthermore Crane had to rely on loose, episodic structure—except once or twice he would never use any other. And no passion such as revenge or love or greed could dominate the fable. If in these unpropitious circumstances he achieved in *Maggie* a sense of inevitability, one may well wonder how he did it. The word Howells was to use for this triumph of Crane was a good one, namely, "Greek."

Not Maggie's fate alone but the fates of the others are inevitable, given their misconceptions of each other, themselves, and their world. These misconceptions register as astonishment and rage. Pete and then another man are astonished when Maggie repulses them; her mother is astonished when she succumbs. Jimmie is astonished to learn that his own sister, like others', can be seduced. She is astonished by leonine Pete's sudden submissiveness (to Nell), then by his desertion. Everything is exactly what we expect but not at all what they expect. It is not that they lack moral ideas but that these ideas either are the perverted ones common to their conditions or are simply unable to make headway against their conditions' weight. The first moral idea in the book is introduced in the first sentence and the last is fulfilled in the last sentence, and the delicacy and completeness of the deterioration from one to the other, Crane standing aside, account for the fable's power. The small boy standing on a heap of gravel for the "honour" of Rum Alley impresses us as natural; loyalty and bravery may begin so. But this defiance and an attempt later the same evening to prevent his father from stealing a can of beer (with which, empty, his father then hits him on the head) represent the highest point Jimmie's morality will touch. His parents are far below this already, and the saturnine parody of a forgiveness-scene with which *Maggie* ends concludes a sort of demonstration in the geometry of needless agony.

Self-indulgent, brutal, self-pitying, none of these people can help each other. Even when a decent action is advocated, the reason is wrong. "Why deh blazes don'cher try teh keep Jim from fightin'?" the mother bellows at the father, and why? "Because he tears 'is clothes, yeh fool!" Shamefacedly one day Jimmie tries to get her to let him bring Maggie home, because "dis t'ing queers us! See?" One note of sentimentality or reproof, by the author, would destroy the work, but Crane never falters or insists. "It seemed that the world had treated this woman very badly. . . . She broke furniture as if she were at last getting her rights." The characters are left to their illusion that they are working out their own fates, and the reader is left to draw his own conclusions. In the brilliant analysis of Jimmie's progress towards nihilism, all Crane says is: "He became so sharp that he believed in nothing." If the mother's self-pity apes affection, crooning drunkenly to her children about "yer poor mudder" just before she beats them up again, Crane does not explain that it does. At most, over certain moments of their aspiration, irony permits the tone to lift. The young man wanders hilariously into a mission and comments freely, but confuses the speaker with Christ: "Momentarily, Jimmie was sullen with thoughts of a hopeless altitude where grew fruit." And for all his police record, his seductions and desertions, "he had, on a certain star-lit evening, said wonderingly and quite reverently, 'Deh moon looks like hell, don't it?'"

Of the compassion that plays unseen over the story, we catch glimpses only once or twice, as toward the "meek freaks" in a dime museum Pete takes Maggie to—and at once we learn that Maggie "contemplated their deformities with awe, and thought them a sort of chosen tribe," for his heroine's misconceptions are spared as little as anyone else's by Crane in this confident and stern little work. Only her good faith distinguishes her from the others, who deceive themselves with their simulations of good faith. And after her fall, the timid girl "imagined a future rose-tinted because of its distance from all that she had experienced before. . . . Her life was Pete's, and she considered him worthy of the charge. . . . She did not feel like a bad woman. To her knowledge she had never seen any better." Nervously leaving the music-hall with him then, because other men eye her, she shrinks aside passing two painted women and draws back her skirts; very much as, after her suicide (but not because of it), Pete drunk in a saloon "laid stress upon the purity of his motives in all dealings with men in the world, and spoke of the fervour of his friendship for those who were amiable. Tears welled slowly from his eyes. . . . 'I'm goo' f'ler, ain' I, girlsh?'" Crudity in stylistic detail *Maggie* sometimes shows, but in originality of conception, energy, instinct for exclusion and for the tacit, consistency of ironic execution, it as little solicits allowance on the score of its author's youth as the *Disparates* of Goya do on the score of his deafness and age. *Maggie* is like a *Disparate*.

His statements about it are less impressive. It tries, he said in an inscription to Lucius Button, "to show that environment is a tremendous thing in the world and frequently shapes lives regardless. . . ." This suggests a Naturalistic novel, and *Maggie* has often been traced to *L'Assommoir* (1887) of Zola. It would be interesting to know when Crane read *L'Assommoir*, because one would like to be able to say definitely whether American Naturalism owed its origin to French Naturalism. About Frank Norris there is no doubt, but as *Maggie* appeared Norris was just, in his fourth year at the University of California, transferring his enthusiasm from Walter Scott and Kipling to Zola and beginning to plan out a book that would be published six years later as *McTeague*. Unfortunately we do not know just how early Crane conceived *Maggie* and it is not quite certain that he ever read *L'Assommoir* at all. Four kinds of influence are in question: first and most important, the general conception of a kind of material for art, then attitudes towards the material, then artistic method, and finally the actual material (incident, character, and so forth). In method Crane owes nothing to Zola—not even so much as the irony of detail from *Sevastopol* when on page three of *Maggie* as the urchins depart they "began to give, each to each, distorted versions of the fight." Crane had probably observed this himself but he had learnt from Tolstoy to say it. As for attitudes, the determinism of *Maggie* we have seen Crane himself relating to Howells, not to Zola (to whom in fact he never related anything and whose work he apparently did not admire); and another motive for this determinism will appear. Zola's scientific attitude he has nothing of. The worship of force (strong men, and even better than strong men, machines) Crane's work shows a perfect contempt for, here and everywhere. This doctrine crucial to Naturalism may be studied in Chapter VI of *L'Assommoir*; the courtly Norris took it over wholesale and was writing rapturously in 1893 of "that splendid, brutal, bullying spirit that is the Anglo-Saxon's birthright"—no irony, either. Upon the evidence so far,

Crane was a very imperfect Naturalist indeed and cannot possibly be seen as a disciple of Zola.

Nevertheless he probably read *L'Assommoir* and was influenced by it. A general resemblance, pointed out by Norris in 1896, between Maggie's story and the sallying forth of Nana, is rather tenuous. According to Beer, Crane invented his plot—only two incidents were from life, the saloon fight and the destruction of the lambrequin. Furthermore, and contradicting this, after Beer's study was published Frederic Lawrence wrote to him saying flatly that both *Maggie* and *George's Mother* were "drawn from our own observations and adventures." But the circumstance of Maggie's being driven from home on the evening of her seduction seems to have been suggested by the circumstances that force Gervaise's return to Lantier (end of Chapter VIII), and Maggie's mother like Nana's, after the daughter's fall, explains that she boozes out of grief. Small points; taken together with some similarity in the degradation of Coupeau and Crane's George Kelcey, however, they increase the antecedent likelihood that the young American, whose two works at all naturalistic both deal continually with liquor, would have come at some point on the nineteenth century's most celebrated investigation of that subject. The most interesting question of influence must evidently remain unsettled. If the present account of this matter is acceptable, that is, we can feel no confidence that Crane read Zola before he determined upon the subject of *Maggie*, and no confidence that he did not. It may be germane that Howells, who in the 'eighties was reading "everything of Zola that I can get my hands on," never mentions him in this connection; and that Crane, who though not invariably candid was unusually so, never mentioned the debt, had small regard for Zola, and intensely resented, later on, assumptions that he was indebted to the French. He had besides a motive in *Maggie* not yet mentioned.

Following the sentence about "environment" in the inscription to Button comes one quite different: ". . . If one proves that theory one makes room in Heaven for all sorts of souls, notably an occasional street girl, who are not confidently expected to be there by many excellent people. . . ." This will not fail to appeal to the reader, in its ironic insistence, as *romantic*, and *Maggie* is a romantic book. What conceals the romanticism is the technical "distance" of its impressionism, the handsome representation of the insensitive and brutal in the environment, the guzzling and scrapping. But the girl is as nearly perfect as Crane's honesty could let her be. Only not attractive sexually, and no one fears her as his later heroines are without exception feared by their lovers. She was created to be made a harlot and sent to Heaven.

So *Maggie* went on sale—at Brentano's, that is, which took a dozen copies and returned ten. Other dealers would not handle it. It was not reviewed and not advertised, unless we credit a legend that the penniless author hired four men to ride about the city's streetcars prominently reading it. He gave away copies to his brothers, friends, creditors, anybody. "Miss Wortzmann," one is inscribed: "This story will not edify you or improve you but I owe your papa $1.30 for tobacco. S. Crane." The copy posted to Hamlin Garland just said: "The reader of this book must inevitably be shocked, but let him keep on till the end, for in it the writer has put something which is important." Garland was sharply interested and guessed the authorship at once, more from the congruity of the style with Crane's conversation, perhaps, than from a description of workingmen (in Chapter VII) rather like the parade-story which he had seen. Getting the boy's address from Avon, he wrote accusing him. Crane pale and thin marched up to Harlem, where Garland had rooms with his brother, to confess. He seemed at first very depressed, but after being given, besides praise, a steak and coffee, he chortled and sang strolling about the room, talking freely—"always with precision and original tang." Garland suggested too that he send a copy to William Dean Howells.

Crane was roaming the city as he would be doing now for two years, dropping in on friends to lounge and chat or write: Willis Brooks Hawkins, Senger's cousin the painter Corwin Knapp Linson, Acton Davies, Walter Dunckel, John Hilliard, dozens. He had started a short novel eventually to be called *George's Mother*, laid a little more respectably among the ordinary working class but otherwise a counterpart and continuation, as it were, of *Maggie*: a son and mother living alone, the mother this time a pious devoted dreary woman driven gradually to despair and death as her son takes to drink. A delightful summer story "The Reluctant Voyagers" Linson illustrated "on spec," Crane posing comically for the tall man, and this manuscript was lost in some magazine office. He held dead cigarettes and listened. He was the author of a book; he was waiting. Privation gained. One cold night stumbling to Lakeview, he felt his arm taken with "You seem to be in a pretty bad way, boy," and a farmer helped him along the country road until they could see Edmund's lights. For a time now too, Beer says, he couldn't write at all: everything seemed false. A day of February he drifted into Ed's office, which was in New York, to borrow five cents. Crane's courage, we are told, seemed to him silly later on, since two of his brothers believed in him and had room for him. Certainly he was sardonic later on about the self-satisfaction sometimes involved. The young impressionist painter in *The Third Violet*, describing to the heroine his earlier studio life, responds abruptly to a biographer's word in her mouth: "Brave? Nonsense! Those things are not brave. Impression to that effect created by the men who have been through the mill for the greater glory of the men who have been through the mill." Nothing was safe from this author, least of all his own courage. But there is attitudinizing here as well as modesty; Crane had to be on his own, and those things *are* brave. The piles of yellow *Maggie* brooded on the floor. A bitter day Jennie Creegan gathered up some to light a fire downstairs; Crane grinned and helped her. On March 1st, however, toward the end of his second winter of it, he was desperate. Answering an ad in the *Herald*, he took a job—as a clerk in a Bleecker Street wholesale house—for a week.

About now he came rummaging among old *Centurys* in Linson's studio, looking up the series of articles on "Battles and Leaders of the Civil War," and complaining angrily. "I wonder that some of those fellows," he said to the painter, "don't tell how they *felt* in those scraps. They spout enough of what they *did*, but they're as emotionless as rocks." One day in the studio of William Dallgren, a young actor named Acton Davies, who was posing, insisted on his looking at Zola's *Le Débâcle*. Davies adored Zola and was irritated when Crane threw it aside. "I suppose you could have done it better?" "Certainly." This sounded confident enough, but Crane was still desperate, and it may have been the sensation made by the French war-novel that determined him to try a pot-boiler. He borrowed bound *Centurys* from the Mrs. Armstrong whose nephew he had buried once with a canteen of whiskey still on him, and set to work. Her father told him they were accurate. He tried; but unfortunately he was an artist, and on April 2nd he returned the volumes with a note: "Thank you very much for letting me keep these so long. I have spent ten nights writing a story of the war on my own responsibility but I am not sure that my facts are real and the books won't tell me what I want to know so I must do it all over again, I guess." Whether anyone ever saw this story is unknown. Months later when he showed Louis Senger some chapters of *The Red Badge of Courage*, Crane told his friend about it: "I deliberately started in to do a pot-boiler, something that would take the boarding-school element—you know the kind. Well, I got interested in the thing in spite of myself, and I couldn't, I couldn't! I *had* to do it my own way." * He was writing then, as Senger put it, on the paper the meat came home in.

One thing that had helped him was a sudden, startling response to *Maggie* in the middle of March. Garland, moved by the boy's discouragement, had suggested his sending copies to various editors and arranged himself to review it for *The Arena*. Toward the end of the month, Crane wrote the exultant letter to Mrs. Munroe already cited in part: ". . . I wrote a book. Up to the present time, I think I can say I am glad I did it. Hamlin Garland was the first to overwhelm me with all manner of extraordinary language. The book has made me a powerful friend in W. D. Howells. B. O. Flower of the '*Arena*' has practically offered me the benefits of his publishing company for all that I may in future write. Albert Shaw of the 'Review of Reviews' wrote me congratulations this morning and tomorrow I dine with the editor of the 'Forum'. . . ." Now or later there was perhaps a plan for the Arena Company to issue *Maggie* properly, but it fell through, and the uncertainty of these hopes is transparent. More than a year would pass before the *Arena* published "An Ominous Baby"**; no periodical publication of Crane's is recorded indeed for this whole year, 1893. But what mattered was the sense of encouragement, and overwhelmingly the approval of Howells. After some time the critic had received a heartbreaking letter from Crane saying he saw that Howells did not care for his book. Howells in fact had not read it. He now did, with amazement, and invited Stephen Crane to call in 59th Street.

* This is confirmed by a conversation of Crane's later still, reported by "The Rambler" in *The Book Buyer*, April 1896. The pot-boiler was to have been a short story for a newspaper, till he determined to put into it the best work of which he was capable.
** Beer announces that "Flower promptly bought *An Omnibus Babe* [sic] for twenty-five dollars" and his account of these years wanders imperiously back and forth; he places now "An Experiment in Misery" and "The Men in the Storm" also (printed in April and October 1894).

We have had since 1900 no outstanding novelist who is also the country's leading critic and essayist, and the fully established leader of a movement still strongly debated and opposed; so that it is not easy to imagine Crane's feelings on receiving this invitation. William Dean Howells understood himself better than many contemporaries did. "My way is still the byway, not the highway," he wrote privately ten years later, "the minor, not the major means"—and more painfully: "I have often thought my intellectual raiment was more than my intellectual body, and that I might finally be convicted, not of having nothing *on*, but of that worse nakedness of having nothing *in*." But he was sensitive, candid, and serious, still changing from the man who expurgated *Huckleberry Finn*, murmuring in 1869 cf "that safe wildness which pleases me," to the man who would warn Mark Twain in 1904, about the ruffler's autobiography, "Even you won't tell the black heart's-truth. The man who could do it would be famed to the last day the sun shone upon." In 1893, prolific and active, the chief spokesman for Realism, his prestige was immense.* "Here is a writer," he introduced Crane to his other guests, "who has sprung into life fully armed."** And when Mark Twain came up in the talk: "Mr. Crane can do things that Clemens can't." Then he read aloud, from one of her first small volumes, some poems of Emily Dickinson to which Crane, sitting there in a suit of Hilliard's, listened with interest. Afterwards he walked down to the Bowery and into the back room of a saloon, where he watched some drunken Negroes play poker the rest of the evening.

* It continued so; writing of death in 1905, "If [Mother] is living yet somewhere, and I shall see her, what account shall I give her . . . ? Ambitions fulfilled, vanities gratified, and what else? That seems to be the sum of my endeavor." But his dignity survived his power; to Henry James in 1915, "on the whole I should say your worship was spreading among us. I am comparatively a dead cult with my statues cut down and the grass growing over them in the pale moonlight."

** Unless indeed Beer made all this up. Howells wrote that he asked Crane to tea and gives the impression that they were alone. "If I do appear in print some day," said Flaubert, "it will be an appearance in full armor."

These habits of his were already annoying some of his older
or respectable companions. He would pause and talk with an
elderly whore or a tramp, gravely, while a friend fumed. His
appearance too was singular: sallow, handsome, untidy, with
his large intent eyes ringed after poker, or even unringed. In
this month, March, Beer locates the first of certain legends:
Crane was pointed out to a Southerner as the Bowery-haunt-
ing outcast son of an Episcopal bishop.

Slowly a war novel was evolving, with the spring. He was
also writing a series of little things he called the "Baby
Sketches," about the isolated adventures of the baby Tommie
in *Maggie*. In one, "wandering in a strange country" outside
his slum, he comes on children in carriages. "He braced his
legs apart in an attitude of earnest attention. . . . 'Say,' he
breathed softly. . . . 'le' me play wif it?'" It is a pretty child's
fire engine, they war, and the wanderer, his little form curv-
ing with pride, makes off with it down a dark side street.
In another, an Italian reads absorbed by his fruit-stand, and
the baby is "left face to face with the massed joys of the
world. . . . His lips moved. Presently into his head there
came a little plan. He sidled nearer, throwing swift and cun-
ning glances at the Italian. He strove to maintain his conventional manner, but the whole plot was written upon his countenance"—and this time the Italian retrieves the lemon from
the little fingers.

These are good; but the relation of tyranny and adoration,
in a third, between the baby and "A Dark Brown Dog" he
rules, is one of the perfectly imagined American stories. "A
child was standing on a street-corner. He leaned with one
shoulder against a high board fence and swayed the other to
and fro, the while kicking carelessly at the gravel. . . .
After a time, a little dark brown dog came trotting with an
intent air down the sidewalk. . . . In an apologetic manner
the dog came close, and the two had an interchange of
friendly pattings and waggles. The dog became more enthusiastic with each moment of the interview, until with his glee-

ful caperings he threatened to overturn the child. Where-
upon the child lifted his hand and struck the dog a blow
upon the head. This thing seemed to overpower and astonish
the little dark brown dog, and wounded him to the heart. He
sank down in despair at the child's feet." He follows the
baby home and enters the family, where he suffers Eastern
sufferings, until the child learns to protect him when he can.
"So the dog prospered. He developed a large bark, which
came wondrously from such a small rug of a dog. . . . The
scene of their companionship was a kingdom governed by
this terrible potentate, the child; but neither criticism nor rebellion ever lived for an instant in the heart of the one subject. Down in the mystic, hidden fields of his little dog-soul
bloomed flowers of love and fidelity and perfect faith." One
day the father comes home drunk, and the child dives under
the table. The dog "looked with interested eyes at his friend's
sudden dive. He interpreted it to mean: Joyous gambol. He
started to patter across the floor to join him. He was the picture of a little dark brown dog en route to a friend. The head
of the family saw him at this moment. He gave a huge howl
of joy, and knocked the dog down with a heavy coffee-pot.
The dog, yelling in supreme astonishment and fear, writhed
to his feet and ran for cover. The man kicked out with a pon-
derous foot," strikes him again with the pot, and flings him
"with great accuracy through the window. The soaring dog
created a surprise in the block. . . ." And it takes the child a
long time to reach the alley, "because his size compelled him
to go downstairs backward, one step at a time, and holding
with both hands to the step above."

No magazine printed this, so far as is known, during its
author's lifetime, though it was to look well enough in various collections of "Great Short Stories of the World" thirty
years later. Nobody would print anything. Warm weather,
however, was better than cold. When the Pendennis Club
building was sold, he moved with the proprietor to a house
on West 15th Street. Here his establishment was, in a friend's

phrase, "not a success"; so in June he stored three hundred *Maggies* at Mrs. Armstrong's and went out to Lakeview. All plans for *Maggie* had failed. Harper resisted Howells's urging that he re-issue it, Edward Marshall could not get his paper the *Press* to serialize it, dealers would not touch it even though Howells saw them personally. But a review appeared. "It is the voice of the slums," Hamlin Garland declared in the June *Arena*, unveiling the new author, ". . . graphic, terrible in its directness. . . . The diction is amazingly simple and fine for so young a writer. Some of the words illuminate like flashes of light. Mr. Crane is only twenty-one years of age, and yet he has met and grappled with the actualities of the street in almost unequalled grace and strength. . . . Mr. [Richard Harding] Davis will need to step forward right briskly or he may be overtaken by a man who impresses the reader with a sense of almost unlimited resource."

With th's language and Howells's ringing in his ears, Stephen Crane spent the summer slowly producing a fuller version (by no means the last) of *The Red Badge of Courage*, still apparently untitled. He worked in the garret, far into the night, playing football or games with his nieces in the afternoon, reading it to Ed as he went forward. "He told me," his brother remembered, "he did not want my literary opinion, only to know if I liked the story. That was pretty good from a kid fourteen years my junior. I liked the story." He got and took advice, however, from both Edward Marshall in the spring and Edmund now, Beer says, about his heavy adjectives and mushrooming adverbs; and the war novel in fact registers fully an advance first perceptible in *The Reluctant Voyagers* toward a tone, not indeed less emphatic, but more fluid.

It was evidently this summer that he got to Virginia— Fredericksburg and other towns—to talk with veterans, though testimony varies as to how far he profited from it, Fred Lawrence recalling that he was delighted and Edward Garnett that Crane told him he could get nothing out of them but one thing: "We just went there and did so and so."

When he came back to the city in the fall (1893), Crane was wearing rubber boots because he had no shoes, but he might have felt some satisfaction looking back on the first year of his majority. He had formulated a creed, rewritten his book in accordance with it, had it printed himself, and it had gained unqualified praise from precisely the men who counted for Crane. He had found, first as metaphor and then openly, his permanent subject, War, and was deep in a second or third draft of his second or third book. A miraculous skill in small stories had appeared. His eyes were a year wiser. His style was wholly his own and still developing. Not least, he had demonstrated, during his second year in New York, that he could endure for a while what was necessary for a while. His character would let his talent have its chance.

Now he stayed at various studios briefly until R. G. Vosburgh, an illustrator, and two other friends who were setting up a studio together invited him there. This was at 145 (and 143-7) East 23rd Street, in the rambling gloomy former home of the Art Students' League, a building endlessly remodeled, with three entrances, fantastic irregularities, mysterious corridors, its upper floors filled with hungry youth, its landlord himself an artist. Here he was for seven or eight months—and at this address, indeed, for most of the rest of his poverty in New York. At first it looked as if the Arena Company would issue *Maggie*, and there was even a plan of going to Europe, perhaps for the Bacheller Syndicate, but none of it came to anything. He worked on his novel. We are in Vosburgh's debt for a valuable, impersonal account, written later, of Crane in this studio where "He could contribute nothing to its maintenance, but he added very little to the expense, and the others were glad to have him." Three slept in a large double bed (they took turns in the middle) and the first man up was usually the best dressed for the day. Crane wrote at night, from midnight to four or five, and spent his afternoons and evenings studying the war and talking over his work. His friend is definite: "Every incident and phase of character in *The Red Badge* was discussed fully and completely before being incorporated in the story." This was not true of the short pieces Crane was writing also. Most of them were drafted in one night, then put away for two or three weeks, while something else was worked on. "When the story was taken out for revision it would be turned over to his friends for criticism, and Crane would argue with them. . . . He often accepted suggestions for changes, but it always seemed as though these changes were those he had already decided upon himself . . . he arrived at his own conclusions." He read football articles with delight, descanting on military analogies, and would stand for cold hours to watch a warship enter the harbor. Cigarettes wreathed, unsmoked, and on a precarious stove somebody made thoughtful coffee. In the worst weather the bed was warm all day.

There was a narcissism and the faith we know. "His daring phrases and short, intense descriptions pleased him greatly," said Vosburgh. "They were studied out with much care, and after they had been trimmed and turned and changed to the final form, he would repeat them aloud and dwell on them lovingly. Impressionism was his faith. Impressionism, he said, was truth, and no man could be great who was not an impressionist, for greatness consisted in knowing truth. He said that he did not expect to be great himself, but he hoped to get near the truth. Although he did not expect to be a great man, he often declared that he would be famous, and sometimes for hours in the intervals when he was not working he would sit writing his name—Stephen Crane—Stephen Crane—Stephen Crane—on the books, magazines, and loose sheets of paper about the studio."*

* So, no doubt, almost every artist.
"I was, after the fashion of humanity, in love with my name, . . . I
  wrote it everywhere." (Goethe)
  "What am I after all but a child, pleas'd with the sound of my own
    name? repeating it over and over:
  I stand apart to hear—it never tires me." (Whitman)

This was among friends. With anyone else he had a profound usual reticence as well as a fund of bluntness. A monocled Englishman named Bassett Holmes was shocked by the weird boy on the subject of Mrs. Humphry Ward, whom the man had met in London—*Robert Elsmere* was higgling rubbish. But it was only after weeks of occasional meetings and talk, when he went off to Ottawa, that he learned that the boy was a writer. *Maggie* had followed him in the mail, with a note: "This work is a mud-puddle, I am told on the best authority. Wade in and have a swim." Holmes like most other people was fascinated by Crane. He took him to the Holland House to dine, to Madison Square Garden to see Corbett fight (Mark Twain was in a box, so Holmes learned that Crane liked only one of his books—*Life on the Mississippi*); was taken in turn to the Bowery, and listened to disconcerting opinions against marriage ("a base trick on women, who were hunted animals anyhow") and the Episcopal Church and "sin." Crane, who liked to handle things, fondled the conservative's monocle, disliked champagne, and said not a word about the novel he was finishing.

Early in February 1894 it was finished, and he took it to a typist. Suddenly he started writing "lines"—he never called them poetry. It is not clear that he had ever written verse before, and it was not clear that these were verse.

> In the desert
> I saw a creature, naked, bestial,
> Who, squatting upon the ground,
> Held his heart in his hands,
> And ate of it.
> I said, "Is it good, friend?"
> "It is bitter—bitter," he answered;
> "But I like it
> Because it is bitter,
> And because it is my heart."

If they fell into verse, or rhymed, it was plainly accidental. He showed some first to Senger and Linson, then to the "Indians" he was living with, and the Indians howled. The sentiments seemed as queer as the form. He wrote half a dozen a day, taking them out of his head as he found them there; later he revised some, but not to make them more conventional. On the third day or so he wrote nine "lines" or poems, and next morning, tired of his friends' jeering, he put the whole roll in his pocket and went up to 105th Street to show them to Hamlin Garland. To Garland, amazed, impressed, and incredulous, they suggested French translations of Japanese verse or Emily Dickinson or the "savage philosophy" of Olive Schreiner— "and yet they were not imitative." Coming to the end, he asked if Crane had any more. "I have four or five up here," the poet pointed to his temple, "all in a little row." Garland, who wrote a sort of verse himself and had the alertness to the uncanny often found in earnest unimaginative men, told him to go ahead and write one. So Crane sat down at the desk and wrote:

> God fashioned the ship of the world carefully.
> With the infinite skill of an All-Master
> Made He the hull and the sails,
> Held He the rudder
> Ready for adjustment.
> Erect stood He, scanning His work proudly.
> Then—at fateful time—a wrong called,
> And God turned, heeding.
> Lo, the ship, at this opportunity, slipped slyly,
> Making cunning noiseless travel down the ways.
> So that, for ever rudderless, it went upon the
>   seas
> Going ridiculous voyages,
> Making quaint progress,
> Turning as with serious purpose

Before stupid winds.
And there were many in the sky
Who laughed at this thing.

It flowed from his pen, so Garland said, like oil, though Crane told him it had never been on paper before and its words had not been consciously arranged in his mind. But Garland could still not believe the poems original, till he consulted—as he did at once—"my most scholarly friends" and was unable to detect the source of their inspiration. His guesses, though, were better than he knew, or the last one was. Among the influences on these poems the strongest was evidently Miss Schreiner, not so much in her masterpiece (which Crane however had no doubt read and even Crane must have admired) as in her small book of allegories published in Boston the year before, *Dreams*.

Then Crane turned up at lunchtime with a larger roll in the pocket of his ulster—not "lines," but a tale. It still had no name. So far as one can judge, however, it was with minor variations the novel we know. Garland spoke long afterward of a first sentence that fairly took him captive, describing a vast army in camp on one side of a river, confronting with its thousands of eyes a similar monster on the opposite bank. This is indeed perfect Crane; he has the image in several stories, from which Garland probably misremembered it, or it is just a syncopation of the novel's actual, beautiful opening paragraph. "The cold passed reluctantly from the earth, and the retiring fogs revealed an army stretched out on the hills, resting. As the landscape changed from brown to green, the army awakened, and began to tremble with eagerness at the noise of rumors. It cast its eyes upon the roads. . . . A river, amber-tinted in the shadows of its banks, purled at the army's feet; and at night, when the stream had become of a sorrowful blackness, one could see across it the red, eyelike gleam of hostile campfires set in the low brows of distant hills."

The Red Badge of Courage is the story of the mind of a

new young Northern soldier as it accustoms itself to war during two days in and out of his first battle. There is a preliminary debate with himself as to whether he will run away or not. When his regiment is charged a second time, he does; and hides resentfully in a wood, where he meets a rotting corpse in a chapellike place. He joins the march of wounded away from the battle, and comes on a friend hurt horribly, a tall soldier, whom he accompanies to his extraordinary death. A tattered man has befriended him on the march; this man, whose plight is very bad, his mind wandering, the youth deserts in shame, on the question, reiterated, of *where* he is wounded. Then in a flight of the troops he is clubbed with a rifle when he tries to ask a panic-stricken man a question. An unseen man finally helps him back to his regiment. Since it has got scattered during the battle, his shame is unknown; he says he was shot and is cared for by a friend, a loud youth, who bandages his bloody head. He sleeps. Next morning he feels no remorse, and is full of "self-pride" even, when the loud youth reluctantly and shamefacedly has to ask for the return of a packet of papers given the youth, in fear, before the battle. "He had been possessed of much fear of his friend, for he saw how easily questionings could make holes in his feelings." Now "his heart grew more strong and stout. He had never been compelled to blush in such manner for his acts; he was an individual of extraordinary virtues." In the battle of this second day he is a war devil. During the charge, when the color-bearer is killed, he wrenches the flag free and bears it. In hard new fighting he and the loud youth are commended. The regiment takes a fence and a flag, and rests. "He had been to touch the great death, and found that, after all, it was but the great death. He was a man. . . . Scars faded as flowers.

"It rained. . . . Yet the youth smiled, for he saw that the world was a world for him, though many discovered it to be made of oaths and walking sticks. He had rid himself of the red sickness of battle. . . ."

Though the major circumstantial irony survives in this account, Crane's sympathy as he dances near and behind his hero's mind does not, nor does, of course, the imagination of fear and war in the book; together, these produced a thing that was new in literature. It is produced with awful simplicity. Henry Fleming, the meditative, panic-stricken farm boy, is the one character to whom we attend; the tall soldier Jim Conklin and the loud one Wilson are scarcely developed, and the others are mere vignettes, sometimes admirable. Critics have not failed to ask *how* it was produced. Garland, who read the manuscript with amazement, was the first: How did Crane know about war? and "in his succinct, self-derisive way, he candidly confessed that all his knowledge of battle had been gained on the football field! 'The psychology is the same. The opposite team is an enemy tribe!' "

Football was more instructive, probably, than Zola; and some other roots of *The Red Badge* may be mentioned. A relative of Crane's in Port Jervis had told him war stories, veterans had, his brother William was a student of the strategy of Gettysburg and Chancellorsville. The battle is obviously modeled on Chancellorsville (the encampment until April on the Rappahannock with sentries across the river friendly, the pontoon bridges of Chapter III, the character of the Southern attacks—all this he could find in the *Century*, for instance in 1886, xxxii 770 ff.). Henry Fleming, in a later story, is a veteran specifically of Chancellorsville. But the battle is not eagerly geographical and Lyndon Upson Pratt must be right in suggesting that Antietam has influenced it. The conception of the rout, the color-sergeant killed and the colors saved, the loss of more than half the regiment (end of Chapter XIV), and then its slow overnight reassembling, show the marks of Van Petten's Claverack tales of the 34th New York at Antietam. Crane's regiment is a (nonexistent) 304th New York; and this will appear, when we come to examine his practices with names, to have constituted a proof—he simply made the number imaginary by enlarging it, and reduced the regiment to inexperience in order to have Fleming *part* of an ordeal. He may, too, have glanced through an enormous, banal chronicle of 1887, *Corporal Si Klegg and His "Pard"* by Wilbur F. Hinman, though few of the correspondences rehearsed by H. T. Webster look anything but inevitable in two stories, however different, dealing with a recruit's experiences in the Civil War. If he saw the book—which must not be regarded as probable—the brindle cow that Henry Fleming's mother milks may be a memory of it, and another detail or so; but brindle cows occur in nature. More interesting is Crane's Civil War slang. This does not resemble Colonel Hinman's (which is mostly midwestern), but an investigator finds it authentic; evidently the young writer got it from veterans, modified by contemporary rural speech in New Jersey and New York State. Crane had an ear like a trap. Aesthetic influences are more interesting still. Tolstoy's is clearer, naturally, here than in *Maggie*, and as little accounts for most of the book. About Zola it is again hard to say. If Crane had seen Ambrose Bierce's recent, comparatively "realistic" images of the war, they may have encouraged him. This author's whole inhuman, slight way of working is unlike the felt, majestic, *humanly* dreadful art of Stephen Crane. Perhaps the book took its origin really from Mark Twain's young pilot in *Life on the Mississippi*, who hid during his maiden engagement and then was acclaimed.* Who knows how many origins a deep work has? An advance is perceptible at any rate from the fully developed style of Crane's first book to a style much better capable of registering degrees of variation of feeling. The grotesquerie as well is better knitted into narrative, and when let loose, in the

---

* Chapter xxvi. "I had often had a curiosity to know how a green hand might feel. . . . So to me his story was valuable—it filled a gap for me which all histories had left till that time empty. . . . 'All through that fight I was scared nearly to death . . . but you see, nobody knew that but me. Next day General Polk sent for me, and praised me. . . . I never said anything, I let it go at that. I judged it wasn't so, but it was not for me to contradict a general officer.'"

great ninth chapter, this gave him a scene decisively beyond anything he had done before, as well as one of the major scenes in American writing.

Thomas Beer's account, however, which Crane could hardly give, would have answered Garland's question best. How did Crane know about war? "There had been a boy who went confidently off to make war on a world and a city. He had been beaten to shelter and had lurched up a lane in darkness on the arm of some stranger. He had been praised for his daring while his novel, like a retreating army, lay in unsold heaps and the maker of images was sure of his own clay."

During lunch, Garland tried in vain to relate the thing to its author, sitting across from him eager over a steak: sallow, yellow-fingered, small and "ugly." But there was only part of the manuscript: "Where's the rest of it?" The rest was in hock, to the "typewriter," for fifteen dollars. Garland offered to lend the sum if Crane would bring the rest next day. He did, and Garland swung into action with editors. By February 24th, S. S. McClure was so enthusiastic about it for the ambitious popular monthly he had started the summer before, that Crane dropped a note to Holmes: "I have just sold another book and my friends think it is pretty good and that some publisher ought to bring it out when it has been shown as a serial. It is a war-story and the syndicate people think that several papers could use it." But this is a flight of optimism; McClure had not bought it, and for a long time no one would.

He had kept bringing "lines" up to Harlem, though fewer and fewer. One night at Daly's Theatre, where James A. Herne's *Shore Acres* had at last been drummed by Garland and others into a hit and Crane had been given the run of the house, he came into Herne's dressing-room to tell Garland that the last one had been "drawn off." This was called "The Reformer," a poem tremendous in its effect on Herne and Garland, which Crane later lost and couldn't remember. (Crane's carelessness was chronic; the whole manuscript of his poems was repeatedly lost and recovered.) It was months before he could write to Garland: "I have got the poetic spout so that I can turn it on or off. . . ."

Stephen Crane now received a commission. "The Men in the Storm," about a March blizzard, was written at his adviser's suggestion and then sent off by him with "An Ominous Baby" to the *Arena,* which accepted both. But Wilson's Syndicate wanted a lodging-house piece. "An Experiment in Misery" is one of Crane's finest etchings, and the small framework (later omitted) enclosing it as it appeared in the *Press* of April 22nd contained one of his most affecting iterations. "Two men stood regarding a tramp," it began. " 'I wonder how he feels,' said one, reflectively.* 'I suppose he is homeless, friendless, and has, at the most, only a few cents in his pocket. And if this is so, I wonder how he feels. . . .' " An unreprinted "Experiment in Luxury" which followed it shows Crane off his usual ground, admirable. To visit a wealthy college friend, evidently, he enters a great house in New York,—"an invader with a shamed face, a man who had come to steal certain colors, forms, impressions that were not his." They loafed upstairs, chatting. "He was beginning to see a vast wonder in it that they two lay sleepily chatting with no more apparent responsibility than rabbits, when certainly there were men, equally fine perhaps, who were being blackened and mashed in the churning life of the lower places. The eternal mystery of social conditions exasperated him at this time. He wondered if incomprehensible justice were the sister of open wrong." "He stretched his legs," however, "like a man in a garden, and he thought that he belonged to the garden. . . . There had been times in his life when little voices called to him continually from the darkness; he heard them now as an idle, half-smothered babble on the horizon's edge. . . ." Returning downstairs, the splendor of color

* I guess at this word, which stood "re   ely" in the damaged copy in the Newspaper Division of the New York Public Library until later someone tore it still further and destroyed it.

and form swarms upon him again: "it said to him a word which he believed he should despise, but instead he crouched. In the distance shone his enemy, the footman." Crane's hatred too for social matrons as a class was intense, and the mistress of this house was no exception. "Here was a savage, a barbarian, a spear woman of the Philistines . . . here was a type of Zulu chieftainess who scuffled and scrambled for place before the white altars of social excellence. . . . Woe and wild eyes followed like obedient sheep upon her trail." Of the rich, on the whole, he could not see "why they should be so persistently pitied," and he remarked that if this family were indeed "fairly good" this was because they were "not strongly induced toward the bypaths. . . . The more exalted forms of virtue have grown to be utterly impracticable." But the daughters the young man found "adorable" and observed: "Beauty requires . . . certain fair conditions."

His "lines," meanwhile, he had shown to John Barry of the *Forum*, who rushed them off to an experimental-poetry publisher in Boston, Copeland & Day. They seem to have been accepted at once and were to come out this year. The excited Barry also arranged a reading to the Uncut Leaves Society meeting at Sherry's on April 14th. Crane refusing to read himself—in fact, said the *Tribune*, the poet made the assertion that he "would rather die than do it"—or even to attend, Barry read them to a mystified, genteel audience while Crane waited on 23rd Street for Senger and Linson to come back and report. Next day's *Press* printed a review of *Maggie*, with long quotations, and on another page a prominent interview with Howells in which the country's chief critic declared himself: "Mary E. Wilkins, Mark Twain, Sarah Orne Jewett, Hamlin Garland, and George W. Cable are the most strikingly American writers we have today. There is another whom I have great hopes of. His name is Stephen Crane, and he is very young, but he promises splendid things. . . ." Probably the rising star had already flung off to Mrs. Munroe a letter quoted already which goes on: ". . . This winter fixes me firmly. We have proved too formidable for them, confound them. They used to call me 'that terrible, young radical,' but now they are beginning to hem and haw and smile—those very old coons who used to adopt a condescending air toward me. There is an irony in the present situation that I enjoy, devil take them for a parcel of old, cringing, conventionalized hens," and so on angrily, hugging himself, for pages.

This mood was rare, and it vanished sooner than the mood of one dispirited day in the winter when Garland had been assuring him that a man who could write *The Red Badge of Courage* could not be penniless forever. "I'd trade my entire future," Crane said soberly, "for twenty-three dollars in cash." McClure was delaying, McClure would delay for months. The young man's situation, though, was improving; some sales had given him a little independence. Wild for a place where he could write sometimes in peace, without the Indians on his neck, he invested in privacy rather than clothes. "I have not been up to see you," he wrote to Garland on April 18th from 111 West 33rd Street, "because of various strange conditions—notably, my toes are coming through one shoe. . . . I've moved now—live in a flat. People can come to see me now. They come in shoals, and say I am a great writer. Counting five that are sold, four that are unsold, and six that are mapped out, I have fifteen short stories in my head and out of it. They'll make a book." Somewhere among the last ten were three, not taken by the *Press* until October, in which Crane amused himself with his late studiomates: stories of the struggles of Wrinkles, Great Grief Warwickson, and Little Pennoyer to contribute to the *Monthly Amazement*, the *Established Magazine*, the *Gamin*, and so support life around a "fierce little stove" in the grimy fantastic old structure on East 23rd Street. Purple Sanderson "lived there too, but then he really ate," having "learned parts of the gas-fitter's trade before he came to be such a great artist. . . . Once Purple Sanderson went to his home in St. Lawrence county to enjoy some country air, and, incidentally, to explain his life failure to his people." Corinson, whom Grief hates ("His egotism is so tranquil") until he takes them to Thanksgiving dinner, is certainly Corwin Linson, but the others are unidentifiable unless little Penny, the butt of the rest, with "his tiny, tiny smile of courage," is Stephen Crane.

A fourth study of artist-life, much the best though not printed until after Crane's death, may belong here. Crane was wonderful at all periods about his manuscripts, whether submitting them to editors, losing them, or just putting them away and forgetting them; nothing could be more misleading than that handsome tabulation to Garland. "The Silver Pageant" represents an etherealization of the manner of the Sullivan County Sketches, and slight though it is gives us perhaps the earliest first-rate example of the fabulous element in Crane's prose. The subject is Gaunt, who "never heard anything close at hand" and "never saw anything excepting that which transpired across a mystic wide sea. The shadow of his thoughts was in his eyes, a little gray mist, and, when what you said to him had passed out of your mind, he asked: 'Wha-a-at?'. . . . All the younger men, moved by an instinct of faith, declared that he would one day be a great artist if he would only move faster than a pyramid . . . he was watching that silver pageant across a sea." The three in their den near his studio are of the opinion that somebody ought to set fire to him. "He's got pictures in his eyes," says Wrinkles. "Each new flounder by Gaunt made a stir in the den. It awed them, and they waited. At last one morning Gaunt burst into the room. They were all as dead men. 'I'm going to paint a picture.' The mist in his eyes was pierced by a gleam. His gestures were wild and extravagant. . . . If bronze statues had come and danced heavily before them, they could not have been thrilled further. Gaunt tried to tell them of something, but it became knotted in his throat, and then suddenly he dashed out again. Later they went earnestly over to Gaunt's studio. Perhaps he would tell them of what he saw across the sea. He lay dead upon the floor. There was a little gray mist before his eyes." Wrinkles, when they finally get back that night and he has put out the gas, decides: "There is a mistake. He couldn't have had pictures in his eyes."

The ambiguity of this exquisite thing ought to be remembered along with its author's mostly very flat, matter-of-fact remarks about his art. But Crane was not writing stories only, this spring. Garland went off to Chicago and a letter that followed him early in June, with its "we" and "all the struggling talent miss you," suggests that Crane either had some friend sharing his flat—as one would expect—or had moved in again with somebody else. "I am plodding along on the *Press* in a quiet and effective way. We now eat with charming regularity at least two times per day. I am content and am writing another novel which is a bird. . . . I wrote a Decoration Day thing for the *Press* which aroused them to enthusiasm. They said in about a minute, though, that I was firing over the heads of the soldiers. . . ."

A little mystery attaches to this novel. One naturally takes it to be the companion-piece to *Maggie* begun over a year earlier at the Pendennis Club, laid aside presumably for *The Red Badge of Courage*—though a draft may have been finished —and not yet called *George's Mother*. One also naturally takes it to be the same novel mentioned to Garland six months later, in November, as done: "I have just completed a New York book that leaves *Maggie* at the post. It is my best thing. Since you are not here, I am going to see if Mr. Howells will not read it." This almost certainly was *George's Mother*, not published until 1896 but known to Howells by that name in his "Appreciation" of *Maggie* dated 1895; in *Current Literature's* report of July 1895, it is called "A Woman Without Weapons"—one of Crane's several manuscripts then in publishers' hands, "a story of New York life, like *Maggie*, but its scenes are laid on the borderland of the slums."

All this seems reasonable enough, and encounters no difficulty either from another puzzle about the publication of *George's Mother*, which we will come to in due time, or from *The Third Violet*, which was written late in 1895.* But as of the novel Crane was working on in May, it is very remarkable that an anonymous informant of Thomas Beer (who did not use the information) dates just now the beginning of a book not mentioned yet. The informant was obviously James Huneker. One night in April or May of 1894 he ran into Stephen Crane and they were on their way to the Everett House when a kid came up to them in Broadway, apparently begging. Huneker gave him a quarter but then as he tagged along saw that he was really soliciting. Crane, "damned innocent about everything except women," did not understand till they emerged into the glare of the hotel-front and could see the boy was painted, with big violet eyes like a Rossetti angel. Huneker thought his friend would vomit. Shortly, Crane became interested, took the boy in with them and fed him; his name was something like Coolan and he had, of course, a story; Crane quizzed him carefully. Told he was diseased and wanted to be treated, Crane rang up Irving Bacheller and borrowed fifty dollars to give him. He now began a novel about a boy prostitute. Huneker made him read *A Rebours*, which he thought stilted. His book started in a railway station, with a country boy running off to New York—a scene that in Huneker's view Crane never surpassed. It was going to be called "Flowers of Asphalt" and was to be "longer than anything he had done." But Hamlin Garland, when Crane read him some of it, was horrified and begged him to stop. Whether he ever finished it Huneker didn't know. The manuscript has not been traced.

This is not the best attested account in the world, nor the

* Mr. Linson, in a letter, is certain that this was written in 1894, though he admits that Crane made no mention of it then; but this is probably owing to a confusion between the sketches of artist life already mentioned and the second half of *The Third Violet*, which has some of the same characters. See below, p. 122.

pleasantest, but let us consider it on its merits. It is very circumstantial, and the theme of the projected novel was one to absorb Crane, being precisely the theme of *Maggie* and *George's Mother* (and even, up to a point, of *The Red Badge of Courage*): the movement in youth from innocence to experience, seen as a degradation. Crane's passion for assisting outcasts, and precisely for rescuing "fallen" persons, will seem to strengthen as we go on—it was one of the dominant passions of his life. The coincidence of Huneker's dating with Crane's letter to Garland (which Huneker could not have known) is impressive. Beer had no opinion of Huneker's veracity, but he quotes him freely enough upon other subjects, and this was just the sort of information that Beer did not desire. Huneker indeed, as Beer quotes him (cf. page 234 below), was a determined enemy of the scandal that washed about Crane in later years; it is hard to see his inventing this incident. On the other hand, the admirable but naive and extremely credulous Garland was one of the few men close to Crane to credit the scandal. Their relation deteriorated, moreover, on both sides, in a way not easy to understand even as a consequence of this credulity (in Garland's account, or his various accounts rather, of the friendship), but not difficult to understand as a consequence of the unreported shock to the older man of "Flowers of Asphalt" and the resentful acceptance of his verdict by the younger.* Crane's title, finally, is as characteristic as his opinion of Huysmans and the other details, notably (recalling Syracuse) the railway station. If we can ever hope to depend upon anything, we had better accept Huneker's account as

---

* The rare meetings of the two hereafter must await their turn, but one posthumous account may be anticipated. In the paragraphs of critical estimate Garland wrote shortly after Crane's death, there is scarcely a sentence but contains some qualification. And on the other side: "He spoke of you often," Senger wrote to Garland long afterward, "and always with a sense of blame for himself lest you should think him ungrateful. He was never that"—but this is perhaps the state of mind of a man who is unable through old obligation to acknowledge, even to himself, present resentment.

genuine.* It remains to inquire when and why Crane abandoned the novel. But he and Garland were not to meet again for more than a year and we shall come on these questions then. In the spring of 1894 we must see him, apparently, attacking this most unorthodox, pathetic subject, with the rapidity usual to his first drafts and an eagerness reflected by "which is a bird."

Crane's restlessness was growing. One of his sketches for the *Press* in May enjoys a tramp named Billy, "resolved to eat if it cost a life," who rides the rails compulsively to Omaha (after a certain point the trip is "incoherent, like the detailed accounts of great battles") and starts at once compulsively back. Another, of July, takes a bank-clerk Mr. Binks with his family to the country for a day, or a nightmare. But after inconceivable, warlike exertions Mr. and Mrs. Binks reach the top of a hill to watch the sunset: "Slowly there went on the mystic closing of the day . . . the green tints became blue. A faint suggestion of yellow replaced the crimson. The sun was dead." They listen, then, to the trees' song, and as his wife links arms with him Mr. Binks makes a comment. "I wonder why," he says; "I wonder why the dickens it—why it—why——" Meanwhile the author had gone away himself, though only to Scranton where he was to write, Linson to illustrate, an article on coal mines for McClure's energetic monthly, which printed it in August. Besides the caves and ghouls it did not fail to mention, Crane noted the

---

* Crane had not at this date (*pace* Beer) met Irving Bacheller, so someone else must have lent the fifty dollars—a sum, by the way that Crane was as fond of giving outcasts later on as, just now, one would have expected him to find it hard to get. When he and Huneker met is unknown; they were friendly in 1896 and 1898. A divergent report whereby Huneker is said to have placed the incident in October 1898 seems unreliable, Crane being then in Havana. He was in New York for six weeks in November-December, but a date so late would render thoroughly implausible two of the affair's striking aspects: (1) the "longer than anything he had done" (i.e., a full-length novel)—since he had then finished *Active Service;* (2) his acceptance of anybody's verdict. Also Crane watched life: if one can imagine him at 22 ignorant of commercial male homosexuality, at 27 it appears incredible.

owners' voracity of human and animal exploitation on his way to a more general observation, and described the tiny gray slate-pickers who have always before them "the hope of one day getting to be door-boys down in the mines; and, later, mule-boys; and yet later, laborers and helpers. Finally, when they have grown to be great big men, they may become miners, real miners, and go down to get 'squeezed,' or perhaps escape to a shattered old man's estate with a mere 'miner's asthma.' They are very ambitious. Meanwhile they live in a place of infernal dins . . . uncowed." The self-possession of the mules he admired, and spoke of their "fantastic joy" when after years down pit they find themselves restored to light and air. Then these concerns vanish. "The meaning of it all," he blazed, "is in the deep bass rattle of a blast. . . . It is war. It is the most savage part of all in the endless battle between man and nature. These miners are grimly in the van. . . . Man is in the implacable grasp of nature. It has only to tighten slightly, and he is crushed like a bug. His loudest shriek of agony would be as impotent as his final moan to bring help from that fair land that lies, like Heaven, over his head."

Naturalism? His attribution of malevolence to Nature, his concept of a struggle active on both sides (however unequal), are as much at variance with later Naturalist doctrine as the style of his last sentence is unlike Naturalist style. Something else Crane has that the Naturalists have not—humor. "If the red-haired young man with the keen brain and the freckles will meet the mop-headed young gentleman in the mud-colored sweater by moonlight and alone he will hear something greatly to his disadvantage." Most of the *Pike County Puzzle* clowning has faded now, but this notice suggests the gaiety with which it must have been produced—a parody facsimile of a country newspaper, celebrating a camping trip in Pennsylvania late in the summer with a crowd of young people and chaperons. The four pages of its solitary issue (Camp Interlaken, August 28, 1894) seem to have been written mostly by Crane and Louis Senger, who has a lengthy dialogue on the last page together with an ad by "Stephen Crane, Drink Mixer." In a playlet Crane amused himself with his own style. "Scene: Sunset Rock.— The gray rocks and green moss are in the shadows from the crimson and gold death of the sun over behind Pop Curry's barn. . . ." The tenor obviously answered as well as wrote his letter "*To the Editor*: What can I do with my voice?" "In the spring, Stephen, you can plough with it, but after corn ripens you will have to seek employment in the blue-stone works. We have seen voices like yours used very effectively as cider-presses." An editorial is pleasing: "Having in this issue proven ourselves to be earnest, firm and intolerable representatives of the most advanced and exasperating type of rural journalism, we here take occasion to felicitate the universe upon our being present."

Three days after this date, he was in Albany giving two little boys money to have their long curls cut and explaining to his hostess his opinion of *Little Lord Fauntleroy*, according to Beer, who also says it was this summer, at Port Jervis, that Crane worked out two papers on a social theory and slum-charities that Elbert Hubbard bought for *The Philistine* and lost on a train. But *The Philistine* was not to begin for another year, and it is uncertain when Crane first met the busy, banal former soap salesman who entered Harvard at 36, in January 1893, for a little. Beer summarizes the theory from a letter of Hubbard's: old, dull ladies sat about on porches, omnipotent. . . . all Americans were educated by female schoolteachers, dull, limited women, who taught them to cringe . . . there should be more male teachers. If Crane did not share the general misogyny which would be common among American intellectuals of a later generation, we have seen his hatred, as a man well-born but poor, for social pretension in matrons. He understood the main force of his decade in American society,—"The Iron Maiden" of American fiction; it is not the main force of later decades simply because as we lose our veneration for age the women who wield power can be younger. In a letter from Port Jervis a few months later, about December 20th, he described one of these divinities. "There is a feminine mule up here who has roused all the bloodthirst in me and I don't know where it will end. She has no more brain than a pig and all she does is to sit in her kitchen and grunt. But every when [*sic*] she grunts something dies howling. It may be a girl's reputation or a political party or the Baptist Church but it stops in its tracks and dies. Sunday I took a 13 yr. old child out driving in a buggy. Monday this mule addresses me in front of the barber's and says, 'You was drivin' Frances out yesterday' and grunted. At once all present knew that Frances and I should be hanged on twin gallows for red sins. No man is strong enough to attack this mummy because she is a nice woman. She looks like a dried bean and she has no sense, but she is a nice woman. Right now she is aiming all her artillery at Cornelia's new hat. I have been deprived by heaven of any knowledge of hats but it seems to be a very kindly hat with some blue flowers on one side and a ribbon on the other. But we rustle in terror because this maggot goes to and fro grunting about it. If this woman lived in Hester Street some son or brother of a hat would go bulging up to her and say 'Ah, wot deh hell!' and she would have no teeth any more, right there. She is just like those hunks of women who squat on porches of hotels in summer and wherever their eye lights there blood rises. Now, my friend, there is a big joke in all this. This lady in her righteousness is just the grave of a stale lust and every boy in town knows it. She accepted ruin at the hands of a farmer when we were all 10 or 11. But she is a nice woman and all her views of all things belong on the tables of Moses. No man has power to contradict her. We are all cowards anyhow." It was a sketch for Martha Goodwin in *The Monster*.

Other moral forces had been glaring at him, with as little effect. Copeland & Day now had cold feet about *The Black*

Riders, so that Crane had to write from Hartwood, September 9: "We disagree on a multitude of points. In the first place, I should absolutely refuse to have my poems printed without many of those which you just as absolutely mark 'No.' It seems to me that you cut all the ethical sense out of the book. All the anarchy, perhaps. It is the anarchy which I particularly insist upon." He thought some poems unworthy of print and enclosed them, but he insisted that all the poems about God (which they had condemned) be included in the book, and he further refused to write any more, as they wanted: "It is utterly impossible to me."

In the face of McClure's continued, exasperating delay with the war novel, this self-possession was formidable. The anarchist put on white flannels to play tennis and croquet in Port Jervis, went shooting with Will, and romped with his nieces around the corners of the house—they were crooks and he a red-headed policeman after them. "On his return in October," says Frederick Gordon, who was living in the old Art Students' League building, "he took a little room near my place, and began to hunt for a job. Toward the end of a black, cold rainy day he came in to see me, soaking wet, shivering and coughing—utterly done up. He had been down to see [Edward] Marshall, who had refused to take him on the World staff, because he believed the hectic newspaper work would ruin his genius for imaginative writing, but offered to buy special articles from him. Steve hadn't a nickel for carfare—too proud to mention it to Marshall—so he tramped in the cold downpour from the World building to 23rd Street—no overcoat, and literally on his uppers. He was ripe for pneumonia. I got him into an extra bed I had, and in a week he was up, nearly as good as new. My shop was so big that he might just as well stay, and so he finished the Red Badge there, and wrote a lot of other things. . . ."

By the month's end matters were looking up. On October 28th the *Press* printed, besides his three stories of studio life, one yearning westward, about an ex-Nevadan sheriff, and he had an interview with Howells in the *Times*. A week later he pushed through election night crowds, with Gordon, taking mental photographs for a *World* story next morning. The political situation was one that interested some people. After Tammany's landslide of 1892, equal nearly to Cleveland's, such serious frauds had turned up the following year that in April 1894 the State Senate had sent the Lexow Committee to investigate; among other things they discovered that a police captaincy was expensive—one cost $15,000; Croker stayed in England, delicately, throughout, and on November 6th Tammany was defeated at the polls. What interested the quiet young reporter was a crowd before the Pulitzer Building that burst out into a roar "like some enormous acoustic football," the police like chips before a torrent.

"So much of my row with the world has to be silence and endurance" (he wrote to Garland in mid-November) that he was still largely underground; but he was fast coming up. He was excited, briefly, about the just-completed draft of his companion-piece to *Maggie*, mentioned above. Difficulties over *The Black Riders* were ending; he had not compromised; and Fred Gordon was to make the cover design, using the orchid ("with its strange habits, extraordinary forms and curious properties" as Gordon wrote to the publisher) for the floral motive, an idea Crane liked. And he had tired of waiting for McClure. "McClure was a beast about the war story. . . ."

He took the manuscript to Irving Bacheller, told him that Howells and Garland had liked it, and asked for a frank opinion. Bacheller, a blond cheerful young man running a new syndicate, had heard of Crane from Marshall, though he now first saw the "pale slim youth, with blue-gray eyes, a rather dark skin," his head "picturesque and beautiful in its shape and poise." He took the soiled, handwritten manuscript home that night, when he and his wife read it aloud to each other by turns, and next morning he accepted it, to be cut to some 18,000 words for serialization, at ninety dollars. The length was unusual but Bacheller was willing to experiment. *The Red Badge of Courage* ran in the *Philadelphia Press* from December 3rd to 8th, 1894, and then this whole version was got into three pages of the New York *Press* on December 9th.* On the bitter Sunday morning it appeared in New York, Curtis Brown of the *Press* had gone to his office for mail and when he came out met Crane on the wind-swept corner "without an overcoat, but his face, thin and white, lit up when he saw me. He threw his arms around me and said 'Oh, *do* you think it was good?' Fortunately I could guess what he meant, and said 'It's great.' 'God bless you,' said he, and hurried off to anywhere in the sleet." The story affected the staff in Philadelphia so strongly that Talcott Williams and James Duffy begged Bacheller to bring the author down, and its success affected Bacheller so strongly that he sent Crane west to write sketches wherever he liked about whatever he liked, so long as he wound up in Mexico. The young novelist was "amazed" to hear what was said to him when they crowded round in Philadelphia—editors, reporters, proof-readers, compositors—to shake his hand.

A word about this version. In condensation from 50,000 words to 18,000, and twenty-four chapters to sixteen, much even of the essential story disappeared: the youth's parting with his mother from Chapter I, continual speculation, the

* Also, probably, in 200 small city dailies, 250 weekly papers, and as patent insides in some 300–350 more. A curious letter of 1947 from Wright A. Patterson, who was handling the Bacheller material for the Kellogg Newspaper Company in 1894, states that it took him a month to capitalize, punctuate, and paragraph the wholly undivided manuscript that came down to Philadelphia from New York. Crane was a newspaperman; this cannot have been his copy, even done in haste. But it is not likely, either, to have been the work of a Bacheller copyist, and what happened to the famous earlier typed copy (unless McClure kept it) is another minor mystery. None of the innumerable persons who claim to have once had in their possession a manuscript of *Maggie* or of *The Red Badge* has ever produced one. Two pages of the first draft of the war novel are said to be among Cora Crane's papers.

crucial irresolution of XI, and the final chapter—indeed all the last three chapters—are gone; and practically everything else that could be cut away: description, dialogue, narrative.* Nevertheless it seems probable that Crane did the cutting. The great ninth chapter, of the death—the story's center—is all but intact. Most of the magnificent details are preserved, such as "He lagged, with tragic glances at the sky" (in III) and the famous line "The red sun was pasted in the sky like a wafer" —though the first gains emphasis by ending a chapter and the second loses by being run on into what is in the original Chapter X (as well as by a "fierce" before "wafer" that Crane later excised). The new jointing, when necessary, is done with skill, and the story holds astonishingly well. Only it is a different story, much more compact, rapid, external, less brooding and powerful. It is also less realistic, the editors normalizing Crane's dialect until they tired of the job midway, and there were some brilliant misprints or sophistications, the tattered man being made to ask, "Were you hit, old boy?" instead of "Where yeh hit, ol' boy?"—the whole point being the assumption that of course he *was* hit.

Bacheller wanted Crane to leave before Christmas, but he lingered at least until January 10th (1895) when he sent Copeland & Day a *Black Riders* dedication: "To Hamlin Garland." Before departing he also took two of his newspaper stories to Appleton's to see whether they would be interested in doing a book. Ripley Hitchcock, impressed, asked whether he had not got something longer. He mentioned the war story hesitatingly, promised to send it, and did, on December 18th, in "its syndicate form—that is to say, much smaller and to my mind much worse than its original form" (which he had already sent or shortly did send). By February Hitchcock had offered terms, and—with incomparable judgment—only wanted the novel's title changed. The letter reached Crane in Lincoln, Nebraska, and he agreed to the terms, but "I shall

* The "loud" youth Wilson loses his dialogue in II and the story of his packet (III, XV), though he is one of the three chief characters.

have to reflect upon the title." In Galveston on March 8th, he told Hitchcock that he had sent the manuscript from New Orleans (it had been posted to him there—his traveling delayed the book till autumn), with many small corrections. Then he took up the question of the title, drily: "As to the name I am unable to see what to do with it unless the word 'Red' is cut out perhaps. That would shorten it."

West

Crane's western journey in the first half of 1895 was the happiest time perhaps he was to know—an idyl. With all his special capacity for disillusion, the West did not disappoint him. "To Hamlin Garland of the great honest West," he inscribed a book next year, "from Stephen Crane of the false East." Such was the view with which he went, and this was what he thought he found. The passion felt by most American boys, until the West was improved, had been inflamed in this one by the revolver he had had since a lost Wyoming cowboy gave it to him on the Jersey shore, by Frederic Remington's pictures, by the stories of Garland and John Hilliard and a cowboy artist of 23rd Street who went crazy and died. It had been a passion exceptional anyway. Crane needed danger. Privation was interesting and he had enjoyed a good deal of this; but danger was something else, which after imagining it for a masterpiece he needed to feel, and to see what he would do with it. Irving Bacheller, on their way down to Philadelphia, was struck with his excitement over Kipling's ballads, particularly the end of "The Young British Soldier":

When you're wounded and left on Afghanistan's plains,
And the women come out to cut up what remains,

  Jest roll to your rifle and blow out your brains
   An' go to your Gawd like a soldier.

But there were no wars going—the West was as near as Crane might come.

Of course it was a characteristic idyl, beginning with severe dyspepsia, which recurred, and bogging down repeatedly in Crane's generosity or his wonderful incompetence as a traveler. But his health would never be so good again and the moment of this jaunt was altogether lucky. For the first time in his life he was not very hard up for money. He was utterly on his own, and not pining, having got over all early loves. In two and a half years' work since his majority he had written *Maggie, George's Mother, The Red Badge of Courage,* a book of poems, and a set of stories, and he had a new long novel started. Critics had been amazed by the first and readers by an abridgement of the third; at twenty-three, matters were under way, two books were about to appear, and Crane might have felt that he could relax—not that he did. At the same time, no book of his had yet been properly published, he was *not* famous, not bitter nor a laughingstock; these were advantages he would feel very quickly in retrospect. Also he did not during the trip write much, except dispatches, and so was free for a while from anxiety and labor. He was absorbing. The consequence of these six months to his art can barely be measured. He had made astonishing, beautiful stories—a few—but none yet with the manly balance of the mature work to come. D. H. Lawrence, who knew our West better than most of us do, has in his *Studies in Classic American Literature* two remarks that oddly illuminate opposed sides of Crane's mature work. "The essential American soul," he says, "is hard, isolate, stoic, and a killer." And: "There are terrible spirits, ghosts, in the air of America." Not until "The Blue Hotel" will these polar senses blow together; but both this balance, and another kind of human balance that made possible "The Open Boat," Crane moved toward through a development in his thought that occurred in the West. Human nature he found to be something he had hitherto only suspected it was, and the discovery changed his thought.

Crane set out, Beer tells us, with three desires. He wanted to see the Mississippi and watch a cowboy ride and be in a blizzard of the plains. It was a strength that he generally knew what he wanted. "I always want to be unmistakable," he wrote from Lincoln, Nebraska, on February 12th to a college friend who calmly quoted the letter eighteen months later in an interesting article on Stephen Crane for the *Monthly Illustrator*. (By unmistakable he meant not "unlike anyone else" but "incapable of being misunderstood," as we learn from a letter to Hilliard: "My chieftest desire was to write plainly and unmistakably, so that all men (and some women) might read and understand.") "As far as myself and my own meagre success are concerned," he now told Clarence Peaslee, "I began the war with no talent but an ardent admiration and desire. I had to build up. I always want to be unmistakable. That to my mind is good writing. There is a great deal of labour connected with literature. . . ." And next day he wanted to halt a fight in a saloon, where a big man was pounding a smaller one. "But thus I offended a local custom. These men fought each other every night. Their friends expected it and I was a damned nuisance with my Eastern scruples and all that. So first everybody cursed me fully and then they took me off to a judge who told me that I was an imbecile and let me go; it was very saddening." Crane with his vision of justice was no brawler. When a 23rd Street tough named Eddie Mayhew, a real bar-fighter, swore once to "get" him over something, Walter Dunckel remembers that he stayed away.

Nebraska was suffering agony from a drought of the previous July. Visitors, Crane wrote, "have trod lightly in the streets of Omaha to keep from crushing the bodies of babes" —the sort of hyperbole that rings ludicrous or insincere in him to those who, gifted with weak emotions, would never themselves dream of interfering in an unequal fight at the risk of a beating. He sought out Governor Holcomb, who was optimistic and vague, then he moved west into the heart of the stricken territory and rode forty-five miles through the midwinter prairies to talk with farmers, whom he thought "strong, fine, sturdy men, not bended like the Eastern farmer, but erect and agile . . . a fearless folk, completely American." "How did you get along?" he wanted to know. "Don't git along, stranger." From Eddysville in Dawson County with the temperature at eighteen below, a blizzard raging through the gaunt hamlet, Crane sent back East a long story of the failure from relief from "intrigues and scufflings" at Lincoln. The farmers, though, kept their "faith in the ultimate victory of the land and their industry. . . . In the mean time they depend upon their endurance, their capacity to help each other, and their steadfast and unyielding courage." This sentiment of respect is almost new in Crane.

An uncertainty in our chronology henceforward may be illustrated by the circumstance, which would be surprising of anyone else, that on the date of this storm-dispatch, February 20th, he was writing to his publisher from New Orleans and had already composed a whimsical dispatch dated March 1st from Hot Springs. Never mind; after crossing the Mississippi at St. Louis, he was several weeks in Nebraska and then went south, charmed with the heterogeneous resort throng. "No man need feel strange here. He may assure himself that there are men of his kind present. If, however, he is mistaken and there are no men of his kind in Hot Springs he can conclude that he is a natural phenomenon and doomed to the curiosity of all peoples." Even the millionaires seemed "peculiarly subdued and home-loving" in this mecca where "man becomes a creature of three conditions. He is about to take a bath—he is taking a bath—he has taken a bath." He then related an Indian legend about the origin of the baths. The

Kanagawas "handily brained" other savages until a terrible
scourge came, then they "crawled piteously on the pine needles
and called in beseeching voices toward the yellow sunset"; the
Spirit of the Wild, hearing, brought vapors and the pool
turned hot. "The wise men debated. At last, a courageous and
inquisitive red man bathed. He liked it; others bathed. The
scourge fled."

Finally came a saloon legend about the "traveller from the
hat firm in Ogallala, Neb." and the "youthful stranger with
the blonde and innocent hair" which closed with a characteristic joke: "In the back room of the saloon the man with the
ruffled beard was silently picking hieroglyphics out of his
whiskers." Not five funerals here could ruin Crane's spirits.
"It rained," he wrote to somebody, "funerals on me. I was
soaked with lamentations and the hope of widows." New Orleans, except for such matters as "a little terse quarrel of
peasants" in the first act of *La Juive*, he liked less; and, the
rich food giving him dyspepsia again, he stayed only long
enough to run into a "most intolerable duffer" from Akron,
Ohio. Once Lucius Button had taken Crane to call at a house
in 34th Street when a Miss Crouse from Akron was there, so
he brought the conversation round to Miss Crouse—as he
did *not* tell Button when he was inspired to write from San
Antonio, March 12th, describing the duffer. He had "fingers
like lightning rods" pointed continually at citizens: " 'Look
at that fellow!' People in New Orleans don't like that sort of
thing, you know." Invited to visit the duffer, "I modestly replied that while I appreciated his generosity and his courage, I had to die early in the spring . . . but I had an open
date in 1997 and would be happy to see him in hell upon that
occasion. Well, at any rate, I lie, for I was considerate of
him, treated him well at times, and was careful of his childish innocence. . . . Tell Tommie Parson that this is a straight
tip upon the quality of his rivals. I am off to Mexico tonight."

But the young man had sunk into San Antonio, which he
loved from the Alamo monument to the dives, sombreros,

and veils, and he loved Texas altogether. At some point he loafed westward a thousand miles to ride a mule in the Painted Desert of Arizona, listen with mad excitement to the music of the Apache scalp-dance, and collect some silver spurs from a ranch near the Nevada border; but weeks slipped by dispatchless in San Antonio while he looked and listened. His own kind of experience followed him about. The hair of the fellow next him in a saloon trying to draw a revolver—the bartender threw a seidel across—was red. He pulled a little girl out of the river, and emptied his pocket to feed and start back home a lad of sixteen from Chicago who had invested a birthday gift of sixty dollars in a cowboy career and was sobbing on the Alamo Plaza penniless. An uncle met the lad in St. Louis and the money returned by telegraph. "Dear Deadeye Dick: Thanks for sending back my money so fast. The hotel trun me out, as my friends of the Bowery say and I was living in the Mex diggings with a push of sheep men till my boss in New York wired me money. Now, old man, take some advice from a tough jay from back East. You say your family is all right and nobody bothers you. Well, it struck me that you are too young a kid and too handsome to be free and easy around where a lot of bad boys and girls will take your pennies. So better stay home and grow a mustache before you rush out into the red universe any more. Yours sincerely, Stephen Crane." Remarkably gentle and considerate always with younger people, Crane, but a special anxiety in "handsome" suggests the author of "Flowers of Asphalt"; perhaps he had some of the draft of this novel with him.

Ultimately he took the slow train south. If Crane had been sentimental in San Antonio—all his adolescence, Beer says, there frothed to a head—no trace of sentimentality survives in the stories that would eventually form about certain of his western experiences. In part, of course, this is due to the difference between his art, on the one side, and his dispatches and letters on the other. Sentimentality is an excess. In

Maggie a policeman is just mentioned as beating the "soft noses of the responsible horses." The first of Crane's Mexican dispatches printed (sent—maybe—on May 13th) is moving and humorous, but characteristically excessive. "When a burdened donkey falls down a half dozen Indians gather round it and brace themselves. Then they take clubs and hammer the everlasting daylight out of the donkey. They also swear in Mexican. Mexican is a very capable language for the purposes of profanity. A good swearer here can bring rain in 30 minutes. It is a great thing to hear the thump, thump, of the clubs and the howling of the natives and to see the little legs of the donkey quiver and to see him roll his eyes. . . ." Sarcasm is trying openly to push here what irony levers in silence. But the disappearance of sentimentality was due essentially to a change of mind, in which two experiences appear to be central.

The ride from San Antonio to Mexico City impressed Crane very deeply. He had known all his life Nature that delighted and moved and in darkness frightened, but not, until now, Nature that compelled while standing apart. His dispatch is dramatized and begins amusingly with a Chicago capitalist and a Boston archeologist making the trip (the archeologist had gone to school with some Cubans and learnt to swear in Spanish—an odd disguise). Changing money at two for one, the pair "bid good-bye to their portraits of the national bird with exultant smiles." But as sand increases south of Laredo, as cactus "began to grow with a greater courage," as the churches, "small and meek" structures at first, grow more impressive, as color becomes "volcanic," the character of the dispatches changes. At Atotonilco, "a baby, brown as a water-jar and of the shape of an alderman, paraded the bank in utter indifference or ignorance or defiance"—and we pause suddenly on a chief theme of Crane's middle thought. This baby wore an aspect of Nature, not of man. Later this year, when two friends made him read some of the critical work of Henry James, which he liked: "What, though, does the man mean by disinterested contemplation? It won't wash. If you care enough about a thing to study it, you are interested and have stopped being disinterested. That's so, is it not? Well, Q.E.D. It clamours in my skull that there is no such thing as disinterested contemplation except that empty as a beerpail look that a babe turns on you and shrivels you to grass with. Does anybody know how a child thinks? The horrible thing about a kid is that it makes no excuses, none at all. They are much like breakers on a beach. They do something and that is all there is in it." Nature, Crane decided, was not interested in man, even as an enemy. At night the train began its great climb, and then after restless hours there was Nevado de Toluca: 15,000 feet, sun-smitten with gold. It appeared that this peak "was staring with a high, serene, eternal glance into the East at the approach of the endless suns. And no one feels like talking in the presence of these mountains that stand like gods on the world, for fear that they might hear."

The other experience was a fear such as Crane had had no occasion to feel before. As Beer tells it, Crane and his guide Miguel Itorbide were staying over night in a village when a well-known bandit named Ramon Colorado arrived with his followers, learned of the American's presence, and decided to rob him. But some whores turning up on their way to the capital distracted Colorado briefly, so that Crane and the guide were able to creep out of their hut and get away across the plain on their horses, with the gang half a mile behind, until they came on a troop of the *rurales*. Diaz' regime had tolerances: the lieutenant, Beer says, just "sat cursing Colorado while the bandit tried to apologize for having annoyed a friend of the government. This business was delicious to Crane." But "Horses—One Dash" written later this year followed actuality closely, and from Richardson's emotions in the sardonic story we learn something of its author's. Wakened by sounds of a guitar and quarreling in the adjoining room, Richardson hears one voice determined to "ask this

American beast for his beautiful pistol and spurs and money and saddle" and, if he will not give them up, to kill him. He "felt the skin draw tight around his mouth, and his knee-joints turned to bread. He slowly came to a sitting posture, glaring at the motionless blanket at the far end of the room. This stiff and mechanical movement, accomplished entirely by the muscles of the wrist, must have looked like the rising of a corpse in the wan moonlight." The "emotions of Richardson's terror destroyed that slow and careful process of thought by means of which he understood Mexican"; but there he sits, straight and still, until a fat Mexican bursts in with a torch, followed by others even drunker, and halts. They contemplate each other. Not even an insult can make the American move. "He was staring at the fat Mexican with a strange fixedness of gaze, not fearful, not dauntless, not anything that could be interpreted; he simply stared." The Mexicans are disconcerted, posing and swaying: Is this American a great fighter, or perhaps an idiot? "To Richardson, whose nerves were tingling and twitching like live wires, and whose heart jolted inside him, this pause was a long horror; and for these men who could so frighten him there began to swell in him a fierce hatred. . . ." But he sits on like stone, his fingers clenched rigidly on the revolver handle under his blanket, and watches impassive while they beat up his guide, continually turning their eyes to see if they are to succeed in making him begin an action. Then the girls arrive and the Mexicans withdraw for an orgy. After a very dignified delay, Richardson and José "sneaked toward the door. The man who said that spurs jingled was insane. Spurs have a mellow clash—clash—clash." The American's little horse whinnies an enthusiastic welcome. At this point the fundamental relation in the story starts: "Upon the threshold of safety he was being betrayed by his horse, his friend. He felt the same hate for the horse that he would have felt for a dragon." Fumbling at the girth with his hands "in invisible mittens," Richardson is "wondering, calculating, hoping about his horse. . . .

Maybe the little fellow would not feel like smoking over the plain at express speed this morning, and so he would rebel and kick and be wicked. Maybe he would be without feeling of interest, and run listlessly." But as they swing forward, those four feet skim as light as fairy puff-balls. "The houses of the village glided past in a moment, and the great, clear, silent plain appeared like a pale blue sea of mist and wet bushes. . . . The American looked down at his horse. He felt in his heart the first thrill of confidence. The little animal, unurged and quite tranquil, moving his ears this way and that way with an air of interest in the scenery, was nevertheless bounding into the eye of the breaking day with the speed of a frightened antelope."

The story thereafter is rather the horses'—that of this "little insignificant rat-coloured beast" and the heroic black maltreated by the hopelessly terrified guide—than the men's or Richardson's, and a failure of unity of conception prevents its being, notwithstanding psychological and pictorial brilliance, one of Crane's best stories. The third part, for that matter, is as fine as either of the first two. "José harried at his horse's mouth, flopped around in the saddle, and made his two heels beat like flails. The black ran like a horse in despair." Or is it only in context that this slight last phrase —a sort of periphrasis—moves, seeming wholly convincing and pathetic? And the cavalry are waiting serenely behind a ridge as the mob of bandits sweeps over the brow: "When they discerned the pale-uniformed rurales they were sailing down the slope at top speed. If toboggans half-way down a hill should suddenly make up their minds to turn around and go back, there would be an effect somewhat like that now produced by the drunken horsemen." But Crane had been writing as well as this for several years. What is new is the material of the first two parts.

If Nature—a sort of Nature this boy had not seen before— was simply indifferent, not to be warred against, one was thrown back on oneself; it became more important than ever

to find out what one was, how, that is, one would *act*. A
chance occurred. Crane found that he was able to feel terror
and act as if he did not feel terror and *so* survive. This discovery somewhat improved his view of human nature—a view
destined never indeed to wobble towards the optimism of
most men, but from now on much less derisive or dreadful
with tacit scorn. The heroism imagined in the final chapters
of *The Red Badge of Courage* is the element feeblest, least
plausible, in the book. Crane had perfectly imagined his
youth's confrontation with the great death, in Chapter IX,
but over its consequences he falters; his irony fails. Now, in
"Horses—One Dash," the confrontation in the hut, though
beautifully recorded, somehow does not convince; but its
circumstances and its consequences do—irony is live and familiar on them—and henceforth Crane could be an heroic
writer. One immediate triumph he had with the exquisite
Civil War story "A Mystery of Heroism," probably written
in Mexico, for it appeared a fortnight after his return in the
Philadelphia Press (August 1-2, 1895)—whence a young editor named Theodore Dreiser clipped it for his projected *Ev'ry
Month*.

This comes to a creed of *self*-reliance, in spirit altogether
different from the cynical bravado of the young men in *Maggie* and *George's Mother*. Richardson is the first of Crane's
heroes, it is worth notice, not obviously young. But his characters have relied upon others as little as they have calmly relied upon themselves. Faith out has been as absent as faith
in. The confidence Richardson comes to feel in his horse
must reflect Crane's experience, and it is important that this
confidence *surprises* him. "He knew the little animal's willingness and courage under all circumstances up to this time,
but then—here it was different." Here is a crisis, suspending
laws, making everything uncertain:—and then the horse, he
learns, *can* be relied on. Reliance upon a horse is a perceptible way still from reliance upon human beings, but to a
mind so skeptical as the one Stephen Crane brought to bear

upon his fellows the step taken was great, and it was a step in the direction of the interhuman relation we shall find in his supreme achievement.

Another of the Mexican stories presents a semblance of interhuman relation, in the New York Kid's saving the life of the Frisco Kid, but it is semblance only; what matters is a confrontation almost exactly like Richardson's. Beer has misrepresented this story so impressively that he had better be quoted: "The boy of *Five White Mice* stands with a drunkard on each hand and the cloudy group of Mexicans before him, speculating on his friend's attitude after the slaughter. . . . And then he steps forward and the great death steps back. The Mexicans retire up the dim street. Nothing has happened. The emotion has projected its intensity against nonsense, against a posture of some loungers. It is the last point in futility. . . ." (Beer is describing the story with admiration.) The action in the black street begins with Benson's jostling a Mexican gentleman passing with two friends. Benson, whose insensitivity to events just now is grandiose, is being supported home by the scarcely less drunk Frisco Kid and the New York Kid, who is sober because he lost at dice early in the evening and had to take a gang of Americans to the circus. The Mexican burns an insult and then breathes: "Does the señor want fight?" The Frisco Kid, an automaton up to now, suddenly says "Yes." "There was no sound," Crane wrote, "nor light in the world. . . . Into the mouth of the sober Kid came a wretched, bitter taste, as if it had filled with blood. . . . The sober Kid saw this face as if he and it were alone in space—a yellow mask, smiling in eager cruelty, in satisfaction, and, above all, it was lit with sinister decision . . . fascinated, stupefied, he actually watched the progress of the man's thought toward the point where a knife would be wrenched from its sheath." So they face each other, three and three, five with their right hands at their hips. The original, most dangerous gentleman confronts the Frisco Kid in the center, they curse elaborately, and the New York Kid, opposite one curved like a grandee, meditates on death, his own death. He recalls then what shape his friend is in (Benson, of course, unable to fight at all, is safe), and it occurs to him that he can draw his immense, virgin revolver and face the Mexicans down, perhaps. Ultimately he does this, to his surprise, and makes a discovery of great importance, never having dreamed that he did not have a monopoly of all possible trepidations. The fulsome grandee springs backward with a low cry: the Mexicans have been afraid also. Now the Kid, "bursting with rage because these men had not previously confided to him that they were vulnerable," lashes their faces with oaths as thick as ropes, while they slink back, their eyes burning wistfully. The affair is concluded with dignity on both sides, from a distance. "Nothing had happened."

Beer's misunderstanding of the ironic sentence with which Crane concludes the story surpasses his misrepresentation. Nothing has happened except that a young man has learned, first, that he is not isolated in his fear—everybody is afraid; and second, that his fear need not prevent his controlling his fate. A similar naïveté about Crane's *apparently* pointless endings has misled critics of "A Mystery of Heroism" and "The Blue Hotel," to which we shall come in due time.

"The Five White Mice," like the story of Richardson, is imperfectly unified; halves fell apart; but the structure with which Crane tried for unity, though it must be partly responsible for Beer's misunderstanding, is perfectly serious. The New York Kid, "a youth at whom everybody railed for his flaming ill luck," worships the "five white mice of chance." He has a rhyme, intoned to them as he dices, and after they have let him down, when the others banter him, he affirms his confidence in their fidelity and wisdom; presenting "a most eloquent case, decorated with fine language and insults, in which he proved that, if one was going to believe in anything at all, one might as well choose the five white mice." The others point out that his loss hardly makes him a convincing advocate. At the end, when the Mexicans have vanished, Benson comes to and observes with pain that the New York Kid is "shober." Benson "passed into a state of profound investigation. 'Kid shober 'cause didn't go with us. Didn't go with us 'cause went to damn circus. Went to damn circus 'cause lose shakin' dice. Lose shakin' dice 'cause—what make lose shakin' dice, Kid?' The New York Kid eyed the senile youth. 'I don't know. The five white mice, maybe.' " A reader not determined on nihilism will recognize without difficulty that Crane intended something by this rigmarole. The sequence of unforeseeable, fortuitous events has turned out well: the Kid enjoyed the circus, and has had an important experience, and neither of the Kids is dead. He was right to trust the mice. But is it really owing to the mice that things have turned out well? Perhaps in drawing his revolver—Crane says—the Kid "had unconsciously used nervous force sufficient to raise a bale of hay." This is not quite the work of the mice; all they have done is to provide the situation and the soberness. Soberness is an agreeable provision, just here. A disagreeable provision earlier in the story, his losing die, has been mastered by the Kid in a way foreshadowing this climax. He throws it, concealed, on the bar and faces the crowd to bet fifty dollars that it is an ace, with a manner so confident that no one dares. In fact the mice have given him a ten-spot, and the ensuing triumph is his, the bartender's for him, each man's over the cowardice of each man's neighbor. The story is not about casualty but about self-reliance in the midst of casualty. Why, then, the insistence throughout upon casualty? This question is asked in effect by the men's banter: did the Kid really mean to appeal to mice, and why not try other animals—rabbits, hedgehogs? The point, unmentioned by the author, is that the five mice are blind, that is to say indifferent. After providing the materials of a man's fate, they interfere no further; what happens to him is up to himself. The Kid's faith, in substance —Crane's new faith—is in Circumstance as *not* making impossible the individual's determination of his destiny. No doubt this is a faith ironic in one view, but for the author of *Maggie* and "A Dark Brown Dog" and many lines—

A god in wrath
Was beating a man—

it represents a confidence attained.

So much for "futility" as the creed of the young man who was lounging about Mexico City in May and June of 1895, brown and armed, turning gradually Mexican. Bullfights he disliked, for the horses' sake, and would have had a dry word upon this subject for his most famous disciple; but he adored the circus, where the Kid—not "debased" as in the United States by the sight of "mournful prisoner elephants and caged animals, forlorn and sickly"—sat in his box until late, and "laughed, and swore, when past laughing, at the comic, foolish, wise clown." Beer says "The Five White Mice" was invented, not founded on experience. Crane's fancy, certainly, was wandering. Mexican reference is heavy in a little fantasy and three fables published the next year, and he probably wrote these now or shortly after his return. "A Tale of Mere Chance" is the title he gave the fantasy, seeming to refute everything we have been saying: the ironic title. A man murders his rival in love while the little white tiles of the floor whisper to each other, a chair throws itself in his way as he springs for the door, and the bloodstained tiles follow him flying and screaming through the world, murmuring on his trail "like frothy-mouthed weasels." Now they are always there in the jail corridor, "muttering and watching, clashing and jostling. It sounds as if the dishes of Hades were being washed"—and indeed they are. Once he cries out to the tiles to go away, but they doggedly answer: "It is the law." If we have heard in Crane's poems once or twice of "justice," retribution is a new theme. One of the fables pursues it, accounting for the donkey's subjection to man as an outcome of his abominable pride in boasting to the horse that he could emulate

Atlas. Of course this is only a donkey and an amusement, as the other is only a madman (and if hardly a skit on Poe, as one critic has suggested,* hardly worthy, as Edward Garnett thought, of Dostoievsky). Another amusement is the race between two bartenders, in "The Wise Men," evidently the first-composed of three stories about the two Kids in Mexico City. These Kids from the ends of America are inseparable, similar in appearance ("an idiosyncrasy of geography"), and very subtle and wicked. It is hard to say whether Crane had a San Franciscan companion or just split his personality into Eastern and Western—probably the latter, for except when he needs the New York Kid sober or in love he is characteristically unwilling to distinguish between them. But the lazy, alcoholic, gambling life of Americans in a foreign city had never been so well observed before, slight though the stories are, and Benson, the bartenders, and the other characters probably had originals. For one of them Crane varied the name of his indolent brother Wilbur: "Wilburson worked—not too much, though. He had hold of the Mexican end of a great importing house of New York, and, as he was a junior partner, he worked—but not too much, though." Neither, probably, was Crane working. One day an engineer looked up from a New York paper across the table: "Is this poet Stephen Crane related to you?" "I'm him," said Crane, and studied a column of coarse abuse. He drifted south to Pueblo, avoiding pulque, which "looks like green milk and tastes like—it tastes like—some calamity of eggs. . . ." Summing up a year or so later, "The Indian," he wrote, "remains the one great artistic figure," with two creeds: "One is that pulque as a beverage

---

* Miss Whitehead. Perhaps, however, we can look in Poe for the source of the fantasy—at the end of the much-maligned (and uncomprehended) "Berenice," where the *white* teeth of the hero's beloved scatter on the *floor*, he being covered with *blood*. Poe's source in fantasy is more interesting still, but no matter here. "The Tell-Tale Heart" stands also behind Crane's tale; so that the tiles' muttering represents a syncopation, oddly, of the two stories.

is finer than the melted blue of the sky. The other is that Americans are eternally wealthy and immortally stupid. If the world was really of the size that he believes it to be, you could put his hat over it." Then the young philosopher saw an American girl, at his hotel, in a spring gown. He saw her again in the street. He saw her again. She looked like Miss Crouse. He went back to New York.

The ferocity of the attacks on *The Black Riders* has been, if anything, understated, but from the beginning there were powers in opposition. The very influential Harry Thurston Peck, reviewing it in the May *Bookman*, declared roundly: "Mr. Stephen Crane is the Aubrey Beardsley of poetry . . . a true poet whose verse, long after the eccentricity of its form has worked off, fascinates. . . . If Whitman had been caught young and subjected to aesthetic influences, it is likely that he would have mellowed his barbaric yawp to some such note." The little book was just "the most notable contribution to literature to which the present year has given birth." No doubt Peck had seen a *Boston Transcript* interview with Beardsley reprinted by the New York *Press* at the end of the winter. The career of this genius, also consumptive, two years younger than Crane and even earlier cut off, does in its rapid, shocking rise oddly parallel Crane's, as in elegance and conciseness their work has relation. Each had to make his mark rapidly, and did; both scandalized. "The harlot," said Beardsley, "is the woman of the day. . . . Centuries ago it was the Madonna whom people worshipped. "His aim," the Englishman went on, "was to see how far dead white and dead black may be used to give realistic effect," and he quoted Boccaccio: "The grass was so green that it was nearly black"—a sentence that would have been telescoped by Crane. High comparisons these, to Whitman and Beardsley, and there were judges who concurred.

But Crane's poetry is a queer affair. It is written in a strange short-line free verse, so that everything depends upon phrasing; and Crane's ear, angular in prose, was more angular in verse. Even a poem plainly genuine, and large in its final modulation, requires some hearing:

> There was one I met upon the road
> Who looked at me with kind eyes.
> He said, "Show me of your wares."
> And this I did,
> Holding forth one.
> He said, "It is a sin."
> Then held I forth another;
> He said, "It is a sin."
> Then held I forth another;
> He said, "It is a sin."
> And so to the end;
> Always he said, "It is a sin."
> And, finally, I cried out,
> "But I have none other."
> Then did he look at me
> With kinder eyes.
> "Poor soul!" he said.

It is a mistake to hear the two lines before the last as one heroic line; but this curious fact must wait for explanation. Formally, in short, his "lines" maddened his contemporaries.

Their themes were troublesome equally. God is the brutal villain of *The Black Riders*, and some pieces that set against this Old Testament swaggerer an interior pitying God (XXXIX, LI, LIII) went unnoticed. His mother's had been warring with his father's God in Crane's thought. Neither won; both perhaps disappeared and were replaced hereafter in his verse by a notion we shall come to—already now when the little book appeared, some of it had ceased to represent his thought, transformed in the Southwest. But God was not the only villain.

Crane's irony shot everywhere, and against the extreme self-possession of his *manner*, against his confident gleaming dissatisfaction with God, with sages, with churches, with "virtuous" persons, must be set a restless, ironic view of man himself. Courage, Truth, Wisdom, Kindness, are the themes of this poetry; but "coward" is nearly as common a word as "brave," and "lie" and "fool" are commoner than their opposites, and the work burns with cruelty, active or indifferent. It was not perceived in 1895 that the attitude of the poet is hopelessly moral. One is to be on guard utterly—we gather —against what is outside, but one cannot at all trust what is inside either; vigilance, courage, daring, and pity, all are necessary, and they will not be enough, but one must strive for them. Among the rebellions, one hears repeatedly something, however, Calvinist.

> I walked in a desert.
> And I cried,
> "Ah, God, take me from this place!"
> A voice said, "It is no desert."
> I cried, "Well, but—
> The sand, the heat, the vacant horizon."
> A voice said, "It is no desert."

This irony, under contemplation, fades, to reveal a character simpler and more difficult.

Tradition surprisingly looms in the book. As a rule Tradition is a lie. What matters is to rebel and tell the Truth: to dare (XII) and not to pretend to see what others do (XLIX), and

> "Think as I think," said a man,
> "Or you are abominably wicked;
> You are a toad."
>
> And after I had thought of it,
> I said, "I will, then, be a toad."

and

> . . . There was one who sought a new road.
> He went into direful thickets,

> And ultimately he died thus, alone;
> But they said he had courage.

At the same time, there is the longing medievalism of XXVII, a piece not ironic at all but embodying one of Crane's prime conservative obsessions; compare his family sense and the heraldic imagery in his war stories. And there is a grain of sympathy, at first glance mystifying, with the man in V who wishes to range all men in rows—though he too, like almost everyone else, is defeated. Self-mockery is very active. Not only does the writer recognize that he is unable to tell the truth, that truth is "A breath, a wind, a shadow, a phantom"; but in successive poems he acknowledges that he fears truth, and is helpless:

> Tradition, thou art for suckling children,
> Thou art the enlivening milk for babes;
> But no meat for men is in thee.
> Then—
> But, alas, we all are babes.

Other pieces register futility—of virtue (XXX), of "a life of fire" (LXII), of Crane's own striving (LII):

> Why do you strive for greatness, fool?
> Go pluck a bough and wear it.
> It is as sufficing.

> My Lord, there are certain barbarians
> Who tilt their noses
> As if the stars were flowers,
> And Thy servant is lost among their shoe-buckles.
> Fain would I have mine eyes even with their eyes.

> Fool, go pluck a bough and wear it.

But the dramatization of this poem after all replaces the sense of futility, and the necessity of war is definite in a piece following, equally personal:

"It was wrong to do this," said the angel.
"You should live like a flower,
Holding malice like a puppy,
Waging war like a lambkin."

"Not so," quoth the man
Who had no fear of spirits;
"It is only wrong for angels
Who can live like the flowers,
Holding malice like the puppies,
Waging war like the lambkins."

Of the love poems, little need be said save that they are mostly farewells, bodiless, except a fantasy (XL) probably inspired by "L. B.," two earlier poems evidently addressed (in imagination) to Helen Trent, and three more objective pieces in each of which the lover is dead—the loyalty of the maid to her wicked lover being the point in the first, in the last the loyalty of the man to his companion-in-sin. These loyalties recur at the end of LXVII, though the sin-connection is suppressed in the poem. Crane had seen, Beer tells us, a young prostitute cover the head of a drunken procurer with her body while his assailants were trying to stamp his face; when Crane ran for help, the police arrested the girl for cursing.

But of all sadness this was sad—
A woman's arms tried to shield
The head of a sleeping man
From the jaws of the final beast.

The suppression of what, in the light of the other poems, must have locked the image in Crane's mind—the disguise even of drunkenness as sleep—suggests similar suppressions not now traceable, elsewhere.

Places among the stars,
Soft gardens near the sun,

Keep your distant beauty;
Shed no beams upon my weak heart.
Since she is here
In a place of blackness,
Not your golden days
Nor your silver nights
Can call me to you.
Since she is here
In a place of blackness,
Here I stay and wait.

During the months to come these poems accumulated upwards of a hundred parodies, and certain good-natured epithets. Not only were they "absurd," "besotted," "idotic," "lunatic," but they were "hamfat," "garbage," "rot," and also "opium-laded," "bassoon-poetry," "gas-house ballads." Some of this abuse was encouraged by the book's rather precious make-up, printed in capitals without punctuation; Crane liked this, but *Life* for instance jeered: "We used to hear of the poetic ear; it has been superseded by the typographic eye." The abuse was mixed from the beginning, so that by July *Munsey's*, skeptical enough, granted that "Stephen Crane is one of these newly heralded geniuses . . . one of the fads among a certain class," and by the end of the year a little magazine starting in Boston (*The Fly Leaf*) felt impelled to devote its leading article to an attack on "The New Mysticism," "or symbolism, or impressionism," parodying *The Black Riders.** When somebody asked Crane this summer if he admired Mallarmé: "I don't know much," said he, "about Irish authors." He arrived in New York in mid-July a semicelebrity. Calling immediately at a house in 34th Street (nobody was there and he put Miss Crouse out of his mind), he joined the Lantern Club, where at least the ban-

---

* The book was "vituperated" into six printings within a year. In February of 1896 *The Literary Digest* had a new tune, "Is there room for a second Walt Whitman? . . . the star of Mr. Stephen Crane is in the ascendant. . . ." But by then *The Red Badge* was in full career.

ter about his crazy poems would be from friends. "Some of the pills are pretty darned dumb," he conceded, "but I meant what I said."

The Lantern or Lanthorne Club had been organized by a group of young newspapermen and writers—"strugglers towards the literary dawn," as one put it afterward. From an aging Dutchman for fifty dollars they bought a shanty on the roof of one of the oldest houses in New York, in a part of William Street called Monkey Hill, near Brooklyn Bridge, and decorated it as a ship-cabin, with lanterns—Oriental, colonial, and medieval; an old ship's lantern hung outside the door. There were Post Wheeler and Edward Marshall, Irving Bacheller, Richard Watson Gilder, Willis Brooks Hawkins, John Langdon Heaton, the humorists Ned Townsend ("Chimmie Fadden"), Tom Masson, Charles W. Hooke, and a Negro cook Walter who made lunch every day. Bacheller was president, and one of the businessmen taken in to help pay expenses, Don Seitz, was treasurer. They were "good fellows but able borrowers" in Bacheller's memory. Crane was their hero. Most were old friends; they loafed on the red leather lounges and played poker and argued. On Saturday nights they held literary banquets, at which one member each week read out a story and was criticised; encomium and favorable comment were prohibited; the highest tribute was complete silence. Richard Harding Davis came, Mark Twain came once for lunch and monologued without halt over cigars and two hot scotches all afternoon until he had no time to dress for dinner. The club was approached by means of a hanging iron stairway, and (according to Howells, who climbed up for a Thanksgiving dinner when the hired waiters got drunk) its presiding genius was Captain Kidd.

The lunches gave Stephen Crane, still so poor that he is said to have borrowed an extra gun to pad his expense account, one square meal a day when he was in town. He was partly in town, with Nelson Greene at the old place in 23rd Street for a fortnight; and he visited Hartwood, where Edmund Crane had moved with his wife and daughters. For one of Will's girls he had a Mexican opal left—the "Indians" had got the rest. Then he went off to Pike County. Did he guess what was coming? The August *Current Literature* accused him of "Whitmania" and printed most of the fourth chapter of *The Red Badge of Courage*.

Some uncertainty in this chronicle may be illustrated—as we now approach difficulties of an altogether new kind—by a presentation copy of *The Red Badge* now in the New York Public Library. "To W. D. Howells this small and belated book," he wrote and, for once, dated it: "August 17, 1895." On the third flyleaf he wrote out the poem "Do not weep, maiden, for war is kind," dating it also "1895." The book had been long delayed; it would not be published until the very end of September or the beginning of October 1895, but one sees this readily as a prepublication, though "belated," copy. The astonishing poem was published in February 1896; one easily sees it as new in August 1895. What is less easy to see is Crane's delaying for nearly a year to send Howells a copy, transcribing a poem published months before, and giving the year wrong. Yet this is what apparently happened. The book was not ready in August; on August 26, we find Crane writing to Hitchcock from Parker's Glen, Pike County: "The title page proof is all right." And the title-page of the Howells copy reads "1896." Now title-pages of the first English edition, issued late in November 1895, are actually dated 1896, but nothing of the sort is known of the American edition (the bibliography of which has been endlessly examined). We seem bound to suppose that the author, knowing Howells had read the book long before (with disappointment—which may be relevant), somehow neglected to give him a copy until months after the book had become an international sensation. This matters very little perhaps, no more than Stephen Crane's thinking himself twenty-nine instead of twenty-eight on his final birthday, but one would like to have the whole strange story right.

Fame

The *Red Badge of Courage* was published by Appleton at the beginning of October 1895, and Stephen Crane had a quiet autumn. The reviews were good; not so good in New York. The *Boston Transcript* said, "We have had many stories of the war; this stands absolutely alone"; a Kansas City paper agreed; the *San Francisco Chronicle* thought it had no parallel unless *Sevastopol*. The national sale began well. But this was off in the corners a little. In New York the *Critic* called it a strong book and a true book, but his old friend the *Tribune* bludgeoned it, and the *Bookman* called it a far cry from *Maggie*—"so far that he seems to have lost himself as well as his reader." Crane had the "root of literature," but "the root seems to be terribly buried." Typical was the *Outlook's* impression of an "extraordinary bit of realism . . . not pleasant by any means, but the author seems to lay bare the very nerves of his characters." On Christmas Eve, he wrote to somebody: "Mr. Hitchcock tells me that the book does not sell much in New York. It has gone to about 4,500, though, and many of them have been sent west." Very fair, for three months.

Crane was working up a new novel. He had moved his furniture from the city to Edmund's new place at Hartwood, a hamlet north of Port Jervis, and there he stayed, tramping the woods, playing games with his nieces, amused apparently by the reviews as he read them over and over and pasted them in a scrapbook. The novel was a love story, half laid in Sullivan County, then the second half growing out of (though not reproducing) his 1894 sketches of artist-life in the crazy old building on 23rd Street. It went fast. By the end of October he was writing to his publisher: "The story is working out fine. I have made seven chapters in the rough and they have given me the proper enormous interest in the theme." He had "adopted such a quick style" for the story that he thought it wouldn't run over 25,000 words, possibly 35,000: "Can you endure that length?" *The Third Violet* is placed by some, including Mr. Linson, earlier than this fall, but this is obviously a first draft. If these seven chapters are the same as the very short ones into which the book was finally divided, he kept on fast. There are thirty-three of them, and about six weeks later, on a Friday in December, he sent the finished manuscript to Hitchcock to be typed—Hartwood consisting of a store, a blacksmith shop, and a tavern. This is a pace of twenty-five small pages a week, plausible enough for the light, agreeable work. On December 27, 1895, then: "I forward you today my new story 'The Third Violet' in the original manuscript for the typewriting was so bad I am obliged to consider the original better. Moreover as I am considering a start very shortly to some quarter of the world where mail is very uncertain, I am in haste for your opinion. . . ." This was early for an English trip projected in February; but somebody in Boston had asked him to write a play, Crane wanted Indians in it, and he was dreaming of going west again.

What made Crane think he could write effectively at length about a courtship resists inquiry. He stammers on this theme. The beautiful and happy early story "The Pace of Youth" (1893) succeeds, though its young man speaks just twenty meaningless words to the girl, she thirty to him, because it is natural that these timid merry-go-round assistants should be incoherent, because a tyrant (her father) supplies activity, and because Crane created for the fable what Garnett nicely describes as an "airy freshness and flying spontaneity." He never repeated the success. A Civil War story of 1894 tries, "A Gray Sleeve"; so far as it is not a love story, it is very well, but the farther it goes the feebler it gets. Crane knew as a rule perfectly what he could do and what he could not. Perhaps he dared himself in *The Third Violet*; but his friends were becoming urgent, and editors were, with projects, to which sometimes he gave in, as perhaps now. His action is very subtle. William Hawker, a young impressionist painter, is in love with and frightened to death of an heiress, Miss Grace Fanhall; a young writer George Hollanden advises him; perhaps Miss Fanhall is interested in wealthy young Oglethorpe, whom Hawker therefore hates; certainly an artist's model, Florinda O'Connor, adores Hawker in vain; after various half-quarreling, Miss Fanhall raises her eyes to his, and "Later, she told him that he was perfectly ridiculous." Better than the human characters are the wonderful setter, Stanley (William Crane's orange-and-white Chester), and even a certain brook which possesses one sentence: "A little brook, a brawling, ruffianly little brook, swaggered from side to side down the glade, swirling in white leaps over the great dark rocks and shouting challenge to the hillsides." The book is honest, often charming, but produces in many of its human passages an odd, slight sense of *instead*, as if we were not hearing whatever it is that matters. Crane's representing himself, obviously, in both the painter and the writer, did not keep it from being completely undramatic. The studio half is more amusing than the first and also more nearly affecting—one feels gently the model's longing for Hawker, even little Pennoyer's longing for her. If Stanley is lost, there is a stove-pipe that "wandered off in the wrong direction and then turned impulsively toward a hole in the wall." But this second half is hardly able to hold the story in view through a series of sketches. At any rate, he was done with the novel by the time a violent change began in his life, beginning with a dinner the Philistines gave him in Buffalo on December 19th.

Elbert Hubbard had started his magazine *The Philistine* in June, from the village East Aurora near Buffalo. The title, which reflects his opposition to those he called the "Chosen People"—Howells, that is, of *Harper's*, Gilder of the *Century*, Edward Bok of *The Ladies' Home Journal*, and S. S. McClure—seems now better to characterize Hubbard himself; it is odd to find him beating the drum for Stephen Crane. But probably he foresaw a sensation, and beat the drum he did, with a Crane poem in nearly every issue of 1895 (besides continual reference thereafter, a force in Crane's American reputation). By November 10th he had organized a dozen journalists scattered over the country to sign a letter informing the young poet that the Society of the Philistines wished to give a dinner in his honor and asking him to name a date. Setting aside the insulting "poet," Crane replied with some irony that December 19th would do, and went on that date to Buffalo where in the private room of a hotel thirty men did him disorderly honor. Drunken reporters interrupted the speeches until Hubbard, Harry P. Taber, and Claude Bragdon got them into order. After Taber's address on "the strong voice now heard in America —the voice of Stephen Crane," Crane had to get up. He was cool among the strangers (when the Lantern drank a toast to him he was helplessly shy) and responded "modestly and gracefully," according to the *Buffalo News*, "saying he was a working newspaper man who was trying to do what he could 'since he had recovered from college' with the machinery which had come into his hands—doing it sincerely, if clumsily, and simply setting forth in his own way his own impressions." The toasts went on into the night, and the affair was memorialized the following May in an issue of Hubbard's *Roycroft Quarterly* called "A Souvenir and a Medley" where the tributes and regrets of those who had not been able to come were

collected. Some looked interestingly ahead, like the message
from Amy Leslie of the *Chicago News*, "My most gentle
thoughts are tinged with envy of you who are so lucky as to
meet Stephen Crane"; and several still amuse, like Colonel
John L. Burleigh's "I was with Crane at Antietam," Hayden
Carruth's parody "I saw a Man reading an invitation," and
a dry bow from Arthur Lucas of the *Albany Express*: "I have
a profound admiration for a man who, casting to the winds
rhyme, reason, and metre, can still write poetry." There were
also seven new poems by Crane, including "A slant of sun"
and "I have heard the sunset song of the birches." The Philistines' invitation had not mentioned his novel.

The sensation of *The Red Badge of Courage* was made by
the English critics. Crane's publisher Ripley Hitchcock,
Thomas Beer, and others have denied this for fifty years, but
the facts are simple. The book appeared in London two
months later than here, and it was not until early in January
that news of the British reviews came in: the *Pall Mall's*,
George Wyndham's in the *New Review*, the *Saturday Review's*, others'. These were different from the American reviews. Wyndham, one of England's ablest critics, in a long
article on "A Remarkable Book," said simply that "Mr.
Stephen Crane, the author of *The Red Badge of Courage*, is
a great artist," and "Mr. Crane's picture of war is more complete than Tolstoi's, more true than Zola's." The *Saturday
Review* also thought Zola inferior to Crane, mentioned Tolstoy, Kipling, and Mérimée, thought Crane's irony Sophoclean,
and in general seemed to lose its head: the book was "an inspired utterance that will reach the universal heart of man."
"In the whole range of literature," said the *Daily Chronicle*,
"we can call to mind nothing so searching in its analysis."
They vied with each other. To *St. James's Gazette* it was "not
merely a remarkable book: it is a revelation." "Most astonishing"—"no possibility of resistance"—and so on. But let us
make sure of the dates. The issue in which the *Saturday Review* went overboard is dated January 11, 1896. Next day,

Crane posted to a girl a clipping from the *Scranton Tribune:* "*The Red Badge of Courage* has fascinated England. The critics are wild over it and the English edition has been purchased with avidity. Mr. Crane has letters from the most prominent English publishers asking for the English rights to all of his future productions; but the young author refuses to be hurried. . . ." In mid-January, as Beer says, New York began to buy the book; and these were the reasons. The advertisements quoted the British reviews (until 1896 the book went unmentioned or just listed in Appleton ads), people talked of them, American critics fell resentfully or eagerly into line and in ten months of 1896 *The Red Badge* went through thirteen editions in America.

The anomaly was pointed out repeatedly at the time, John D. Barry (the sponsor of Crane's "lines") being perhaps the first to do so. From New York for the Boston *Literary World*, also dated January 11th, he observed: "It is a satisfaction to note that the unique and promising work which Mr. Stephen Crane has done during the past three years has at last won distinguished recognition. I wish that this recognition came from Mr. Crane's own countrymen. . . . I cannot think of the case of another American writer who was accepted as a man of consequence in England before winning marked recognition in his own country, and I doubt if Mr. Crane's recent experience has a precedent. At any rate, now that the English critics are crying out his praises . . ." English fame had always helped, of course,—a few years later Ezra Pound and Robert Frost were to have similar experiences. In February the New York *Bookman* took up the refrain ("Why is it . . . that in America critics are less sure and readers slower to discover a good book in spite of the genius in it?"), and on March 14th the *Literary Digest*: "It is scarcely to the credit of America that this book . . . was first pronounced a work of genius in England, where its success is great and growing. The story has now caught the attention of the American public, and it is said that during the first week in February the publishers were unable to supply the demand." By April 11th it was "now pretty generally admitted that Stephen Crane is a 'genius.' . . ." The English reception was less single-minded, naturally, than it has been represented; the *Academy* in a curt dismissal found the book funny (a discovery it laboriously repented), while the *Spectator* called it an essay in pathology. The American press had praised the book more highly than soon either it or the English press was recognizing; but the essential features of the success are unmistakable. It was inevitable that the truth should have got mislaid here since.

More predisposition to hospitality existed than one might think. *Punch* in this December and January, despite the political crisis over Venezuela, was extolling *Huckleberry Finn* and extending a hand to Howells, while baiting Kipling, Meredith, and Hardy, with articles on "Dude the Diffuse" and rhymes:

Hi, Kipple-Kipple!
Your rhymes cease to ripple;
Your prose too is turning abstruse . . .

There was a biographical misconception in England also, the author being assumed to be a man of some age and experience of war; this was to the book's credit as illusion. And the publisher was energetic and well-connected. But the intense excitement of the English critics, as well as their perspicacity, will be understood better when we remember that they did not see *The Red Badge of Courage* through a maze of imitations, which if they cloud for us its originality also incline to dignify it and above all lend it *plausibility*. The critics saw very well the work's main origins, but they saw its immense difference from these, and its value, and said so. Crane never forgot. Writing to an American editor shortly before his death, he came to the matter again, absolutely: "I have only one pride, and that is that the English edition of *The Red Badge of Courage* has been received with great praise by the English reviewers. I am proud of this simply because the remoter people would seem more just and harder to win."

The past, too, always looks better, but if *The Red Badge* was not one of the six American best sellers in December 1895, Weyman's *The Red Cockade* was, and so were two Ian Maclarens, an Anthony Hope, a Marie Corelli—and a Kipling. It is in the vague light of these novels that H. G. Wells's statement should be read, that Crane's "did, indeed, more completely than any other book has done for many years, take the reading public by storm," English and American. Frederick Pollock might disagree with the younger Oliver Wendell Holmes about it, Barrett Wendell of Harvard call it sensational trash, teachers everywhere balk at its grammar. *The Shadow* (Cambridge, Mass.) decided—"if it be permitted to consider unfavorably a book so unanimously considered great by the critics of to-day"—that "Mr. Crane sneers in rainbow colors. . . . Mr. Crane must tone down this crimson style of his. . . ." But America possessed its greatest war, a million readers ran a boy's fear through, and writers on both sides of the water reflected.

Meanwhile Crane had returned to Hartwood for Christmas, while the transatlantic display was gathering. He must have been in a nervous and open state, unwilling to go to New York but needing someone besides Ed to talk to, and on New Year's Eve he suddenly wrote a long letter to Miss Crouse in Akron, describing the *Philistine* affair and the occasion of his leaving Mexico eight months before. She replied, and during the next two months he wrote to her half a dozen more, endless, unimpassioned—eager to hear from her and to arrange to see her again (he never did)—the egotistical letters of a young man, sometimes naive, but the weary and hopeless letters also of a man who has seen and weighed a deal of essential life. As he reasoned with her about his semi-infatuation, it wore itself out; probably her letters disappointed him; but meanwhile he was undergoing

the terrifying experience of fierce general fame. A last brief
note from Washington in March is bitter and without affectation desperate. The letters, which are not yet available, show
as clearly as any other single source that fame fell, in Stephen
Crane's case, on a developed character. We speak of a man's
"philosophy," but Crane had one.

It was simple, as such things are when they exist. He took
no sharp pleasure in human life, did not expect or wish to
live very long; thirty-five was the age he named to friends. It
was as well to be kind. Kindness, in fact, though a quality
more or less unattainable like justice, was infinitely and actively desirable; so was justice; to the degree that one got
towards these qualities at all, satisfaction was conceivable.
Work and grief made up the context. It was desirable to
keep one's mouth shut, especially where women were concerned, and to be kind especially to women; to mind one's
own business in general. He did not like idealists. The real
enemy, it was necessary to understand, was oneself: one's
laziness and cowardice and self-satisfaction, man's ordinary
lot. The point was, not to *be* true to whatever in oneself was
better than these things, for that was probably impossible,
but to *try* to be true to it; and you found out at death, only,
whether you had won or lost.

A good equipment, and he wanted it. Fame, Father Hop-
kins observed to Robert Bridges, "though in itself one of
the most dangerous things to man, is nevertheless the necessary and appointed air and setting of works of genius." If genius is a capacity for the astonishing, not faked, we may reasonably see in Crane what he was called, a genius; and little
congenial though his genius was to his decade, he was doomed
to be famous. He came to it with a singular outfit of self-
possession, hopelessness, and self-distrust. But he came to it
young. We have seen it growing, very slowly; fame seldom,
even when it comes, comes at once. In January of 1896 however it fully came. He was twenty-four and he lived with it
from now on. The subject has been little studied, for few

bring candor to it, but some operations may be rapidly distinguished. Fame opens up, first, every irony back onto one's past; one is abruptly *valued* by one's *friends*. Then actual envy and malice are hard to ignore. It is difficult just to be watched. There is injury to one's sense of rebellion—pivotal in Crane; it is easier much to feel that "all" are against one, than to recognize strong definite forces for *and* against; one is curiously opened to adverse criticism. One's sense of self-reliance is disturbed. Under the special new conditions, one behaves—at best—at first as before; but this is not adequate. Also the burden of confidence in oneself is to some extent assumed by *others*; and the sudden lightness inclines to overset one. One suffers, finally, at once the intermittent sense that fame is *nothing*, and the necessity—since almost everyone thinks it important (and "affectation" is their readiest charge) —of acting as if it were something. If even the morbid vanity of Tennyson could attain to a sense of the nothingness of fame, it must be intermittently attainable by anyone. He said constantly that "all the praise he had ever received didn't outweigh for the moment a spiteful and unkindly criticism, even though the criticism (he once added) was directed against the straightness of his toe-nail"; yet he could say sincerely one day to Barnes and Allingham: "Modern fame is nothing: I'd rather have an acre of land. I shall go down, down! I'm up now. . . ." This sense becomes a bulwark in the end. But sad forces are at work to baffle its formation, even in a strong character. Tolstoy was over seventy when he told reporters: "Fame is relegated to the rear where there is a consciousness of duty. I certainly was not born in order that people might praise me." Stephen Crane we shall see overset, recover, overset and recover.

On January 12th he went reluctantly down to New York to see McClure (who wanted him to write a new war story and then go to England), Hitchcock (who was dubious about *The Third Violet*), and his friends, who were exultant; passed on to Virginia, and, picking up a mass of letters about *The*

Black Riders and *The Red Badge* on the way, fled back to Hartwood, where on the 27th he penned one of his rare semi-apologies. "My dear Mr. Hitchcock: I fear that when I meet you again I shall feel abashed. As a matter of truth, New York has so completely muddled me on this last visit that I shan't venture again very soon. I had grown used to being called a ―― ass but this sudden new admiration of my friends has made a gibbering idiot of me. I shall stick to my hills. . . . 'The Third Violet' is a quiet little story but then it is serious work and I should say, let it go. If my health and my balance remains to me, I think I will be capable of doing work that will dwarf both books." He was pleased by a letter of Harold Frederic from London in the *New York Times*, about the British sensation, and probably not upset by a broadside against "The Red Badge of Hysteria," by General A. C. McClurg, in the *Dial* of February 1st. Some friends were to sail for England late in February and he thought he might go with them; but then, since people on both sides wanted him to, he thought he wouldn't. He was not writing the reporter-hero story his Lantern friends were begging for, but he had agreed to one more war-novelette for *McClure's* and was working on "The Little Regiment"—"positively my last thing dealing with battle"—interesting himself by setting up the story in a new way, as well as rewriting *Maggie*, which Appleton's would reissue in June. "I have carefully plugged at the words which hurt. Seems to me the book wears quite a new aspect from very slight omissions. . . ." On exactly the day perhaps that Edgar Saltus, in one of Beer's most charming touches,* was reporting that Crane had made twenty thousand dollars, Crane had in mind a smaller sum. "I don't

---

* ". . . the sale mounted so swiftly that Edgar Saltus, who in October wrote that Crane had outdone Zola, Tolstoi, and Kipling in a breath was now, on February 6th, moved to write to Charles Devlin: 'A man sometimes yearns for the power to write vulgar inanity and sell it by the cart-load to fools. I hear that Stephen Crane has made twenty thousand dollars out of his trash.' Devlin called the exquisite's attention to his former praise of the book and their interesting correspondence untimely ceased."

care much about money up here," he wrote to Hitchcock, "save when I have special need of it and just at this time there is a beautiful riding-mare for sale. . . . I don't want to strain your traditions but if I am worth $100.00 in your office I would rather have it now." The publisher showed prompt sympathy, as Crane puts it, but—mysteries of Crane's horses—this was not Peanuts. Peanuts arrived one great spring day in a box-car from East Aurora, fascinating the nieces. Whimsical, Crane was fond of it because he never knew what it would do next, pretending to shy and jumping deliberately over a piece of bark in the road. The little brown horse was bright; he learned to turn the button on his stall-door in order to come out and burrow in the feed-bags; when someone was coming he whicked back into the stall and laid his head over the side, so, innocent. Now Crane skied, on an exceptionally long pair of skis, and snowballed with the little girls. They attacked him, he captured them and marched them around the house, arms up; Edith remembered that once when she got tired and cried, her uncle was disgusted. Agnes was always game. Crane enjoyed target practice more, but hunting and fishing less, than his brother. It was a pastoral life. In describing his literary career in a letter to the editor of the *Critic* on February 15th, he omitted two or three books written but unpublished, and closed: ". . . When I look back on this array it appears that I have worked but as a matter of truth I am very very lazy, hating work, and only taking up a pen when circumstances drive me. I live at Hartwood very quietly and alone, mostly, and think a good saddle-horse is the one blessing of life."

Meanwhile however the work in the upstairs room went on, and *The Red Badge* raged. When "The Little Regiment" was finished toward the end of the month he went to New York again, dodging editors and publishers, planning a Civil War play with Clyde Fitch (it never came to anything because Fitch couldn't see it without a woman and Crane couldn't see it with), and trying to satisfy the passion of his friends to see him. He could take people to lunch now—two friends, ladies of forty, he took repeatedly; and repay debts—paying some twice over while utterly forgetting others; but he was very gloomy at 33 East 22nd early in March and then bolted for Washington, taking with him an unfinished letter to Miss Crouse. McClure had urged a novel about political society. Hurrying about the capital all day and retiring at night to the Cosmos Club, he underwent a severe depression in which he still was when on the 18th he set a final despairing postscript, ashy and impersonal, on the letter to Akron and posted it, closing that relation. Then he pulled himself together, accepted a membership in the Authors' Club, and on the 23rd sounded eager enough to Hitchcock: "I will begin to drive Maggie forward. Is the Red Badge going yet [=still]? Greeley by the way told me yesterday that it had been filed in the 'archives' of the war department." He was "gradually learning things. . . . I want to know all the congressmen in the shop." One week later: "You may see me back in New York for good by the end of this week. These men pose so hard that it would take a double-barrelled shotgun to disclose their inward feelings and I despair of knowing them."

Crane was swinging to and fro, and a reason was that he found he could not trust himself. He went straight back to Hartwood. But the self-possessed way in which he had dealt with two further, serious embarrassments with his publisher showed that he would hang on. "Of course eccentric people are admirably picturesque at a distance," he wrote to Hitchcock shortly after arriving in Washington, "but I suppose after your recent close-range experiences with me, you have the usual sense of annoyance. After all, I cannot help vanishing and disappearing and dissolving. It is my foremost trait. But I hope you will forgive me and treat me as if you still could think me a pretty decent sort of chap. . . ." The same technique, of blanket arrogance (Crane thought Hitchcock arrogant himself, which is material) *preceding* concession, had to be more strenuous on March 23rd: "I have not told you that I am beset—quite—with publishers. . . . If I make ill terms now there may come a period of reflection and so I expect you to deal with me precisely as if I was going to write a *great* [twice underscored] book ten years from now* and might wreak a terrible vengeance upon you by giving it to the other fellow. And so we understand each other. . . ." He then explained that (under the pleading of a close friend, Harry Thompson) he had given Edward Arnold to publish "an old thing, strong in satire, but rather easy writing—called Dan Emmonds. You know of course that my mind is just and most open but perhaps in this case I violated certain business courtesies. . . . My only chance is to keep away from them." This was evidently the old short novel, *George's Mother*, which Arnold published—Crane's only work he did publish—early in June, a week before the reissue of *Maggie* by Appleton's; so that he must now have been revising and retitling it.** Having made the blunder, under importunity, Crane avoided a recurrence with a judgment and address remarkable in a man twice his age, any age. But we must begin to measure dreadful pressures.

Malice was busy with celebrities in the Nineties on three subjects: alcohol, drugs, women.† Nowadays it prefers the last subject, since drinking is universal and narcotism recognized as implausible, but the force of attacks in any of the kinds must be felt in relation to 1896. Somebody, on the book's way to the public, removed with horror "for he had known women of the city's painted legions" from a sentence towards the end of the third chapter of *George's Mother*, and the *Literary World* found *Maggie* "repulsive" in August. "Something" (it went on) "really must be done about Mr. Stephen Crane." Ladies in Port Jervis wondered to William

---

* Still within the age of thirty-five, it will be noticed.

** Finishing it, Beer says. The title is puzzling: "A Woman without Weapons" in 1895, "George's Mother" to Howells that year, now "Dan Emmonds," and in two months *George's Mother* again.

† Much less often than now, on homosexuality. This topic, happily, Crane's biographer is spared.

Howe Crane whether it would still be proper for them to receive his brother. A letter from Gilder to Crane's agent, Paul Reynolds, on October 24th is just amusing. The *Century* had bought "A Man—and Some Others," gotten panic-stricken over the scandal around the author's name, held the story for months, and was now finally going ahead. But: "I am particularly sorry he did not change that 'B'Gawd! . . . I am a sincere well-wisher of the author. . . . I particularly ask him through yourself to omit that expression, for his sake as well as yours. . . ." The story was delayed three months more, and then the ghastly oath was gentled to "B'G——"!

Such was the decade, and so to the charges, of which Crane did not escape one. First, that he drank. Crane seems to have drunk very little; he did not need alcohol. The testimony of his friends and people he lived with is uniform. Very surprisingly, there is no reasonable evidence of his having, even once, got drunk, except when he was ill in Cuba. He held drinks in his hand, usually beer, dark beer, as he held cigars and cigarettes. But he certainly understood drunkenness to the heart, and it is not astonishing that readers of *Maggie* or of the matchless bouts in *George's Mother* (IV and VIII-IX) were prepared to regard their author with dismay. George Kelcey "was about to taste the delicious revenge of a partial self-destruction. The universe would regret its position when it saw him drunk." "Kelcey fell with a yellow crash. Blinding lights flashed before his vision. But he arose immediately, laughing. He did not feel at all hurt. The pain in his head was rather pleasant," so "with a show of steadiness and courage he poured out an extravagant portion of whiskey. With cold muscles he put it to his lips and drank it. It chanced that this addition dazed him like a powerful blow. A moment later it affected him with blinding and numbing power. . . . He was at first of the conviction that his feelings were only temporary. He waited for them to pass away, but the mental and physical pause only caused a new reeling and swinging of the room. Chasms with inclined approaches were before him;

peaks leaned toward him. . . . At last he perceived a shadow, a form, which he knew to be Jones. The adorable Jones, the supremely wise Jones, was walking in this strange land without fear or care, erect and tranquil. Kelcey murmured in admiration and affection, and fell toward his friend." "As for his legs, they were like willow-twigs." "He ate the greater part of his breakfast" (after a lesser occasion) "in silence, moodily stirring his coffee and glaring at a remote corner of the room with eyes that felt as if they had been baked." Crane had a habit too, Beer relates, of defending himself with "Oh, I'd have to get too drunk to write that" from the people who crowded around him now with "stories" that he ought to write; so, naturally, he wrote only when drunk. A note to McHarg when he got back from Washington shows him alive to the slander: "When people see a banker taking a glass of beer in a café, they say, There is Smith. When they behold a writer taking a glass of beer, they say, Send for the police!" But this was only annoying.

One Thomas McCumber had perhaps, according to Beer, started the drug story, on February 22nd: Crane took morphine. McCumber may have met Crane, as a man about town. It spread like a flood. Most of his friends were flatly incredulous; not all. Two years later he wrote from Key West to England: "I owe Harold [Frederic] an apology for laughing when he said they would tear me in pieces the minute my back was turned. Hi, Harold! I apologize! Did you know me for a morphine eater? A man who has known me ten years tells me that all my books are written while I am drenched with morphine. The joke is on me." Crane's publisher had at once asked his opinion of drug-taking. He disapproved; he had seen its end on the Bowery. The best account is Richard Harding Davis's, long after. No love was lost between these stars, and they were very cordial. "I was never intimate with Crane but his best friends assured me that the story was false and they were not men to lie. He had a decided prejudice against drug-taking which I heard him express frequently at dinners and at the Lanthorn Club. But appearances were against him. He smoked constantly and he was very sallow and very thin. To see him through the smoke of a restaurant and to be told that he ate morphine would not have surprised me. But I know a great deal about the signs of the drug habit and Mr. Crane had none of them." What Crane had was insouciance incredible. Who else, under attack, would have composed a circumstantial account of "Opium's Varied Dreams" for the *Sun* of May 17th (always 1896) and then followed it with the story of "Yen-Nock Bill and His Sweetheart" in the *Journal* on November 29th? His friend Ned Townsend had an opium den in *A Daughter of the Tenements* (which was at least once reviewed with *The Red Badge* and preferred to it), but Townsend was older and happily married and not Stephen Crane. In the fall story there is just one vivid desire ("Swift Doyer was a good fellow, but he used to remark that Bill's voice made him wish that he was a horse, so that he could spring upon the bed and trample him to death") and one generalization ("A most peculiar truth of life is the fact that, when a man gets to be an opium-smoker, he has ill-fortune"); but the sketch for the *Sun* is worth display. The rumors about himself may have led Crane to investigate the subject.

There were some twenty-five thousand smokers, he found, in New York, formerly gathered in two great colonies in the Tenderloin and Chinatown, but now splintered. It was hard to find, not being noisy like whiskey, and smokers were hard to recognize. "An opium smoker may look like a deacon or a deacon may look like an opium smoker. The fiends easily conceal their vice." The ordinary smoker spent a quarter a day, for pinheads; some a dollar a day, indulging in high-hats. "Habit smokers have a contempt for the sensation smoker. . . . There are more sensation smokers than one would imagine. It is said to take one year of devotion to the pipe before one can contract a habit; but probably it does not take any such long time . . . when a man talks pipe persistently, it is a pretty sure sign. . . ." Crane probably tried a pipe, he tried almost everything.* After one's first trial, "If he had swallowed a live chimney sweep he could not feel more like dying." Chinatown dens were now "bare, squalid, occupied by an odor that will float wooden chips," and the pipe was notable for the way in which it did not resemble its drawings in print. He described the "yen-yen," the craving that will make an addict do all but "buck through a brick wall to get to the pipe. . . . When the victim arrives at the point where his soul calls for the drug, he usually learns to cook," and he described the process. "He has placed upon his shoulders an elephant which he may carry to the edge of forever." "If a beginner expects to have dreams of an earth dotted with white porcelain towers and a sky of green silk, he will be much mistaken. . . . The influence of dope is evidently a fine languor, a complete mental rest. . . . The universe is readjusted. Wrong departs, injustice vanishes: . . . a quiet harmony of all things—until the next morning." "Opium holds out to them its lie, and they embrace it eagerly. . . ." The article was unsigned, but the style was one of the best known in America, and its author's obvious contempt would be lost in the fact of its subject. It cannot have allayed the slander that dogged him until his death—his death not from smoking and drinking and doping but from tuberculosis, hardship, exhaustion on reporting two wars, and extracting from himself fourteen books in eight years.

Crane was very romantic in some senses of that mysterious word. Everything suggests that he was peculiarly interested in prostitutes, like Beardsley and other artists, modern or older. "The idea of prostitution," wrote Flaubert to his mistress, "is a meeting place for so many elements—lust, bitterness, complete absence of human contact, muscular frenzy, the clink of gold—that to peer into it deeply makes one reel. One learns so many things in a brothel, and feels such sadness, and dreams so longingly of love! Ah, makers of elegies, it

* See p. 146 below.

is not amid ruins you should linger, but on the breasts of these laughing women!" Crane was indeed a maker of elegies, and brothels were probably part of his rebellion. If this was exaggerated at the time and later by some of his "friends" (early this year he observed that three men knew him really well), it was denied altogether by others and has been dissimulated since. Beer has a weird, thoroughly implausible tale to account for his meeting with the Englishman Bassett Holmes, whereas what Crane wrote to Sanford Bennett on August 29, 1899, was just: "Met him in a whorehouse in New York when we were kids." And then Crane expressed opinions, not romantic, with incautious freedom. "This girl in Zola is a real streetwalker," he wrote to a woman. "I mean, she does not fool around making excuses for her career. You must pardon me if I cannot agree that every painted woman on the streets of New York was brought there by some evil man. Nana, in the story, is honest."* And to a friend: "most streetwalkers would be 'demimondianes' [*sic*] if they had money. Lots of women are just naturally unchaste and all you jays know it."

This was the background for scandal, which did not need it. There seem to be three stories. Early in 1896—Beer tells the first—a disreputable Mrs. Bowen (quondam Doris Watts), whom Crane had met before as the wife or mistress of an acquaintance, came up to him in Mouquin's restaurant one night and appealed to him for fifty dollars. Acton Davies warned him that he would never see it again but he borrowed a blank check from Clyde Fitch and made it out for some figure. Cowboys, runaways, loose women—Crane was an easy touch. She wrote letters then, explaining that she needed money in order to reform, and he sent her various small checks coming to some hundred and fifty dollars, till she threatened to invade Hartwood, when he went to New

---

* Not that he liked the novel. "Zola is a sincere writer but—is he much good? He hangs one thing to another and his story goes along but I find him pretty tiresome."

York and called in West 48th Street to deal with her. "I leaned on the door," he recalled the visit, "and told her to drop this nonsense. There was one of those horrors called Turkish corners in the room with a shield stuck full of knives. She lost her temper and grabbed a knife from the shield. It flew over my shoulder and stuck into the wood beside my ear and quivered so that I can still hear the noise." She fainted in the arms of her Negro maid while he went off without his hat to borrow a friend's cap in 30th Street and retire to Hartwood. In August she turned up at a lawyer's to sue for support, but the four letters she had to show were formal and called the checks "loans," and the case was refused. A court then declined to issue the warrant she wanted for Crane's arrest. This seems to have been the end of it, except that by July and thenceforward Crane had notoriously seduced somebody either poor and virtuous or otherwise interesting, and abandoned her and his child. It was this story, in splendid versions, that caused him trouble in the spring and summer. The other two belong later in the year and must wait.

Crane had taken a room in the middle of the shopping district, at 165 West 23rd Street, and written the address on a bank-book—perhaps his first, since he preserved it. He was here during part at least of April and May, in an enormous room at the top of the house, with war trophies about, impressionistic landscapes on the tinted walls, a green writing table inordinately large, paper, no books, two chairs, and a sofa near the window. "I am engaged on the preface," he wrote to Hitchcock. ". . . The proofs make me ill. Let somebody go over them—if you think best—and watch for bad grammatical form and bad spelling. I am too jaded with Maggie to be able to see it." Nothing more is heard of this preface, but from a letter of the fall we can guess at its direction. "I will try to answer your questions properly and politely," he wrote to Miss Catherine Harris. "Mrs. Howells was right in telling you that I have spent a great deal of time

on the East Side and that I have no opinion of missions. That
—to you—may not be a valid answer since perhaps you have
been informed that I am not very friendly to Christianity
as seen around town. . . . A person who thinks himself superior to the rest of us because he has no job and no pride
and no clean clothes is as badly conceited as Lillian Russell.
In a story of mine called 'An Experiment in Misery' I tried to
make plain that the root of Bowery life is a sort of cowardice.
Perhaps I mean a lack of ambition or to willingly be knocked
flat and accept the licking. The missions for children are another thing and if you will have Mr. Rockefeller give me a
hundred street cars and some money I will load all the babes
off to some pink world where cows can lick their noses and
they will never see their families any more. My good friend
Edward Townsend—have you read his 'Daughter of the
Tenements'?—has another opinion of the Bowery and it is
certain to be better than mine. I had no other purpose in
writing 'Maggie' than to show people to people as they seem
to me. If that be evil, make the most of it." A sentimental zeal,
a dogma, he never got on with. "I was," he told somebody
later, "a Socialist for two weeks but when a couple of So-
cialists assured me I had no right to think differently from any
other Socialist and then quarrelled with each other about what
Socialism meant, I ran away."

His anxiety about the grammar of *Maggie* gives pause to
a legend. Crane spelled as badly as Yeats and spoilt many
fine infinitives, but it is not clear how dogmatic he was about
it. In *Godey's* for September, Rupert Hughes ("Chelifer")
filled nearly two columns with flagrant errors from *The Red
Badge of Courage*, observing justly that "Of all the writers
in real renown, Mr. Crane has the most manifest faults to
correct"; he is at a critical stage, Hughes went on, recom-
mending hard work, merciless self-criticism, vigilance. The
advice was good, and was offered to a writer who had been
practising it for a long time. There were lapses, certainly,
even before the driving anxiety and physical uncertainty of

Crane's final three years. "Sketches dashed off in a few hours," Beer writes, "were issued with all their imperfections just as first seen in the *Press* and the *World*." Sometimes this happened, and the generalization that follows is valuable: "Enormous holes appear in his egotism, and his failure in grooming himself for the general gaze is a thing too curious." But we know the intense care with which he studied his phrasing; its perfection through page after page early and late corroborates Vosburgh's testimony. If he went stale on particular works, so does everyone, and Crane wrote—in relation to the time he had to write in and the concentration of what he wrote—much. Too much, like everyone who writes for a living. After *The Third Violet* was serialized this fall Crane refused to rework it for Hitchcock—as "dishonest," since it had been seen already. But by then he must have recognized an irremediable failure with the subject. In general he did work hard, criticized his work, and was vigilant. It cannot be affirmed that his grammar greatly improved. The point is worth a moment. Crane's grammatical sins consist mostly of difficulty in agreement, in reference, and in word order. The third produces sometimes a gruesome awkwardness; but this is sometimes what he wants. This writer does not aim, as a rule, at smoothness, and of his oddest sentences some seem calculated. We probably now take a more reasonable view of modern grammar (and, for that matter, of Shakespearian grammar, which was flexible and quite different from that of the Victorian editions of Shakespeare we still read) than did the Nineties. The early editions of Crane's prose, moreover, are slovenly. We would feel more sure that on page 74 of *Active Service* we have an auctorial barbarism —"In this matter of war he was not, too, unlike a young girl embarking upon her first season of opera"—if we had not encountered on page 73: "he could not be cynical of war, because he had seen none of it." Still, those negations!

By the end of May the metropolis was too much again for the grammarian and he had withdrawn to Port Jervis. "I shall try to remain here, for I am certain unable to withstand the fury of New York. Are you bringing out *Maggie* soon?" She came out in June and was in a fourth printing by November when Appleton's were finishing the collection of six Civil War tales, *The Little Regiment*. Edward Arnold brought out *George's Mother* too in June, and Crane had the summer in which to enjoy the insulted reviews—lying on a couch, clipping, or shooting across the brilliant hills with his brother and the delightful setter, Chester, and stopping to ask: "Will, isn't that cloud green? . . . But they wouldn't believe it if I put it in a book." The power of transatlantic approval was strongly felt, though there were notes that would haunt his American notices to the end: the tepid, the grudging. These reviews long afterward moved a graduate student to eloquence: "he was considered a promising young writer of the animalistic school. Critics felt it was too bad he had the power to portray the types he insisted on portraying." But there was also a peculiar and personal ferocity that was new to Crane, new even to the author of *The Black Riders*. A champion of that book, Harry Thurston Peck, after explaining that *George's Mother* was an incoherent fragment, probably very early, and denying that it was realism at all (the denial was pejorative, not classificatory), added that Crane "ought not, as a matter of self-respect, to rake over his literary ash-barrel and ask us to accept his old bones and junk as virgin gold." To the *Tribune* the book "bristles with coarseness and dulness, but there is no vitality anywhere which makes them anything but coarseness and dulness." These observations are eloquent, studied, and the tone kept on until, for the *Nation* in 1899, "Whether he can distinguish between the spirit of a gentleman and the spirit of a hoodlum is . . . the only burning question suggested by *Active Service*." Of the native comment he received from now on, much simply resembled insult. It must specially have resembled insult to an author specially insistent, as a man, upon the value of family and breeding, even upon natural aristocracy (Crane

143

is explicit in a letter that cannot be quoted), and upon the duties of a gentleman—so long as fine talk about ideals and so on was omitted. When he had later to read of his young gentleman Hawker, that "The hero has a taint of commonness which he cannot shake off," Crane must have ground his poor teeth behind his smile. In the summer of 1896, riding Peanuts and idling, off to Sullivan once more, he recovered a little from the winter and spring and tried to get used to the new condition.

British magazines had been very hospitable to his work; four of six war stories appeared abroad. And then he was doing his duty. A letter of early September from the city (141 East 25th Street) shows him at it, good-natured, funny, kind, honest. "Dear Miss Walker: I think the motif of the story is properly strong. 'You will never hold the cross toward me.' That, I think is very effective. One thing I must say at once: Take the diamond out of that man's shirt immediately. Don't let him live another day with a diamond in his front. You declare him to be very swell and yet you allow him to wear a diamond as if he were a saloon proprietor or owned a prosperous livery stable. It is of the utmost importance that you remove the diamond at once for our fin de siecle editors will never tolerate a diamond in the shirt-front of a man like that. Frankly I do not consider your sketch to be very good but even if you do me the honor to value my opinion, this need not discourage you for I can remember when I wrote just as badly as you do now. Furthermore there are many men, far our superiors, who once wrote just as badly as I do today and no doubt as badly as you." A week later he was in serious trouble. We come to the second story involving a woman, which is distorted, briefly, by Beer. It involves also the police.

Fifty years later, when we know enough of foreign police, and something of our own, we still can spare some surprise for that florid era. "What's The Matter With New York's Policemen?" a headline had wondered in July of 1891; on successive days of the following January a Brooklyn girl and a Swiss seamstress charged patrolmen, plausibly, with rape; and throughout the decade the police were almost incredible. If the graft was bad, it was less bad than the negligence and the bullying. Top officials came and went, they even improved, but "the Finest" went on. Crane had watched them for years as a reporter, with dislike. He was now learning about them from the Police Commissioner, Theodore Roosevelt— at whose house he dined in July—and meant to write about them. "In the autumn," the September *Book News* said, "he will publish a new series of stories, or a long story, he has not definitely decided which, in which will be presented the life of the metropolitan policeman." The sketch "An Eloquence of Grief" may have been related to this project, which was interrupted.

Late at night on September 16th, while leaving the Broadway Gardens of which he was reporting the opening, Crane escorted some chorus girls into the street and was in the middle of Broadway handing one up to a streetcar when a plainclothesman arrested the other two. He threatened to arrest Crane as well when Crane remonstrated, but in the end didn't, and at the station let one of the girls go after she passed into hysterics. A similar arrest by this officer, nominally for soliciting, had lately been discredited by reporters and the girl released. Charles Becker his name was, a policeman famous enough long afterward and executed for murder. Next morning, in Jefferson Market Police Court, Crane testified to the innocence of the girl held. "I was strongly advised by Sergeant McDermott not to," he admitted; "I well knew I was risking a reputation that I have worked hard to build . . ." but "The policeman flatly lied." The girl was a Dora Clark, twenty, of 137 East 81st Street, and had been arrested before "because a policeman insultingly spoke to me and I repelled him. He arrested me then" and "told the other policemen." There were headlines ("Stephen Crane As Brave As His Hero") and some authentic dialogue as he tried to describe to reporters the girl: " 'Why, she was really handsome, you know, and she had hair—red hair—dark red—' 'Yes?'—'And she was dressed, I am pretty sure, in some kind of shirt waist,' he concluded desperately."

But the consequences were not amusing at all. It was a kind of thing, first, almost impossible to get straight. "Mr. Howells was greatly distrest by the incident," one friend recalled in 1924, "until I put the matter before him in its true light." Worse than scandal followed. Crane had been observing in court just the day before, and Magistrate Brann took his word; then there were complications. The police wrote to Crane. He did not reply—newspapers reported the moves— the letter had been misdirected to another Stephen Crane. The right one was staying with Fred Lawrence in Philadelphia, who remembered going out with Crane one morning to send an immense wire to Roosevelt saying that he was coming over to prefer charges against Becker—"with the result that an aroused and resentful police department bent all its unscrupulous energies to discrediting Crane and making New York too hot for him to live in."* The enthusiastic Commissioner had lined up the ranking members of the force to read them the telegram and harangue them on their treatment of women. Policemen marked Stephen Crane. Dora Clark brought an action in October, Crane testified for her again, the police raided his room,** Dora Clark became celebrated, the case was lost, and Crane was never long in New York again.

The third story follows directly on this. In November, Amy Leslie was in New York. She had been so lucky as to

---

* Frederic M. Lawrence to Thomas Beer, November 8, 1923 (after Beer's study appeared). The hero of *Active Service* is on a black road in Greece between the armies: "He half vowed to himself that if the God whom he had in no wise heeded would permit him to crawl out of this slavery he would never again venture a yard toward a danger any greater than may be incurred from the police of a most proper metropolis."

** Finding an opium layout, newspapers said, according to Garland. Perhaps they brought it with them.

meet Stephen Crane, and she had no gentle thoughts about
him: he owed her money. Amy Leslie had been Lillie West,
who graduated with honors from a Catholic school when
Crane was four, and had an opera bouffe prima donna career
in various soprano roles of Offenbach and Audran. A husband
had been dead for years. Since 1889 she had been the dramatic critic of the *Chicago Daily News*. What she was doing
in the East is obscure. But on November 25, 1896, Crane's
friend Willis Hawkins, the whimsical editor of *Brains*, received from him five hundred dollars with instructions to pay
it to Miss Leslie in installments, which he began to do.
Christmas Eve he had a night letter from Crane in Jacksonville: "Leave soon. Telegraph frankly Amy's mental condition. Also send fifty if possible. Will arrange payments from
Appleton. Troubled over Amy." Hawkins sent the fifty, and
by February 5th (1897) he had paid four hundred to Miss
Leslie, who was living with her sister, a Mrs. O'Brien, in
West 25th Street and badgering him constantly; some later
payments may be unrecorded. On April 27th Crane sent a
hundred dollars from Greece. "Dear old man: I enclose a
pony* for Amy. Give her my love. There is lots more coming. Just off again to see fight. I love Amy. Yours, S. Tell Fairman go to hell." One Leroy Fairman had acted as Miss Leslie's agent—apparently—at least once with Hawkins. But
Hawkins had had enough; he returned the money (he said
later) and refused to act. Something went astray, because
Crane wrote to Miss Leslie from Ireland in September about
the hundred dollars, and she set a lawyer on Hawkins, who
explained. Early in January then (1898) ᵗʰe sued Crane for
$550, charging that on November 1, 1896, she had given him
$800 to deposit for her: he deposited it not in her account
but in his: and he had only repaid her $250. What happened
thereafter has vanished; presumably he paid her whatever he
owed her.

* British slang for £25 (Athens was full of British correspondents), and
referring perhaps to the American "pony up," to settle an account.

Crane's life seems to be turning into cops and robbers. An absconder? But difficulties bristle in this curious series of events. On one hand we have Crane's clear sense of indebtedness, his "I love Amy," her apparent need, and his delays. On the other we have his inquiry about her mental condition, his payment always by intermediary and in installments (as if he thought her untrustworthy), his angry rejection of her intermediary, and her misrepresentation of the amount she had been paid. Whether there had been a love affair does not appear; it is not known that he ever tried to see her again. "I love Amy" does not in context sound exactly romantic. Upon evidence so incomplete, confidence is impossible. Accepting her date, however, November 1st, what can we say of Crane's circumstances? The week before, he had a large story (on Sing Sing, weirdly) in the *World*; *The Third Violet* had just started running in *Inter Ocean*, was on the point of starting in the *Evening World*; money would seem to have been flowing; and on an unknown day about now Bacheller sent him south with a belt of Spanish gold to try to get to the insurrection in Cuba.

On November 29th Crane wrote from Jacksonville to Will: "I was off to Cuba before I had a chance to even inform you of it from New York. I fooled around town for over a month expecting to go at any time," then "suddenly received orders to skip and I left New York that very night." On November 7th he was in Cambridge reporting a Princeton football victory for the *Journal*, and he must therefore have gone to Jacksonville *twice*, because he seems to have been there on November 4th.* We are moving back to November 1st.

---

* Among his widow's papers there is said to be a note to her on a flyleaf torn from a book, signed by Crane and placed, with this date given in full. A copy of *George's Mother* (now at Dartmouth) is inscribed: "To an unnamed sweetheart Stephen Crane, Nov. 4/96." This must therefore be Cora Taylor also, and the place Jacksonville; the book was afterwards Edward Garnett's (a later English friend of Crane's), who might or must have been given it by Mrs. Crane after her husband's death but could hardly have come on it otherwise. Stephen Crane's dating was so spirited that

There were the New York police, and his eagerness to see a war, to drive him. If Amy Leslie's date is right, perhaps this was also "that very night" when he fled south—and the letter to Will (his letters to his brothers are scarce and indirect henceforward) refers to the first flight. November 1st was a Sunday, Crane's twenty-fifth birthday. All these circumstances are unusual and mysterious. Any hypothesis must be tentative, but we can be content with any hypothesis less fantastic than the notion that Crane (a) put her money in his account, (b) sent three weeks later $500 to a friend to be doled to her, (c) inquired a month later about her mental condition, saying "Troubled." Nobody acts thus. At any rate he ran back north, to the game forgotten perhaps or to testify, and ran back south. Crane moved fast from now on, or buried himself somewhere, and seldom explained. Fame wouldn't do at all.

---

neither of these items would count for much alone, but together they are irresistible: he was in Jacksonville on November 4th and had already met Cora Taylor.

Florida

We learn more perhaps about the extraordinary woman Lady Stewart or Cora Taylor, and about her relation with Crane, from a prose-poem she made about it later, sentimental as this is, than from the circumstance that when they met late in 1896 she had left her husband, a son of the former Commander-in-Chief in India, and was now mistress evidently of a brothel in Jacksonville.

There was a woman—young, world-worn, selfish, floating on the swift stream of desire, never able to reach the smooth sea of satisfaction—until one day—

He came, and with him came once again melody in the notes of birds. . . . Out of the glare they went into a quiet spot touched tenderly by sun-fingers stretched down through leaves of ancient oaks. . . .

He was a painter and his canvas glowed with colors that only love's brush may mix. He was pure of heart and soul, and he loved the woman. Under this gentle tutor her nature changed, softened, grew. She became gentle, firm, seeking to do good.

They looked into each other's eyes, and the woman said: "This is heaven," and the man replied: "This is heaven indeed."

But at once we have four incongruities—her first marriage, her profession, her sentimentality, and her regeneration—to assemble; and a puzzling figure to try to understand.

She had been Cora Howarth, a New England girl who broke from her family and married, very young, Captain Donald William Stewart, C.M.G. After an early brilliant military career in the East, he vanishes from sight for a decade until this year, when he was a political officer in Africa; and of where they met, of what the marriage was like ("severely wounded," he was perhaps an invalid), we know as little as of her history after separating from him. She came to Jacksonville as a yachtsman's mistress and persuaded him to set her up with a place called the Hotel de Dream—she was a politician's mistress—so the stories drift, unverifiable. When she met Crane, perhaps at her house, perhaps at a hotel dance, she was a woman in her late twenties, not tall and not slight in figure, whether in the elaborate wasp-waisted evening gown of one photograph or in the heavy war correspondent's kit of another.* Her attractive face was too broad and firm for beauty—"half handsome," somebody called her. Her hair, blonde (touched with red, according to one), and her eyes, were another thing. "Her hair was the honeyiest I have ever seen," a friend of Crane's remembered, "and finer than any floss. . . . Cora Crane's eyes were blue!" An English girl to whom she was kind remembered lovely arms. She was rebellious, energetic, ambitious, improvident, kind, managerial, devoted. Everything suggests that she fell decidedly in love with Stephen Crane at once and loved him until he died.

As for Crane, he had met his fate, and he seems to have recognized it. His brief early notes to her speak only of the sadness, evanescence, and death of love. When in some of the poems called "Intrigue" he seems to address her, the love is a doom.

* These pictures are reproduced by Ames W. Williams in the new bibliography of Crane (page 100 facing) and *The New Colophon*, April 1948 (opposite page 118); they are excellent. The photographs in the old magazines are very poor.

Thou art my love,
And thou art the ashes of other men's love,
And I bury my face in these ashes,
And I love them—
Woe is me.

* * *

Thou art my love,
And thou art a skull with ruby eyes,
And I love thee—
Woe is me.

* * *

Thou art my love,
And thou art death,
Ay, thou art death,
Black and yet black,
But I love thee,
I love thee—
Woe, welcome woe, to me.

Or if in that one beginning

Tell me why, behind thee,
I see always the shadow of another lover?

we hear a muffled protest against the fate, it is accepted all
the same. Perhaps we can discriminate themes of the fate:
seniority, social position, prostitution—and another one:res-
cue. Seniority has become familiar to us in a succession of
women: Miss Trent, Mrs. Munroe, Amy Leslie; with a
younger woman (if she was younger, Miss Crouse) Crane
could only correspond. And Thomas Beer, in one of his most
acute remarks, is explicit: "He was so sensitive to attentions
of people more ancient than Stephen Crane that the trait
lends itself to psychiatric description.* Many of his letters
were written to two ladies fifteen years ahead of him, on

* Working under the influence, the stylistic influence even, of Van Wyck
Brooks's *The Ordeal of Mark Twain* (1920)—that critic's best book—it is

whom he lavished luncheons in his prosperous spring of 1896. He would turn from the prettiest girl in a crowded room to chat with an elderly lady."* The social position of Mrs. Munroe and others we recall. We are also familiar with Crane's absorption in prostitution, and especially the protection or rescue of prostitutes—a matter in which he had risked his reputation. That this was not soft-hearted merely, but compulsive, we may have begun to guess from his hard-headed comment on "real" prostitutes. Fate, who was never indifferent to Stephen Crane, had made a wife ready for him.

Not that they talked of marriage this fall, so far as is known; there was reason not to. The one view that we have of them together—perhaps unreliable—shows them happily illicit at midnight over quail and champagne, Cora Taylor patting her poet with quiet joy and filling glasses, while he slouches in slow, acrid, amused talk with a doctor sowing oats whom she has invited in to help entertain him. Crane liked this man's Christian nomenclature, Ezekiel Adoniram.

Jacksonville was full of correspondents with eyes trained on a dream of Cuba; drawn, as one of them wrote, to "the colorful field of Spain's clumsy effort to prevent an insurrection becoming a revolution, with its side-lights of filibustering expeditions and the delicious mysteries of Junta headquarters in New York and midnight conferences in Jacksonville and Key West." The American Navy patrolled halfheartedly, and every second man in the coast ports might be a Spanish spy. Even the word "filibuster" in this sense has disappeared, but

---

remarkable that some reluctance or some essential vagueness in Beer drew him in his biography of Crane so far the other way. Brooks labors and over-labors; Beer will only, only suggest. The contrast is worth emphasis because these are among the most brilliant American biographical studies of that period.

* An omitted sentence is less valuable: "Favors of middle-aged folk had some special meaning for the final child of a long family, used to petting and scolding from brothers and sisters who had been longer living." Beer confounds his natural deference to certain older and well-known men (Garland, Howells, Huneker, Frederic) with his special and *masking* deference to older women, to be explored later.

in 1896 it represented a magic, a tricky, and ought to have represented a silent, business. "If it were not for the curse of the swinging tongue," Crane observed, ". . . the filibustering industry, flourishing now in the United States, would be pie"; and "Twenty brave men with tongues hung lightly may make trouble rise from the ground like smoke from grass. . . ." Crane's tongue was not hung lightly. He disappeared every day from the St. James, and haunted day and night the back room of a waterfront saloon, watching, waiting for the possibility of a sailing, nursing beer and listening to the talk of oilers, deckhands, sponge fishermen, wharf-rats and dock-thieves—"a sombre, silent member, contributing no adventure of his own." He was not listening as a correspondent. To Charles Michelson, down for the *Journal,* whose account we are following, we owe also the best explanation of Crane's intermittent failures as a journalist. "He hated to ask questions, got no glow of adventure in landing a news story, resented the importance of policemen, and was insulted at the ruthlessness of copy-readers, who slew his words. . . . His writing was painfully slow from a newspaper standpoint. . . . In short he had every quality that made reporting a misery." One famous dispatch aside, he sent little to Bacheller.

Instead he was reading *War and Peace. Peace and War* Crane called it. "He could have done the whole business in one third of the time and made it just as wonderful. It goes on and on like Texas." Less predictably, he read *Under Two Flags,* which he not only rather liked (to his surprise—Crane never expected to enjoy anything) but wrote about for the January *Book Buyer.* He had supposed Ouida outgrown. "I thought that I recognized the fact that her tears were carefully moulded globules of the best Cornish tin," but he found he admired Cigarette, who was imperfect—"it is very nice to come upon a good, sound imperfection when one is grown surfeited with the company of gods"—and he liked one thing about the book as a whole. It was a song of the brave, where "Pain, death, dishonor, is counted of no moment so

long as the quality of personal integrity is defended and preserved. Certainly we may get good from a book of this kind.
It imitates the literary plan of the early peoples. They sang,
it seems, of nobility of character. Today we sing of portières
and champagne and gowns. . . ." Crane seldom walked as
a critic, but there is something charming here: he knew himself. History, grammar, gods, an elaborate society, were nothing. A hero, so long as you didn't call him one and concentrated on his hanging shirt-tail, was worth having.

He hadn't liked Jacksonville at first. "The town looks like
soiled pasteboard that some lunatic babies have been playing
with," he wrote to somebody, pursuing then two of his obsessions. "The same old women are sitting on the hotel porches
saying how well the climate suits them and hurling the same
lances with their eyes to begin bloodshed. . . . I went down
the shore some distance yesterday and watched the combers
come counting in. Sometimes their addition changes to mul-
tiplication and the music is confounded, like a war of drum-
merboys." He had defined music as "addition without pain,"
convulsing a New York dinner-party, and stuck to it—a singular remark that made James Huneker regard Crane henceforth as an intuitive natural philosopher. He missed New
York. His last publication this year was a nostalgic piece on
Minetta Lane and Minetta Street (once "two of the most en-
thusiastically murderous thorofares in New York . . . other
streets ran away and hid") with their heroes of "the razor
habit."

But he was seeing Cora Taylor, waiting, listening, and
hoping southward. On Christmas Eve he worried about Amy
Leslie, as we have seen, and was expecting to leave soon.
He must have been by now in touch with Edward Murphy, the
young master of the famous tug *Commodore*, who agreed to
take him on as a seaman. After more delay, on the afternoon
of New Year's Eve she was slowly loaded with bundle on
bundle of rifles, box on box of ammunition, while a crowd of
excited Cubans on the pier demonstrated with ballads and

farewells to the Cubans who were going on the *Commodore*, under a leader named Delgado, to fight in the island. It was strangely open, unlike any previous filibustering. Spanish threats were shouted at her crew (Thomas Beer says) and two men were heard in Spanish on the dock: "It is all fixed. She will sink."* The revenue cutter *Boutwell* lay perfectly quiet down the river; it was even to prove helpful. The only hitch was a detention of the ship's officers and the Cuban leaders at the customhouse, so that it was twilight before she swung clear of the dock.

Yet nothing about the voyage was auspicious. In a heavy fog the *Commodore* grounded in the mud of the St. Johns less than two miles from Jacksonville and was there all night, until the *Boutwell* came up at dawn and dragged her off. Crane, excited, and also unwell with some intestinal complaint, had not slept. She was cheered, then, down the river from the shore and passing ships, but beached again at Mayport, changing pilots. She would not answer the wheel, and treachery was suspected. When she dragged herself off and headed at last for the open sea, there was a strange ceremony that Crane reported. Captain Kilgore of the cutter grew curious and hailed: "Are you fellows going to sea today?" Captain Murphy called back, "Yes, sir." Then as the whistle of the *Commodore* saluted him, Captain Kilgore doffed his cap, "Well, gentlemen, I hope you have a pleasant cruise," and this was their last word from shore.

The second night Crane tried to sleep in a lurching bunk, expecting momently to be "fired through a bulkhead," failed, and decided to talk with the cook, who woke and "delivered himself of some dolorous sentiments: 'God,' he said in the course of his observations, 'I don't feel right about this ship, somehow.' " He joined the man at the wheel then, and was on

---

* The explanation of the openness is unknown. Beer's statement that Crane thought the ship unseaworthy seems to rest only upon the description of the *Foundling*, filibustering out of Boston in Crane's story about Flanagan; detail cannot be pressed this way without evidence.

the point of going to sleep in a corner of the pilothouse when the chief engineer rushed up the stairs to tell Murphy, who had just come on duty, that something was wrong in the engine room. This was about three A.M. on Saturday, the 2nd. There was a leak, and the pumps would not throw water. The captain hurried below and came back while Crane was drowsing to tell the Cuban leader in a little room behind the pilothouse, one Paul Rojo, to get his men to work, bailing. Rojo told Crane to go help, and he went down to the stifling, swashing, chaotic engine-room.* Crane and a young oiler Billy Higgins were the only Americans who sweated then with the Cubans under their leaders, passing the buckets up a chain of men. The poet heard complicated statements and understood that there was a general, sudden ruin in the engine-room. Higgins forced the Cubans to bail; after moving under orders to a more favorable position on the windward side of the ship, they hesitated when they were ordered back into the fire-room, Crane said, until Higgins dashed down. Instead of fainting, presently Crane went on deck where he heard talk of lowering the boats, of a rocket. Air revived him. The cook, C. B. Montgomery, saw him on the bridge sweeping the horizon with glasses for a sight of land, and once, when he mounted the rigging to get a better view, "I thought sure that he would be swept off as the vessel rolled from side to side, her yards almost touching the water as she rolled down.

* It was a scene, he wrote in his account a few days later, "from the middle kitchen of hades. In the first place, it was insufferably warm, and the lights burned faintly in a way to cause mystic and grewsome shadows. There was a quantity of soapish sea water swirling and sweeping and swishing among machinery that roared and banged and clattered and steamed, and, in the second place, it was a devil of a ways down below." This can be compared with what art did with it later in "Flanagan." "Now the way of a good ship on the sea is finer than sword-play; but this is when she is alive. If a time comes that the ship dies, then her way is the way of a floating old glove." In the stoke-room "Water was swirling to and fro with the roll of the ship, fuming greasily around half-strangled machinery that still attempted to perform its duty. Steam arose from the water, and through its clouds shone the red glare of the dying fires. As for the stokers, death might have been the silence in this room. . . ."

One of the Cubans got rattled and tried to run out one of the boats before time, and Crane let him have it right from the shoulder, and the man rolled down the leeway, stunned for the moment." Crane himself simply reported that there was no panic at any time.

He was impressed by what he saw next, however. "Returning with a little rubber and cloth overcoat, I saw the first boat about to be lowered. A certain man was the first person in this first boat, and they were handing him a valise about as large as a hotel. I had not entirely recovered from my astonishment and pleasure in witnessing this noble deed when I saw another valise go to him" and yet again something like an overcoat. Crane and the chief engineer, leaning out of his little window, had a brief, vivid conversation. This first boat, loaded thus and with twelve Cubans, was got away; one had pulled a knife on Montgomery—"Go with the Americanos." By Captain Murphy's direction the Cubans steered for Mosquito Inlet, near New Smyrna, about twenty miles away (some 120 south of Jacksonville), made it, and did not send back help. Sixteen men, including all the Americans, were left. The lifeboat on top of the deckhouse was now ordered cleared. Higgins, Graines (first mate), two colored stokers, and Crane "wrestled with that boat, which, I am willing to swear, weighed as much as a Broadway cable car. She might have been spiked to the deck. We could have pushed a little brick schoolhouse along a corduroy road as easily." The captain, who had broken his arm, ordered others to help them. Others did, the first mate Graines lost his head and temper, and by some fantasy the boat seems to have been got away with just four men in it, all Cubans. These two boats would have carried them all. The *Commodore's* whistle was blowing now in the rolling darkness, blowing "as if its throat was already choked by the water."

The captain was seeing the third boat launched away in the darkness aft, when Crane worked his way up to him. Montgomery had come to Crane earlier and asked: "What are you going to do?" "I told him of my plans, and he said: 'Well, my God, that's what I'm going to do.'" Now the captain asked him, and Crane told him; Murphy knew the cook had had the same idea, and ordered Crane forward to be ready to launch the ten-foot dinghy, turning around to swear at a colored stoker done up in life-preservers like a featherbed. Crane worked forward with a water-jug, and when the dinghy was launched he went over to fend it off the ship with an oar. The cook and the novelist sat in the darkness waiting, without indifference, for the captain. Finally they heard his hail: "Are you all right, Mr. Graines?" and the mate's "All right, sir." Then the captain came. As he was about to swing over, Higgins appeared, and they came down together, the captain with forty yards of lead line attached to the rail. They were going to wait, he said, as they swung back to leeward, till the ship went down.

The strange possibility must be mentioned here that there were not four men in this dinghy, but five. In the cook's first account (next day) he said: "Captain Murphy, Stephen Crane, the novelist and correspondent; Higgins, myself and one other sailor took to the ten-foot dinghy at the last moment." In the cook's second account (next day) he said, of their battle at the end in the surf: "Crane was a good swimmer, and he really saved one of the sailors, as the man could not swim a stroke, and Crane had to keep him up by the aid of an oar." These give us a fifth man both at the beginning and at the end. One sees the reason for simplification in the story of the dinghy Crane wrote later; but also in the New York *Press* account of the sinking he wrote four days from now there are only four men, and this is less easy to understand, if the cook was right. It is hard—putting the matter very gently—to see how either could be wrong. But we have seen Crane censoring the Cubans' revolt. The facts suggest strongly and weirdly that, whether consciously or unconsciously, he censored in his dispatch, as well as in an immortal story, the man he saved.*

Four men or five, they waited on the end of the line, headed into the wind, seeing on each rise the swaying lights of the dying ship, till dawn. Then the ship herself appeared, "floating with such an air of buoyancy that we laughed when we had time." Then they saw men on board. Then the men saw them. The third boat had foundered alongside, Graines called, and they'd made rafts: would the captain tow them? Besides the first mate and the old chief engineer, there were three white men and the two Negro stokers—seven silent faces above the stern-rail in the gray light, pitching. "All right," the captain said. The rafts were floating astern. "Jump in!" Crane observed then "a singular and most harrowing hesitation. . . . Four men, I remember, clambered over the railing and stood there watching the cold, steely sheen of the sweeping waves." Captain Murphy called again, and the old man jumped first, landing on the outside raft, which he gripped. The dinghy, which had loosened its line earlier and dropped off leeward, had now rowed back, not too near "because we were four men in a ten-foot boat, and we knew that the touch of a hand on our gunwale would assuredly swamp us." A stoker followed the engineer over. Then the first mate "threw his hands over his head and plunged into the sea." He had no life belt and Crane "somehow felt that I could see in the expression of his hands, and in the very toss of his head, as he leaped thus to death, that it was rage, rage, rage unspeakable that was in his heart. . . ." The seaman Crane had talked with at the wheel jumped to a raft. The last three stood, and looked out in silence at the dinghy. "One man had his arms folded and was leaning against the deck-

* One fact more. There were twenty-eight men on the boat. Twelve Cubans and four Cubans is sixteen Cubans. In "The Open Boat," the sole reference back to the ship that had gone down is: "this captain had on him the stern impression of a scene in the grays of dawn of seven turned faces." Sixteen and seven are twenty-three, leaving five men. The captain listened to Crane's story as he was writing it, and corrected it.

house. His feet were crossed, so that the toe of his left foot pointed downward." There was a silence.

"The colored stoker on the first raft threw us a line and we began to tow. Of course, we perfectly understood the absolute impossibility of any such thing; our dinghy was within six inches of the water's edge, there was an enormous sea running." Crane was at an oar, facing the rafts, Montgomery holding the line, when suddenly the boat began to go backward, they saw the white-eyed stoker pulling madly hand over hand, and the cook let go the line. They rowed around to try to get a line from the engineer, and then in the terrible silence the *Commodore* sank. "She lurched to windward, then swung afar back, righted and dove into the sea, and the rafts were suddenly swallowed by this frightful maw of the ocean. And then by the men on the ten-foot dingy were words said that were still not words. . . ."

A lighthouse stuck up like the point of a pin in the east, and they rowed.

"None of them knew the colour of the sky. Their eyes glanced level, and were fastened upon the waves that swept toward them. These waves were of the hue of slate, save for the tops, which were of foaming white, and all of the men knew the colours of the sea. . . . Many a man ought to have a bathtub larger than the boat which here rode upon the sea. These waves were most wrongfully and barbarously abrupt and tall, and each froth-top was a problem in small-boat navigation." Crane when he entered the dinghy had been awake and active most of some forty nerve-racked hours. "He rowed as well as the others," said the cook, "notwithstanding he was so worn out that he could hardly hold his oar straight in the terrific seas." "Shipwrecks are apropos of nothing," Crane commented: if men could train for them, rest, eat, "there would be less drowning at sea," and he mentioned that the oiler had just worked double watch. He and the oiler rowed, the injured captain in the stern. An onshore wind helped. They put up an overcoat, and sailed, till the wind died. They rowed. Land had appeared—thinner, certainly, than paper—and they talked of the life-saving station near Mosquito Inlet (there didn't happen to be any).

The dinghy was an egg-shell. When gulls "came very close and stared at the men with black bead-like eyes"—one hovering near Murphy to his horror—instead of taking the heavy painter-end to it he "gently and carefully waved the gull away." When they had to change seats, rowing, each "slid his hand along the thwart and moved with care, as if he were of Sèvres." A devotion to the captain, and a subtle brotherhood, developed themselves in the men; and their comradeship "the correspondent, for instance, who had been taught to be cynical of men, knew even at the time was the best experience of his life."

"Slowly the land arose from the sea. From a black line it became a line of black and a line of white—trees and sand. . . . Slowly and beautifully the land loomed out of the sea." In an hour they might be in. Crane found cigars in his coat, some dry, somebody found matches, and they puffed away and "judged well and ill of all men. Everybody took a drink of water." They waited to be seen from shore, and waited. "Funny they don't see us," the men said, and said other things. Finally the captain decided to make a try, before they should all be too tired to swim when the dinghy swamped. They exchanged addresses, and headed in. "If I am going to be drowned—" Stephen Crane was reflecting, "if I am going to be drowned—if I am going to be drowned, why, in the name of the seven mad gods who rule the sea, was I allowed to come thus far and contemplate sand and trees? . . . But no. . . . She cannot drown me. Not after all this work." The waves were high, roughening, the shore afar. When the oiler judged the boat would live three minutes, they were too far to swim, and he turned her and took her safely out again. They rowed, and waited. At last a tiny figure on the beach seemed to see them, waved a coat, kept on waving it. This maddened them. They saw something on the beach they thought a lifeboat, and people. One of them made it out finally: an omnibus. "That's just a winter-resort hotel omnibus that has brought over some of the boarders to see us drown." Waiting, they rowed, and the land disappeared in the dusk. They heard the surf.

"A night on the sea in an open boat is a long night. . . . The plan of the oiler and the correspondent was for one to row until he lost the ability, and then arouse the other from his sea-water couch in the bottom of the boat." Minute he stopped rowing, his teeth chattered wildly, but the dinghy was so small that he could partly warm his feet, rowing, under the others. The lighthouse to the south shone gold, and a bluish gleam came out at the water's edge on the north: "These two lights were the furniture of the world." Otherwise there were waves. A big shark came and whirred around the boat for a long time, left, and came back. The captain, drooped over the water-jug, was awake though Crane did not know it. The gray, sore little man in the blackness aching at the oar had a feeling of Injustice. "Other people had drowned at sea since galleys swarmed with painted sails, but still—— When it occurs to a man that nature does not regard him as important, and that she feels she would not maim the universe by disposing of him, he at first wishes to throw bricks at the temple, and he hates deeply the fact that there are no bricks and no temple . . . if there be no tangible thing to hoot, he feels, perhaps, the desire to confront a personification and indulge in pleas, bowed to one knee, and with hands supplicant, saying 'Yes, but I love myself.' A high cold star on a winter's night is the word he feels that she says to him. Thereafter he knows the pathos of his situation." Into his worn mind sprang a verse, never thought of since, he had had to memorize at school:

> A soldier of the Legion lay dying in Algiers;
> There was lack of woman's nursing, there was
>   dearth of woman's tears;

But a comrade stood beside him, and he took that
comrade's hand,
And he said, "I never more shall see my own, my
native land."

He saw this soldier, now, and the low square forms of the
city in the distance. He was sorry for the soldier. "Pretty
long night," said the captain.

When light moved on the waves again, and the dunes came
back, the men looked inshore with interest. The beach was
empty. They held a conference, and decided. The oiler began to back the dinghy in. The combers roared. The dinghy
reared, and plunged. Water swarmed in, they bailed, till at
a great wave's coming Crane called to the captain to jump.
It swallowed the dinghy. These two were thrown out on the
same side, Crane partly under the upset boat, and the cook
saw Murphy catch Crane's collar with the uninjured hand to
save him. The dead-winter water was cold. "The coldness of
the water was sad; it was tragic. . . . The water was cold."
They swam, Higgins ahead, in the terrible surf, except the
captain who was hanging on the boat, to the keel, like a gym-
nast. Slowly and slowly the shore neared them all. Montgomery had a life-belt on; "for an hour almost," he said, "we
battled for life." Crane seems to have been immobilized for
a while in a current, and then, toward the end, to have been
thrown by a wave completely over the boat. He saw a man
come running down the beach, and "as he ran the air was
filled with clothes" as if he had "pulled a single lever and
undressed."* This man went to the cook, then to the captain, who was standing now in the water and waved him to
Crane. Then they saw Higgins face down in the shallows.
His head had been crushed by a timber loose in the surf and,
while the others were being cared for on the beach by some
of the hotel people who had finally arrived, the oiler died.

* This image from Crane's dispatch is better, uniquely, than the sentence
in his story.

They had come ashore in the morning of January 3rd at Daytona. (Some reports, even, said at noon—they may have waited a long time before their desperate second try in the surf; and Crane's dispatch said they were thirty hours in the dinghy.) Aid was asked from Jacksonville, but no trains ran on Sunday and nothing in port could stand the seas except the government tug *Three Friends*; so Washington had to be wired at four in the afternoon for permission to send out the tug with revenue officers aboard. No reply came, and the Treasury Department, a senator, a cabinet member, and the President were involved before the *Three Friends* was allowed to steam out at 6:30. There was wide resentment over this delay, and the press asked angrily next morning why the idling cruiser *Newark* had not been sent. Meanwhile news of the loss of Stephen Crane had been flashed north and abroad. It was corrected in a day, but magazines were going to press and later he could read his obituaries in the London *Academy*, the *Philistine*, and elsewhere.* Hubbard was marvelously ridiculous: "I have gibed Stephen Crane, and jeered his work, but beneath all the banter there was only respect, good-will—aye! and affection. He is dead now—Steve is dead. How he faced death the records do not say. . . . Within the breast of that pale youth there dwelt a lion's heart. . . . *He died trying to save others.* So here's to you, Steve Crane, wherever you may be! You were not so very good, but you were as good as I am—and better in many ways. . . . And so, Stevie, good-bye and good-bye!" Over a page, "LATER: Thanks to Providence and a hen-coop Steve Crane was not drowned after all—he swam ashore."

He was not exactly saved, though. Seventy or eighty hours more or less foodless and sleepless, unwell, the engine-room, the deck, a death, the foundering, deaths, the day and night of the boat, the surf, the final death, these had their effect, and, when taken with his unabated habit of sparing himself

* Six months later Mark Twain made his much-misquoted comment from London: "The report of my death was an exaggeration" (*Journal*, June 2nd).

165

nothing, and with the tuberculosis probably now developing, suggest that from now on Crane was a young man who lived actively with death, a man more than usually a-man-dying. William Howe Crane thought his health never returned.

In some sense, however, he pulled himself together with great rapidity, because three days after he sprawled on the beach, "striking the sand with each particular part of his body," he wired Bacheller from Jacksonville his extended, careful, self-possessed dispatch about the voyage and loss of the *Commodore*—itself, for a writer readier than Crane, three days' stiff work. It filled, with the author's picture, nearly the whole front page of the New York *Press* on the morning of January 7th. And the story of the open boat must have been working already in his mind, for the dispatch says only, near the end, "The history of life in an open boat for thirty hours is not to be told here," and beaches the men quickly at Daytona. An old Asbury Park friend, Ralph D. Paine, dining in a café alcove one night, heard a familiar voice reading aloud in the next alcove, and then breaking off to say, "Listen, Ed, I want to have this *right*, from your point of view. How does it sound so far?" It sounded all right to the big young captain, this draft, and if Crane looked sallow and haggard to Paine when he joined them, he always had looked sallow, and his thin face (with a straggling new mustache) brightened as he and Murphy talked of getting another ship to try again.

Bacheller, whose gold had drowned, was fed up, and Crane seems to have signed now with Hearst, still expectant, writing "The Open Boat," and seeing Cora. By mid-February "The Open Boat" was done. *Scribner's* offered his agent $300 for it on March 5th; Reynolds prodded them for more (Crane had wired his publishers urgently for money ten days before), failed, and sold it. "That and 'Flanagan' were all I got out of Cuba," he told H. G. Wells later, so he probably wrote this second filibustering story, or began it, during February. Mostly he was trying to get to Cuba, and doubtless

wasted money in schemes now undiscoverable. Sylvester
Scovel, a main ally, had been there already once; but if he
and Crane were active, so by now were the searchlights of
naval patrols. "I have been for over a month," he wrote to
his brother Edmund on March 11th, "among the swamps
further South, wading miserably to and fro in an attempt to
avoid our derned U.S. Navy. It can't be done. I am through
trying. I have changed all my plans and am going to Crete."
    What the plans were it is useless to inquire; henceforth
he has six plans to one action. The Turkish island, armed by
a Greek secret society, was at last in a state of insurrection
more advanced than Cuba's; a Greek expeditionary force
had landed in mid-February, and Crete was, when Crane
wrote, just nine days away from its proclamation of au-
tonomy. Crane did not go there, either, as the international
situation developed. But he moved: by April 1st he was
crossing from London to Paris on his way to Greece itself,
which was crowding, fantastically, into a war with Turkey.
    This gives him just twenty days between Jacksonville and
Paris, and he was some time in both New York and London.
He was going for Hearst. Of Cora Taylor, presently.
    His health was bad, worsened by the swamps, and spirits
low, during his few days in New York; he sailed with a bad
cold. The habit of reticence was strong on him; still he
must have known he was exposing himself to scandal more
violently than ever and suffered from the need for tacit de-
ception. Whether he confided in anyone except Scovel about
Cora Taylor is uncertain. Apparently he did not visit either
Hartwood or Port Jervis, and he seems to have mentioned
her to no one in New York except Linson, and then not by
name, saying merely that he intended to marry. There
were always now too his friends the metropolitan police. But
one of the clearest views we ever have of him is one of
these nights in New York, from a young *Journal* man,
Robert H. Davis, who had tried desperately to meet
Crane the year before and failed. Now he was told to his

joy to settle some matter of transportation and cabling with the celebrity, and made an appointment at the Hoffman House by telephone; Crane broke it. Towards midnight though, mid-March or so and cold, Davis was lounging with a reporter at 33rd and Broadway when he saw a small thin young man in a pulled-down black felt hat and loose rusty overcoat with collar turned up, his gaze bent on the sidewalk, coming up Broadway in the wind. He seemed familiar, and when as the man passed the reporter told him softly who it was he begged to be introduced. "Oh, Crane! . . . Here's a man who can't sleep until he meets you." After shaking a thin veal-like indifferent hand, Davis delivered Chamberlain's instructions, wondering how to make the trio a duet, till the reporter took himself off uptown, and he could begin an awkward conversation with some remark about Lord Byron's love for Greece. Crane thought love indifferent to the reporting of a war. "Greece means nothing to me, nor does Turkey. After Cuba it will be cold over there, I imagine. By the way, this is a hell of a town. I never come here without feeling the necessity for taking immediate steps to go elsewhere."

"Hardly the place for a minister's son," said Davis subtly.

"Well, for that matter, is there any place exactly suited to a minister's son?" Davis revealed that he was similarly afflicted and then tried to turn the talk to *The Red Badge of Courage*, but "in spite of my long reportorial training I found it hard to get anything out of Crane about himself. He seemed more interested in the fact that we were both ministers' sons. 'Have you ever observed,' said he, 'how the envious laity exult when we are overtaken by misfortune?' The cigarette that hung from his lips performed like a baton to the tempo of his speech. 'This is the point of view: The bartender's boy falls from the Waldorf roof. The minister's son falls from a park bench. They both hit the earth with the same velocity, mutilated beyond recognition.' . . . Failing in my efforts to unchain Stephen Crane's tongue I made a

careful examination of his characteristics. . . . I was struck
by the weakness of his chin and the paleness of his lips. The
nose, while quite thin, was delicately molded, the nostrils
dilating slightly when he became animated. The eyes, about
which I had heard much, did not seem to be in any way remarkable." He agreed to have a drink with Davis at the Imperial bar, on his way to the Herald Square Restaurant
where he was looking for friends; would he try a novelty, one
part amer picon and three parts ginger ale?

"Sure I'll try it—with your belly."

In the middle of their laugh Davis lost Crane's attention.
A girl in a light blue cloak with sunny hair had come out
from under the shadow of the Elevated structure, stopping
in the light on Broadway, and looked at Crane. "Straight-
way," Davis remembered, "he detached himself from my
side, tossed his cigarette into Greeley Square, placed his left
hand upon his heart, removed his hat, and made a most gallant bow. I have never seen a more exquisite gesture of chiv-
alry than this youth sweeping the pavement with his black
felt. Under the flickering shadows of the arc-lights . . . I got
for the first time a blinding flash of the romantic Crane. A
lock of soft hair lay upon his high, white, and shapely forehead. There was a fulness about the temples, and over the
eyes; the modeling exquisite. Crowning the cheek-bones was
a tone of light coral accentuated against the sallow dominant
tone . . . there seemed to be a tawny note in his hair, which
was soft and long and in disarray. Around the mouth hovered
an elusive smile, while the whole posture of the body suggested the dancing-master about to begin a minuet. I was
not a hero-worshipper. My whole newspaper training had
been toward the development of composure. Nevertheless at
that moment I discerned an almost indescribable luminous
beauty in the eyes of this modern Villon. They were large,
the iris seemingly out of proportion to the pupil, blue in
general tone, brilliant, flashing. . . . 'A stranger here?' inquired Crane with the utmost delicacy in his speech as though

addressing one lost in a great city. The girl stood there . . . lured by the beauty of his eyes and forehead or startled by the weakness of his chin and the poverty of his garb. She caught her breath. 'Well, suppose I am a stranger. Can you show me anything?' 'Yes . . . I can show you the way out, but if you prefer to remain——' Crane made another gesture with his felt and bowed with an air of magnificent finality. The girl suddenly found an extra button at the throat of her coat and fastened herself in. The light seemed to go out of Stephen Crane's eyes . . . 'You shouldn't hang out here, kid,' said Maggie in a throaty voice. You look cold. You can't stand it. This fat guy can.' . . . The girl sauntered off utterly indifferent . . . 'This is a long cañon,' said Crane. 'I wonder if there *is* a way out.' "

They went to the Imperial and with their feet on the brass rail Davis told the author of *The Red Badge of Courage* what Ambrose Bierce had said to him about the book in San Francisco. "This young man," said Bierce, "has the power to feel. He knows nothing of war, yet he is drenched in blood. Most beginners who deal with this subject splatter themselves merely with ink." Crane made no comment whatever, sliding his glass of whiskey up and down. Later he asked whether Davis had read Bierce's "Occurrence at Owl Creek Bridge." "Nothing better exists. That story contains everything. Move your foot over," and he wanted to know what Bierce was like personally—especially whether he had plenty of enemies. "More than he needs," Davis said. "Good," said Crane. "Then he will become an immortal," and shook hands, just shaking his head when Davis gestured toward his untouched whiskey. They went out into Broadway, Crane on uptown. Nobody ever believed Davis, naturally, about the whiskey, so for nearly thirty years he never told about the streetwalker.*

Crane, who had no desire to live very long, had made a will before he went to Florida. William Howe Crane was to

* The story is confirmed in Part V, below.

be sole executor and have a third of the estate, Edmund a third, Townley and Wilbur to divide the rest. Peanuts was not to be sold: "I would prefer that he be kept in easy service at Hartwood and have him cared for as much as possible by Ed himself," he wrote to Will from Jacksonville in November when the will was lost, "or by somebody whom it is absolutely certain would not maltreat him." Howells, Garland, Hawkins, and Hitchcock were to be literary executors. The gathering of his stories "will make considerable work, but there are some of them which I would hate to see lost. Some of my best work is contained in short things which I have written for various publications, principally the New York *Press* in 1893 [1894] or thereabouts. There are some 15 or 20 short sketches of New York street life and so on which I intended to have published in book form under the title of 'Midnight Sketches.' That should be your first care." Since November he had written "The Open Boat"; other of his greatest stories, short and long, were to come. But the experiences of his life, for art, were moving toward completion when he sailed from New York in mid-March of 1897. A man he would meet later, half a dozen years his senior, would put Crane's case perfectly when he wrote: "I am persuaded that our intellects at twenty contain all the truths we shall ever find, but as yet we do not know truths that belong to us from opinions caught up in casual irritation or momentary fantasy." If Yeats's conviction will do for anyone it will do for Crane, and Crane knew his truths with terrible precocity. Even his life was entering a final stage. He would live on a while now, celebrated, furtive, and driven, make a good deal of biography, and suffer much, but essentially it would matter less. "Stevie is not quite at home with us," a woman said to Hubbard in 1895. "I think he'll not remain so very long."

Greece

Crane hovered in England four days, arriving late Sunday night, March 28, 1897. London was a porter and a cabman in the dark, and when his horse slid gravely down an iced and dipping street to fall in its harness, a top hat was among the rescuers. "Now," said the Bohemian, "in America a young man in evening clothes and a top hat may be a terrible object. He is not likely to do violence, but he is likely to do impassivity and indifference to the point where they become worse than violence." This top hat used the strength of his back and gave advice, and Crane was enlightened. He was deposited at his hotel then, asked his nyme, sent up in a lift with an ancient elevator-boy, and put in his room overlooking "a great sea of night, in which were swimming little gas fishes." Next morning he was thrice impressed. He was impressed by the silence of London—"When a magazine containing an illustration of a New York street is sent to me, I always know it beforehand. I can hear it coming through the mails." He liked the accent, in which every word was "cut clear of disreputable alliances with its neighbours." And the expert on New York's police preferred London's: traffic "was drill, plain, simple drill. . . . I looked at one constable closely and his face was as afire with intelligence as a flannel pin-cushion."

Calling on his publisher, Heinemann, he arranged to report the war for the *Westminster Gazette*. His moves were noted by a correspondent of *The Critic*, who was impressed himself by Crane's lack of self-advertisement, his "extreme and refreshing modesty" amid the lionization. Harold Frederic, the big, energetic *New York Times* chief in London, was his main introducer; he led him into the Savage, somebody said, as if he had invented the boy.* This early champion of *The Red Badge of Courage* had issued, at the height of the fame of that book, his own best book, *The Damnation of Theron Ware*, in March 1896 and it had gone through half a dozen American editions by December; we shall hear more of him. Richard Harding Davis contributed a lunch for Crane at the Savoy on Wednesday, to which besides Frederic came Anthony Hope, J. M. Barrie, back from America, and Justin McCarthy, who had not only written a novel about Greece but had visited the country. Thursday afternoon the two correspondents crossed to Paris together, Frederic coming to Dover and handing Crane over to a tall shy Canadian, Henry Sanford Bennett. He took no more interest in Notre Dame than he had in the Houses of Parliament—or than another storyteller took next year, Chekhov, in the ruins of Rome. Paris was Crane's failure except for some children Bennett helped him talk with in the Luxembourg Gardens. Language suddenly harassed. He tried to get up some French on the train, and by Basel was very depressed, writing to somebody: "I now know that I am an imbecile of rank. If nobody shoots me and I get back alive through those Indians in London I will stay home until there is a nice war in Mexico where it does not matter what you talk so long as you can curse immoderately. Willie Hearst has made a bad bargain."

It has been a commonplace of the legend, since, that Crane was right. His failure as a war correspondent was "prompt and flat," Beer writes. H. G. Wells who knew him later was as

* So Beer. Frederic, who had resigned from the Savage years before, now belonged to the National Liberal.

interesting on this as on other matters. "Since Crane had demonstrated," he wrote, "beyond all cavil, that he could sit at home and, with nothing but his wonderful brain and his wonderful induction from recorded things, build up the truest and most convincing picture of war; since he was a fastidious and careful worker, intensely subjective in his mental habit; since he was a man of fragile physique and of that unreasonable courage that will wreck the strongest physique; and since, moreover, he was habitually a bad traveller, losing trains and luggage and missing connections even in the orderly circumstances of peace, it was clearly the most reasonable thing in the world to propose, it was received with the applause of two hemispheres as a most right and proper thing, that he should go as a war correspondent, first to Greece and then to Cuba. Thereby, and for nothing but disappointment and bitterness, he utterly wrecked his health. He came into comparison with men as utterly his masters in this work as he was the master of all men in his own."

But the imperious phrase and the brilliant picture, alas, neglect what happened.

It *is* pathetic that he went to these wars, these boring, false wars, away from the passionate private real war in his mind, but the truth is that he was not merely cajoled and applauded to them, not merely drawn to them by need of money: he drove himself to them. Having written so much about war, he told William Heinemann, he thought it high time he saw a little fighting; and the joke went around London. "I am going to Greece for the *Journal*," he wrote to someone, "and if the Red Badge is not all right I shall sell out my claim on literature and take up orange growing." This lightness is deceptive. Stung by the continual gibe that he did not really know what he was writing about, he *had* to find out. The absolute confidence of an older writer, Flaubert, was given expression only when, halfway through the composition of *Madame Bovary*, he had pushed observation as far as he could. "Everything one invents is true," he sang to a friend, "you may be perfectly sure of that. Poetry is as precise as geometry . . . after reaching a certain point one no longer makes any mistakes about the things of the soul." To Crane at twenty-five, with his lifelong subject still unobserved, this confidence was inaccessible. We have seen that he worked from observation as well as imagination. He had expended life, since ambition formed, watching human beings and animals and landscapes and skies and objects, and listening. Into the motives that fastened him on war it is not yet time to inquire, but we have observed their strength. Until this subject had been mastered in observation, he could not move on.

Crane's whole achievement as a correspondent must be reviewed later. Of this first campaign it must only be insisted here that his sense of failure was comparative and personal, in a man accustomed to excel. He was not yet Davis or Frederick Palmer or the London *Chronicle's* Henry W. Nevinson or Reuter's veteran W. Kinnaird Rose; he covered the war less fully than the *Journal's* own Julian Ralph and John Bass—all of whom were with the Greek army. But these were the age's stars; Crane, despite illness and ill-luck, ran them close. It is necessary to distinguish between what he sent to New York and what he sent to London. His *Journal* dispatches, written on the spot, were chaotic and egotistical; loose, and crammed with "I" because Crane thought it honest, as usual, to set down his impressions simply as his own. The war correspondent arises, he wrote once, to become a "sort of cheap telescope" for the people at home: "there have been fights where the eyes of a solitary man were the eyes of the world; one spectator, whose business it was to transfer, according to his ability, his visual impressions to other minds." These dispatches are too diffuse and ill-written to be interesting to us now, but they made their effect in May 1897. One judges by the reaction. J. B. Gilder's *The Month* was amusing in June on "Our Correspondents in the East," K-PL-NG, D-V-S, and CR-N-: "my favorite color, red . . . huge yellow oaths . . . a pale green rumble . . . red and brown and green ants. . . . A short Greek by his side looked blue for a minute, and then at a remark from the youth he changed color." But much brighter was some Maine wit reprinted in the New York *Tribune* as the tiny campaign ended:

> I have seen a battle.
> I find it is very like what
> I wrote up before.
> I congratulate myself that
> I ever saw a battle.
> I am pleased with the sound of war.
> I think it is beautiful.
> I thought it would be.
> I am sure of my nose for battle.
> I did not see any war correspondents while
> I was watching the battle except
> I.

Crane actually had reported that the roll of musketry was "beautiful as I had never dreamed," and instantly added "This is one point of view. Another might be taken from the men who died there." George Washington, for that matter, used the word "beautiful" for the sound of firing, after his maiden engagement. Still, "I" is everywhere in the hasty and eager accounts, and because of Crane's personal fame his "I" was much more striking than the other correspondents'. "The *London Times* says the Turks are mild, woolly lambs," but he had seen a headless Greek officer: "I do not consider the Turks as woolly lambs." And "It was the great sudden evacuation of Volo which I had the luck to prophesy to you two weeks ago" (sent on May 11th).

His pieces for the *Westminster Gazette* are deliberate and impersonal, written later (they did not appear until June). They so nearly approach the condition of art that what one regrets in them is precisely the absence of "I," a dramatic point of view, a personal narrative. There is a little wayside stone shrine, for instance, with a chromo of a saint and a lamp, before which a column of infantry is kneeling and praying as it passes slowly by on the way to the front. Suddenly a great, hootling shell strikes the base of the shrine and lifts the structure in the air. It falls with a ringing smash —demolished. Men scurry off, their fingers still at their chests. The men in the rear of the column coming up then, finding no shrine, pray quietly facing its ruin.

This is admirable, but there is no one, so to speak, to observe it; it ought to be in a story, or in "lines." Crane obviously could not satisfy himself; he never collected these pieces. Actual battle was confusing, and yet he was not free to invent or imagine. "The Turks did not come like a flood, nor did the Greeks stand like adamant. It was simply a shifting, changing, bitter, furious struggle." This would do as a deliberate momentary relaxation in *The Red Badge of Courage,* but of course it is not a battle. Palmer remembered Crane's puzzled mood in an Athenian café, over brandy ("of which he was given to taking too much," naturally, "in the E. A. Poe part of his genius"), and Crane wrote to someone: "I guess that I expected some sublime force to lift me in air and let me watch. Well, no! Like trying to see a bum vaudeville show from behind a fat man who wiggles. I have not been well either." But his expectations were high, unreal.

It is not clear that his employers were disappointed: the *Journal* reprinted the *Westminster Gazette* articles, and he continued to write for both papers for months after he got back to England. Of course his American paper tried to dramatize him. But Crane was not much of a hero to look at or listen to. A friendly fellow-correspondent off Cuba a year later describes him on his way to war as "one of the most unprepossessing figures that ever served as a nucleus for apocryphal romances; shambling, with hair too long, usually lacking a shave, dressed like any of the deck hands, hollow-cheeked, sallow, destitute of small talk, critical if not fastidious, marked with ill-health—the very antithesis of the conquering male." The famous costumes, happiness, and self-love of Richard Harding Davis* were equally missing. So when John Bass, head of the *Journal* contingent, duly studied "How Novelist Crane Acts on Battlefield" for Hearst, all he could report was a pale thin face, smoking casually, saying, "The interesting thing is the mental attitude of the men," and then, as the Turkish artillery neared, "amid the singing bullets and smashing shells the novelist stopped, picked up a fat, waddling puppy and immediately christened it Velestino, the Journal Dog."

The puppy rivals in interest this war, in which—as Bierce put it from San Francisco—a feeble nation was making an unjust war against a strong one. The Turks had German coaching and modern arms; it lasted one month. While Davis idled in Florence, Crane seems to have gone straight out to Athens, where he was writing an article on April 16th and sending money to Amy Leslie on the 18th. The war began on this day, with a general advance in the north of Thessaly and a bombardment of Arta, at the south of Epirus. North-south mountains split Greece into Epirus (west) and Thessaly (east); Athens is southeast and did not recognize the seriousness of the action in Thessaly for some days. Crane moved to Arta and was on his way north to Janina when word came of fighting in the east. Doubling back to Athens, here he met "Imogene Carter"—if they had not met before since America. Both sent dispatches from Athens to the *Journal* on the 29th. He traveled north with the other *Journal* people under Bass, Julian Ralph, Franklin Bouillon, Edward Abbott, Langdon Perry, and presumably her, together with

---

* "I was a beautiful sight at the Levee," wrote Davis without a shred of irony on June 2, 1897. "I wore a velvet suit made especially for me but no dearer for that and steel buttons and a beautiful steel sword and a court hat with silver on the side and silk stockings that I wore at Moscow and pumps with great buckles. I was too magnificent for words and so you would have said." When a photograph of Davis in war-kit was published in New York, an excited public controversy followed, partly on its beauty, partly on the question of how he was going to draw one object through another in case he needed it.

Davis who had turned up. The mystery of "Imogene Carter"
let us defer a moment. The Greek art of retreating began at
Larissa. All the correspondents went on to Volo, a port and
railway supply base covered at Velestinos by the right flank
of the Greek army, except Bass and Davis, who stopped in
deserted Velestinos, took over the mayor's house, and went
to bed. They were awakened—"you can imagine our joy and
excitement," said Davis—by cannon, and had the battle all
to themselves for eight hours.

Exhausted by the trip from Pharsala to the coast, and
"rather laid up," Crane turned back inland toward the high
bold naked hills and hurried, but it was noon of the second
day of the battle (apparently May 5th) before he got there.
On the yellow highway he met a Greek soldier coming away
wounded, dignified, with a ridiculous knot of linen bandage
on the top of his head over his red face—a product of the din
behind him, the enormous factory of the battle. Crane joined
a mountain battery, and studied the infantry in their
trenches below the crest, facing the great plain, across which
the Turks were attacking. Shells hooted and whistled like
the flight of empty beer-bottles, or just whined and sang "in
a sort of an arc of sound, an arc both in volume and in key,"
or went "like immense birds flashing across the vision. . . .
The rapid flapping of their wings was perfectly convincing."
Olympus was visible snowy in the north. The Turks were just
black ants crawling across the plain, hobgoblins, and Crane
was moved to resentment of an army that wore "a black velvet mask of distance." But: "A soldier in the trenches suddenly screamed and clasped his hands to his eyes as if he had
been struck blind. He rolled to the bottom of the trench, his
body turning twice. A comrade, dazed, whistling through
his teeth, reached in his pocket and drew out a bunch of
bread and a handkerchief. It appeared that he was going to
feed this corpse. But he took the handkerchief and pressed
it to the wound and then looked about him helplessly. He
still held the bread in the other hand because he could not

lay it down in the dirt of the trench. . . ." A hard attack was made at the foot of the height, one of eight that day. It too was repulsed. The Greeks fought well, and that night under the moon, as persistent shells came over from the Turko-German batteries, there was satisfaction on the height; mountaineers in great cloaks sang wild minor ballads. The Greeks fought well next day also, and in the afternoon Crown Prince Constantine ordered a general retreat upon Domokos, giving up Volo. The commander, Smolenski—wrote Crane with feeling—bit his fingers and cursed, and the army sullenly retired.

Crane was with a crowd of seven hundred that fled to Arcos, a town consisting of six houses already crowded. It was a river of fear. "Many made gestures, painting their agonies on the air with fingers that twirled swiftly." He got gradually back, losing the dog Velestino and recovering him in Chalkis from the servant of an English correspondent; the dog was a famous character by the time it reached Athens. Then dispatches, then he was in the north again, though both he and Davis (who had vanished to Florence) missed the decisive battle at Domokos on May 17th, which was reported by Bass. On that day Crane with "Imogene Carter" took over a boat that Sylvester Scovel had chartered and left again for the front. Next day he was with a transport of wounded leaving Chalkis for Athens. Smolenski was ordered to hold Thermopylae; and the soldiers (not officers), and Crane, and very few others, still had hope. On May 20th the armistice was signed.

A letter written by Scovel the day before throws more light on "Imogene Carter" in Athens than anything hitherto published. She was Cora Taylor, of course, or Lady Stewart. It is stated by Beer that she followed Crane to Greece, even that she followed him because she heard that he was ill. But "Imogene Carter" was a war correspondent in Greece for the same paper, the *Journal*, with a dispatch sent on the same day from Athens, April 29th, as Crane's earliest dispatch, and appearing in fact on the same page. Crane must have been out before her; for a week he had been trying in vain to get a dispatch back to Athens. "I was with the Greek army in its campaign toward Yanina," he writes, ". . . when I heard the first rumor of hard fighting in Thessaly," and now was on his way there—"quicker by Athens than overland, so I see another burst of popular enthusiasm"; while all she says is that "I start today for the front of the Greek army to see how the men fight." Nurses are returning "because the Turks fire on the Red Cross flag with the same enthusiasm with which they fire on the line of battle," but she is going (she continues) anyway. They had apparently made some arrangement either in Florida or in New York, or by correspondence; but it seems likely that Crane arranged her job, either with Chamberlain in New York or more probably later with John Bass, who was in charge of the *Journal's* war correspondents in Greece. Whether she was in New York at all does not appear; perhaps she went out directly from the south; they certainly did not travel together in Europe, Crane went down from Paris with Richard Harding Davis. Probably she had with her a much older woman, a Mrs. Ruedy, who seems to have been her constant companion hereafter.

And now for a minor puzzle. Though she was known later in England to H. G. Wells and others as "the first woman war correspondent," possibly it was not Lady Stewart (Cora Taylor) who wrote the dispatches for the *Journal* signed "Imogene Carter," but Crane himself. There seem to be only two,* and though prominently displayed they are very slight, so that one has little to judge by; but the second sen-

---

* Ames W. Williams (in *The New Colophon,* April 1948, p. 116) finds only two, and the present writer had found only these before he came on Mr. Williams's article. The reliability, by the way, of an unpublished sketch of Cora Crane, by Carl Bohnenberger, may be judged from its impressions that the name used was "Imogene Clarke", that Crane went for the *Herald,* and that she reported the war much better than he did; nevertheless the present writer was indebted to this sketch for the suggestion to hunt.

tence just quoted from her sounds exactly like Crane, the coincidence of dispatch dates is suggestive, and the paucity of her reporting is. A letter Crane wrote to his agent later from England ought to be conclusive: "You might go to Curtis Brown, Sunday Editor of the *Press* and say how-how for me. Then tell him this *in the strictest confidence*, that a lady named Imogene Carter whose work he has been using from time to time is also named Stephen Crane and that I did 'em in about twenty minutes on each Sunday, just dictating to a friend. . . ." On the other hand, a photograph of Cora Taylor in her war correspondent's kit has already been mentioned, which was taken in Athens and inscribed on May 22nd "To me old pal Stevie with best wishes—'Imogene Carter.' " Just what arrangement the two had made is probably not now to be discovered—moving as they were, unmarried, in the full glare of Crane's helpless prominence. In view of Cora's literary ambition later, it is hard to see why Crane should have had to write her trivial dispatches, if he did, and why in any case "Imogene Carter" wrote so few. The only one after her first was by courier to Athens, and thence on May 9th, saying: "I returned to Volo tonight (Thursday) from Velestino after witnessing a hard fight there. . . . I was among the last of the correspondents to leave the field. . . . Our train was shelled on the way to Volo." * Yet she *was* in Velestino—was even in danger there, when a shell exploded near her—and was later in Turkey with Crane.

Crane certainly was ill with dysentery briefly, and she

* Another mystery is the full-page story "A *Journal* Woman on the Battlefield in Greece" in the *Journal* on May 9th, by Harriet Boyd, dated from Volo, May 5th. Where did *she* come from? She had left Athens's port on the transport *Thrace* with eleven Greek nurses nine days before; that is, well before the men who went north with Bass, Crane, Davis, and presumably Cora Taylor. There were English nurses in Greece—Nevinson speaks of them, for one; Miss Boyd's dispatch is nursish. Perhaps Bass, having promised the public a woman war correspondent, when "Imogene Carter" did not work out, dragooned a nurse, writing her story if necessary himself. Bass was an attractive young Harvard man and keen about his job.

nursed him, but just when is not clear, and already before the war's end they, or she, were engaged in social life in Athens. Scovel's letter of May 19th observed that Lady Stewart was widely received, perhaps would be received by the Queen. Scovel, who liked her very much (though he commented on the irony of that possibility), was changing his mind about the alliance. He had been afraid she would ruin Crane. Now he wrote to his young wife that Cora's effect on his friend so far had actually been excellent. He was only sorry for them in what seemed a hopeless situation: "She urges him along, but even if he wished to, he can't marry her, as her husband . . . will not divorce her. . . ."

And so Crane lingered a little, anomalous in the despairing capital, bored with architecture but ardent suddenly about Henry James (*The Portrait of a Lady*) and *Anna Karenina* (which was "bully" though too long because Tolstoy "has to stop and preach"). He was so flush, for a change, that he took a note for $300 from one American and lent nearly as much to another. But Athens emptied fast of foreigners; most of the correspondents were English, hurrying to get back for the Jubilee. There was nothing to keep Crane, and something to drive him away. He hated Greek food, which hacked at his stomach, and the interminable incomprehensible jabber about him wore on his nerves. In the supremely bad novel he wrote later about Greece he explored metaphors: "When these men talked together Coleman might as well have been a polar bear for all he understood of it," and interpreting was as satisfactory as "looking at landscape through a stained glass window"—a typical depth-metaphor.

He had been excited at the outset. "Say," he said later to an Englishman in the special dialect he sometimes adopted for Englishmen, "when I planted those hoofs of mine on Greek soil I felt like the hull of Greek literature, like one gone over to the goldarned majority. I'd a great idea of Greece. One catches these fleas at Syracuse, N'Yark." But what he mostly came to like was our North Carolinian minister in Athens, Eben Alexander, of whom he drew an amiable portrait in *Active Service* and to whom he dedicated the American edition. Ill, nervous, tongueless, he was as out of place as Peza of "Death and the Child," a Greek come as a correspondent to the war from Italy, who wants after all then to fight for his country. Officers take him on and drop him. He wanders over the battlefield, "sunk in a great mournfulness, as if he had resolved willy-nilly to swing to the bottom of the abyss where dwelt secrets of this kind, and had learned beforehand that all to be met there was cruelty and hopelessness. . . . It was as if Peza was a corpse walking on the bottom of the sea, and finding there fields of grain, groves, weeds, the faces of men, voices. . . ."

Early in June he caravaned away towards England, taking with him two Greek brothers as servants, Velestino the dog, Cora Taylor, Mrs. Ruedy no doubt, Scovel, and some bitterness. "*The Red Badge* is all right," he said in England, but there is no doubt that he had suffered a disappointment. His eagerness now to get to other wars reveals it; and for a man indifferent equally to Greece and to Turkey he took the Greek disaster hard; the Germans are "hired assassins" in one dispatch. There is not a page of fighting in his Greek novel, and he laid in Greece just one odd story. Somewhere in the West of our country there is a grave of a right hand, with a stone commemorating the loss of the pianist's hopes. Crane might have set up stones too for his hopes, on the Florida coast, in Greece.

England

Stephen Crane was seen in the Strand on June 10th, a columnist reported to the New York *Critic*. For several weeks English critics had been doggedly rapturous over *The Third Violet*, and he inscribed a copy for a friend of Harold Frederic's, "Dear Mr. Harris: This book is even worse than any of the others. Stephen Crane, London, June 1897." The American reviewers were more reasonable: they all attacked it, except one who observed with justice that the little book was "an idyll, and a very pretty one," and Gerald Stanley Lee who took occasion for some intelligent remarks on the author's general situation. "He compels discrimination," Lee wrote, "before his readers are really quite ready to make it. People have to say something—or they think that they have to say something. So the furor of the superficial dins in our ears, and in Mr. Crane's ears. . . . There is one quality in Mr. Crane's work which, by all historic precedent, entitles him at the hands of his judges to the most sincere and conscientious and deliberate and constant benefit of the doubt"—and this was a "challenging quality in all that he does. He makes men take sides. He inspires the question mark."

His summer has inspired a question mark since Thomas Beer blotted it out; but Harold Frederic supplies a key. In this burly racy confident man of forty, long settled in London but with a familiar careless American manner still, Crane came for the first time on a writer with whom he could be intimate. Even as an author he probably liked Frederic better than he'd liked Garland or Howells. If *The Damnation of Theron Ware* "could have been written a darned lot better," as Crane confessed, this penetrating ironic chronicle of the degeneration of a young Methodist clergyman was and remains a tougher-minded book than any that the others had produced. It had been published at the height of the fame of *The Red Badge of Courage*, Frederic was now replacing Crane as the American most widely read in England, and their friendship shows not a shred of envy either way. Certain reaches of the imagination were closed to Frederic, he admired Stevenson and detested James, his literary advice to Crane was atrocious; for an artistic equal, as friend, Crane would have to wait a little longer. But then this equal would not be *intimate*—artistic peers seldom are. It was as a man that he valued Frederic—self-educated like himself, like himself a newspaper veteran, indefatigable, extravagant, generous, frank, oathful—"God's trousers!" he used to shout.

Crane and Lady Stewart evidently passed as married—no doubt in Greece—from their first arriving in England, early in June. There was no such flouting of opinion as in the liaison three years before of H. G. Wells's; Wells and his mistress had been determined not to marry, until—tired of servants' impertinence and neighbors' rudeness—when Wells's divorce went through they did. Like Ford Madox Hueffer and Violet Hunt some years later, Stephen and Cora Crane simply came from the Continent as if married; and it is very remarkable that of the half-dozen novelists whom Crane was to know best in England, three (all thoroughly decent, rather normal men—much less rebellious by temperament than Crane) should have lived like him in this common-law relation. Various sources have the Cranes staying with an American lawyer and his wife resident in London, Hoyt de Fries, who told Rupert Hughes of a dog the Cranes loved like a child, or at Mill Cottage on Limpsfield Common; but these stays must have been extremely brief because early in July Frederic had found them a small villa and in a primitive way they were sufficiently settled in—with Mrs. Ruedy, one of the Greek brothers (Adoni Ptolemy) as butler, and Velestino—to entertain Scovel when he showed up just too late for the Diamond Jubilee. Ravensbrook House it was called, in the valley at Oxted, Surrey. "Mr. Stephen Crane has settled down in this country," said the August *Bookman* (London), "for an indefinite period. . . ." Rumors of wars chase themselves through letters to his brothers. In July to Edmund: "Expect to hear from me in the Soudan. The S. A. fight is off." Then he wanted to go to India for a frontier row, but newspapers told him it would be over before he could get there. To Will in October he wrote still that he is going to the Soudan in about a month and has accepted moreover a commission from Bacheller to go to the Klondike afterwards, where he hopes to be able to do a service for Ted. It is very possible, however, that these plans were not altogether real. In any event they came to nothing. Crane was in England now for most of ten months, a householder, an expatriate. Ravensbrook was overlooked from Woldingham by the house of Robert Barr, a young Canadian novelist whom Frederic and Crane liked, and Frederic was not far away.

The last character we should expect in the motives for an artist's expatriation is simplicity. The European vigil of Henry James seems temperamental and spiritual enough now, and is represented so. But his friend Howells, in papers death left unfinished, put it differently. James, he says, was "a constant sufferer, tacit and explicit . . . he ate nothing then [that is, as a young man] or ever, except the biscuit he crumbled in his pocket and fed himself after the prescription of a famous doctor." "The cause of James's going to live abroad"—Howells is definite—"was that he was a man who was less a sufferer in Europe than in America." Of course this is not the whole story either, but it is part of the story. So are both the attracting and the repelling motives by now familiar in Crane one part of the story of his expatriation. They appear successively in the long letter to Will: "You know they said over here in England that The Open Boat (*Scribner's*) was my best thing. There seem so many of them in America who want to kill, bury and forget me purely out of unkindness and envy and—my unworthiness, if you choose." This second sentence is worth all possible emphasis; we shall hear of it again. But early in the triumph of *The Red Badge* Crane had been warned (by T. W. Higginson) not to let British admiration induce him into exile—which had "dwarfed" Bret Harte and "diluted" Henry James. The fact of what during this first period of English residence Crane wrote, besides much journalism and despite a state of mind increasingly violent, answers Higginson. He wrote in astounding succession *The Monster*, "The Bride Comes to Yellow Sky," "Death and the Child," and "The Blue Hotel." We must distinguish Crane's expatriation from the expatriation of James and Whistler and others, who certainly moved in part for cultural reasons. Crane's indifference both as a man and as an artist to "culture," in the ordinary sense, was absolute; nor was he interested in English society. The celebrated rehearsal, in James's *Hawthorne*, of the defects of (an earlier) American society would have left Crane cold. At most he found England intellectually freer. "Englishmen aren't shocked as easily as we are," he told a lady later in New York. "You can have an idea in England without being sent to court for it." There was also Frederic, and presently Conrad; and it is easier to stay abroad than to move there. There was nothing unusual in the settlement—fifty thousand Americans were settled in London. In New York there were the police, and anywhere in America his celebrity, to keep him from working. Crane's move was essentially one for personal reasons, with his materials already in his head, like Kipling's settling at Brattleboro earlier until a personal quarrel drove him away. The grand reason, no doubt, besides all these was his situation with Cora.

It was clear that Crane could not take her to New York. Somebody was sure to investigate her past; even the police might; life would be a nightmare. At Ravensbrook it needn't be, and Crane had for the first time his own home. With little furniture and less money, but able to borrow and free to work, he could look forward to his first stretch of settled independent life. He must have looked to it with relief. Velestino sickened at once, nothing they or a vet could do helped, and in Cora's bedroom "with all the pillows under him which our poverty could supply" on August 1st he died. Crane's feelings for dogs and horses was indescribable, so the letter he wrote to Scovel an hour later omits his emotion: "tonight Cora and I want to speak to you because you are the only one will understand. . . . For eleven days we fought death for him, thinking nothing of anything but his life. He made a fine manly fight, with only little grateful laps of his tongue on Cora's hands. . . . we are burying him tomorrow in the rhododendron bed in the garden. He will wear your collar in his grave." Then, driving over for a luncheon party on Frederic's birthday, the 19th, a horse improperly harnessed ran away with their man and nearly killed them; they arrived covered with dust and blood. Kate however was a Christian Scientist: "They, dear people, took us in"—Cora wrote—"and cured us and then carted us off to Ireland where we had a delightful three weeks in the wilds. . . ." Three weeks would bring them to September 9th. On September 9th Crane wrote to Edmund from Schull (County Cork) that he had "finished a novelette of 20,000 words—'The Monster.'"

One reason these dates are of interest is that Beer gives as a letter from Paris on September 2nd to Sanford Bennett the following: "Frederic and Mr. Heinemann have been urging me to stay in England for a time. So my wife—after practicing nine days I can write that without a jump—and I will be hunting a house or an attic in London pretty soon." Since Beer has hopped straight to this letter from Greece, the marriage he implies might have taken place there or in Paris or anywhere. Unfortunately neither Crane's circumstantial letter to Edmund, nor a very long one of October 29th to Will, mentions marriage or Cora or any settlement in England; both say to address him in care of Heinemann. To Scovel, who knew in Greece *why* they had not married, Cora's long letter of October 17th, from which we have just been quoting, mentions no marriage. A thrice unmentioned run from Cork to Paris and back seems very implausible. In short, Beer's account must be supposed doctored. On the other hand, Bennett was indeed abroad all these months; with a young bride who might be offended, he couldn't— perhaps Crane thought—be taken into a confidence which we have no certainty was extended to *anyone*, except Scovel; the phrasing sounds Crane's; and the letter may be genuine (whether candid or not), written from Paris early in June or from anywhere anywhen. Whether it is sufficient evidence for a marriage of Stephen Crane and Lady Stewart is another matter. We seem bound to suppose that no marriage took place, Captain Stewart persisting in his refusal of divorce*, or that if one did take place it was bigamous—the second alternative being the feebler.

Now Scovel's "even if he wished to" must be set, together with all Crane's independence and social rebellion, against Linson's witness to Crane's intention of marrying Cora, together with all his odd social conservatism, sense of personal honor and obligation, and passion to "rescue." The crucial testimony against this is Scovel's testimony in Greece that Captain Stewart "will not divorce her"—surviving

---

* The propriety of the title Cora used is doubtful, by the way. Stewart became Sir Donald only later, it appears. The title would have been a courtesy matter anyway.

Crane, this gentleman never recorded *any* marriage in *Who's Who* (1901–1905) and the impression thus made of obstinate disillusion rather supports Scovel. Evidently the Cranes, like some other excellent people, did not marry.

Stephen Crane's state of mind is what matters this summer, when he wrote *The Monster*. If Crane's work had not remained inaccessible for a quarter-century after his death, and accessible in so limited a way since, this study of a society's fear, stupidity, persecution, might be now recognized as a major American story. The Negro coachman of a small-town doctor is mutilated while saving the doctor's little boy when the house burns; faceless and harmlessly insane, he is preserved by his master against the whole sentiment of the town: first as a boarder at another Negro's whose family he frightens silly, and then, after he once escapes to make terrifying gentle appearances here and there about town, at the new house of the doctor himself, whose practice and position are thus gradually destroyed. The Negro and the boy have been devoted to each other, and to the doctor, "who was the moon." These three are created by Crane with swift light sympathy in the opening chapters (a charming irony reserved for the Negro, who is a great dude when he makes an evening call on his girl) and held so throughout. The doctor comes on his son in the yard entertaining his comrades with the delicious risk of daring to go up and touch the monster, who is sitting on a box by the stable, veiled, crooning to himself. The doctor comes on his wife in the drawing-room, at the end, crying: she has a headache. "A headache?" he repeats, in surprise and incredulity. Then he sees the cups and plates on the table: it is Wednesday, when she receives. One woman—she finally tells him—came. "Glancing down at the cups, Trescott mechanically counted them. There were fifteen of them. . . . As he sat holding her head on his shoulder, Trescott found himself occasionally trying to count the cups. There were fifteen of them." The story is about as long as *Maggie*, more affecting, and very different.

For it initiates a revolution in Crane's aesthetic. It is deliberately normal in style, much less colorful than his early work, bristling with names, and a *social* study, in which the Antagonist is not implied as in *Maggie*, nor interior as in *The Red Badge of Courage*, nor natural and fatal as in "The Open Boat," but human, multiple, dramatic. A chapter like the straight, masterly, *normal* narrative of XXI (where the doctor, asked to take a colleague's case, calls and is cursed) he had never written before. Details of the exceptional, the colored, the fantastic, the cursory, will indeed be found; but on the whole he attacks his subject directly, and the change is great. Crane must have been thinking hard during the months preceding, agreeing with himself to give up half his tools and try something new. The story is ambitious in a new way: it studies not one individual or two, and a dog or a horse, but an entire community: Negroes and whites, doctors, a judge, a police chief, wives, boys, a barber, loungers, girls. And the emphasis over this range is even, never spasmodic as one might have expected. If the spinster Martha Goodwin in XIX is ridden hard, she embodies a theme, and in the preceding chapter there is the chief of police, one of the most intelligent, decent people in town. So far could Crane master his prejudices.

Obsessions were another matter. For of course his mind was swarming with fear and rage, and we are interested, sharply, in the materials of *The Monster*. Its theme is rescue-and-punishment. For trying to rescue the boy, the Negro is punished with mutilation and idiocy, he becomes a "monster" and has to hide his no-face. For rescuing the Negro, the doctor is ostracized. For trying to rescue Dora Clark, Stephen Crane had been beaten out of New York, and he was now making up his mind to do the same thing again, to "rescue" Cora Taylor by (as it were) marrying her. But the theme is more definite still. In the opening sentences of the story, the boy Jim is playing engine on the lawn and destroys a peony: "Number 36 . . . looked guiltily at his father, who . . . had his back to the accident." The boy tries to "resuscitate" the "broken flower," fails, confesses, and is forbidden to play any more. For attempting to rescue, that is, he is punished. Wishing to *"efface"* himself, the "disgraced one" goes to the stable for solace from his friend the Negro hostler, who has also for "crimes" been reprimanded by the doctor: they are two "who had committed similar treasons." Crane has therefore represented his anxiety in all three, but the father is something else as well. The story essentially *confesses* and *reassures*. As a confession, it is a propitiation of the spirit of the Reverend Jonathan Townley Crane (on page one occurs the image: "The doctor was shaving this lawn as if it were a priest's chin") for the crime done against the family by his son's resolve to rescue a "broken flower." As a reassurance, it represents the father as imperturbably protective of the criminal, in spite of the community's terror, disapproval, and power. Crane has his father in effect say: I am with you; go ahead.

He calls this community Whilomville, or former-town. The name might be descriptive (meaning, where I once lived) but perhaps it is dogmatic: *where I will live no more.* The town is based on Port Jervis, as the "monster" was suggested (one niece says) by a Port Jervis refuse-collector whose face was eaten with cancer; but it is any New York town. Odors, assailing the Negro as he plunges downstairs in the burning house, "seemed to be alive with envy, hatred, and malice." "There seem so many of them in America," we saw Crane writing to Will a little later, "who want to *kill, bury* and forget me purely out of unkindness and envy." This powerful feeling governs the story. Its author imaged his rescue-and-punishment situation in all three figures—father, Negro, son—and the watching crowd tells itself that all three are burned to death. As they are carried off on cots, "Whilomville paid them a deep respect . . . three prospective graves."

But the chief Crane-mask is evidently the Negro, whose death the morning paper announces with a reverent editorial —Crane had been moved to more than amusement by his

obituaries of ten months before—while two pages later the
Judge is saying to the doctor, "No one wants to advance such
ideas, but somehow I think that that poor fellow *ought to
die*." It is a chorus thereafter: "he should have let him die."
The name of this Negro who handles horses, the rescuer, the
faceless lunatic, is Henry Johnson—the essence of commonplace, and very interesting as given to him by Stephen Crane,
who when he wanted a nom-de-plume for his *Maggie* (Maggie Johnson) chose "Johnson Smith" (error made it "Johnston"), who called his young hero in *The Red Badge of Courage* Henry Fleming, and who has singular Henrys and Johnsons to come. Crane's strange practice with names dominates
also what seems to be a reappearance of the "broken flower."
It is just before the climax of the rescue, when Johnson enters
the doctor's laboratory with the boy in his arms. "The room
was like a garden," Crane writes, "in the region where might
be *burning flowers*. Flames of violet, crimson, green, blue,
orange, and purple were *blooming* everywhere. There was *one*
blaze that was precisely the hue of a delicate *coral*." The italics
are mine, but the audacity (unless this weird allusion to Cora
was unconscious) is all Crane's, like the audacity that mentions three times near the story's end a woman named "Mrs.
Howarth."

To have no face, to be veiled, is to hide one's face, to be
ashamed. So much is clear, like the persecuted sense that
people wished him dead, even buried; when the door of
Johnson's room at the Negro's swings back, the light discloses
a room "six feet one way and six feet the other way," and the
Negro's family watch this door with "the homage due to a
corpse or a phantom." But the visitation of lunacy on himself
requires a little development. This began after reviewers'
attacks on *The Black Riders* as "crazy," and was conceivably
an ironic reply to them. It occurs in several of his new poems.

Forth went the candid man
And spoke freely to the wind—

When he looked about him he was in a far strange
    country.

Forth went the candid man
And spoke freely to the stars—
Yellow light tore sight from his eyes.

"My good fool," said a learned bystander,
"Your operations are mad."

"You are too candid," said the candid man.
And when his stick left the head of the learned by-
    stander
It was two sticks.

This is still extremely aggressive. In another piece the role is
accepted more fully:

"I have heard the sunset song of the birches,
A white melody in the silence,
I have seen a quarrel of the pines.
At nightfall
The little grasses have rushed by me
With the wind men.
These things have I lived," quoth the maniac,
"Possessing only eyes and ears.
But you—
You don green spectacles before you look at roses."

But there is more than ironic acquiescence in this visitation on
Henry Johnson of madness.

A madman is irresponsible: he cannot well be blamed for
what he does. Now Crane was considered irresponsible by
many who knew him slightly—"He seems a genius with no
responsibilities of any sort to anyone," Richard Harding
Davis for instance had written irritably home in May—and he
must have known this. Very well: if he was going to pay the
price, he would have the advantage: he would agree to be insane, but he must not be blamed. The terrible fire in *The*

Monster is like the extraordinary union itself—extraordinary from Crane's traditional Methodist family point of view. The language used for it is extraordinary. The flames rearing at the windows are "like bloody spectres at the apertures of a haunted house. *This outbreak had been well planned, as if by professional revolutionists.*" But if the chief revolutionist was insane he was not responsible, not even for the fantastic second sense of the word "revolutionist" which leaps to view a page later. When Henry Johnson enters the house on his mission of rescue, what he sees is, instantly, this: "In the hall a lick of flame had found the cord that supported 'Signing the Declaration.' The engraving slumped suddenly down at one end, and then dropped to the floor, where it burst with the sound of a bomb."

So Stephen Crane "rescued" Cora Howarth (Taylor) Stewart. He pretended to marry—and nothing happened. Not a word of scandal seems to have got into print; his family would not retort for nearly forty years. *The Monster* ends in despair, with the grand exception of his father's fantasied protection. The marvelous story written next, "The Bride Comes to Yellow Sky," defiantly brings the subject into the open. Jack Potter, town marshal of Yellow Sky, is bringing his bride—"not pretty nor was she very young"—home from San Antonio on the train. They are shy and awkward and happy until Potter, reflecting, begins to find "the shadow of a deed weigh upon him like a leaden slab. . . . He was bringing his bride before an innocent and unsuspecting community . . . he felt he was heinous. He had committed an extraordinary crime. Face to face with this girl in San Antonio, and spurred by his sharp impulse, he had gone headlong over all the social hedges." This is certainly the "outbreak" of *The Monster*. But then "A sense of mutual guilt invaded their minds and developed a finer tenderness. They looked at each other with eyes softly aglow. . . ." In the event, the town is deserted as they sneak to his house—deserted because Scratchy Wilson is out drunk and shooting, chanting Apache scalp-music. The ominous power of the community is only this drunk, who meets them and wants to fight. It is Potter who keeps this drunk regularly in order, but now he has no gun, and as he says so to Scratchy, somewhere at the back of his mind floats "all the glory of the marriage, the environment of the new estate." Scratchy finally perceives the bride at his side and lurches amazedly off. So they had got away with it; and the superb good-humor, simplicity, clarity of this tale were Crane's celebration.

Perhaps Crane was happy for a little. " 'The Bride' is a daisy," he wrote to Reynolds, "and don't let them talk funny about it"—but he was generally thus with agents. We learn more from an uncharacteristic metaphor in an article written about his flying trip to Glasgow (early fall) in a vermilion engine ahead of white and bottle-green coaches. The engine-driver feels the beauty of the business, he said, but the emotion "lies deep, and mainly inarticulate, as it does in the mind of a man who has experienced a good and beautiful wife for many years." And though he detested tourist Ireland, he recited with half-mocking delight what one could find off alone: "The joys of the pig-market, the delirium of a little taproom filled with brogue, the fierce excitement of watching the Royal Irish Constabulary fishing for trout," and wit able to cut an Englishman's skin into strips—"the ancestral dagger of fast sharp speaking from fast sharp seeing." He acquired there a little of Harold Frederic's diminishing political eagerness on the Irish side and perhaps merged a tall intrepid girl Nora, whom he watched in a black kitchen, with Cora and Amy Leslie for the tall Irish dancer* in a novel about Greece that Frederic wanted him to write.

When he started this book is uncertain. He wrote to Will late in October that he was at work on it, but to Reynolds in

---

* Nora Black is her name. In the Irish Note "An Old Man Goes Wooing," Crane actually uses "black" twice and "dark" twice in the eight lines about this kitchen; even her last name may have emerged so. Harriman, not very plausibly, says that this sketch was one of Crane's favorites.

December that he hadn't begun yet; the second must be right, planning and possibly note-making aside. *Active Service*, whenever he began it, never went well. The theme is Crane's—a rescue—but the hero seldom touches his imagination, and there is no conflict that is not artificial. A friend should have begged him to give it up at the end of any chapter whatever. Frederic was now writing, very rapidly, superficial and slovenly novels about English life, and seems to have understood Crane's talent as well as he understood English life: when he listened to *The Monster* later, in December,* he advised its author to throw it away.

But Crane was making rapidly now other friends, and he seems to have met half the writers in England, including tiny Swinburne who asked him to tea and translated an old French manuscript to him. Crane was polite about this, naturally—the scene presents itself as remarkable even for Putney—but both he and Cora were often outspoken and they made an impression. At a luncheon with Edmund Gosse, some American "became very long-winded on the subject of a reported quarrel between an Exalted Personage and his Mistress. The possible consequences of this rupture were discussed more than exhaustively, and we were all close on madness when Mrs. Crane said, 'Well, if the Prince *has* left her, I suppose we must all just grin and bear it.' This ended the matter . . . she seemed to me very vivid and agreeable. . . ." When Victorian neighbors called one day however at Ravensbrook, with their young cousin Vera, to thank Mrs. Crane for a cold cure she had sent over to the girl, and during chat one of them asked about Mr. Crane's illness in Athens, they were graveled by her bland reply: "Dysentery." Stephen Crane's dryness about the adored, departed Stevenson was as little acceptable

* Beer's date for this reading is right, because Sanford Bennett had only just returned to England and he was present; but the statement that Crane had just written the story (and in "a whole week of interrupted evenings") rests on some wrong memory. The story had been in America for months; Crane may have revised it somewhat in December.

in London. "Mr. Stevenson," he commented in a letter, "has not passed away far enough. He is all around town." Word about him, and about her, traveled; what word, who knows? "All the tongues were wagging," Stevenson's widow wrote to a friend in November. Before bewildered witnesses, and without saying a word, Crane was snubbed by one of the two moguls of British fiction, George Meredith, on the steps of a club.

Crane's Anglophilism—it was probably that, for a time, in this autochthonous character—scaled itself in resentment rapidly down. "They will believe anything wild or impossible you tell them," he raged in a letter home to Huneker, "and then if you say your brother has a bathtub in his house they— ever so politely—call you a perjured falsifier of facts. I told a seemingly sane man at Mrs. Garnett's that I got my artistic education on the Bowery and he said, 'Oh, really? So they have a school of fine arts there?' I had, you see, just told Mrs. Garnett while this mummy listened all about the Bowery— in so far as I could tell a woman about the Bowery—but that made no difference to this John Bull. Now I am going to wave the starry flag of freedom a little even if you condemn the practice in one who knows not Balzac and Dostoy- what'shisname. You Indians have been wasting wind in tell- ing me how 'Unintrusive' and 'DELICATE' I would find English manners. I don't. It has not yet been the habit of people I meet at Mr. Howells or Mr. Phillips or Mrs. Sonntag's to let fall my hand and begin to quickly ask me how much money I make and from which French realist I shall steal my next book. For it has been proven to me fully and carefully by authority that all my books are stolen from the French. They stand me against walls with a teacup in my hand and tell me how I have stolen all my things from De Maupassant, Zola, Loti and the bloke who wrote—I forget the book." Perhaps *La Chartreuse de Parme*, which he had never come on. Crane knew very little French writing and in exasperation would deny knowing any, even to Edward Garnett. One day the young critic took Crane over to meet Ford Madox Hueffer at Limpsfield where Hueffer had a cottage, new but built of huge lumps of rough stone which Crane—who was nothing if not obsessed— took to be the remains of an ancient fortification. Setting out a rose tree for Hueffer, he was pleased by an outside fireplace: "That's a bully ol' battlement!" Talk came on to writing and Garnett remarked that Crane must have read the French writers a good deal. "I never read a word of French in my life," Crane said with his usual defiance and some ambiguity. But Garnett persisted, especially regarding Maupassant. Finally Crane admitted, "Oh well, I've read ol' man James's"— a critical work that Hueffer couldn't recall when he described the day, no doubt the essay on Maupassant.

In the *New Review* this fall was running a work that seems to have excited Crane more than anything since his early passion for Tolstoy: *The Nigger of the Narcissus.* "It is a crackerjack," he wrote to Garland, and when his editor at Heinemann's, Sidney Pawling, asked him again in October whom he wanted to meet, he named this other Heinemann author— the only man since his admirer Frederic six months before. To Joseph Conrad, much older but just beginning (he was a discovery of Garnett's, as a reader for Unwin of *Almayer's Folly* in 1895) and also an admirer of *The Red Badge*, this news came with no casual force. Pawling had them to lunch. They were still talking when he left at four, they wandered over London talking, and finally at ten o'clock Crane demanded insistently to be told "in particular detail all about the *Comédie Humaine*, its contents, its scope, its plan, and its general significance, together with a critical description of Balzac's style"—Huneker had urged him to read Balzac. Never mind, said Conrad, but over dinner at Monico's till eleven he had to hold forth.

Long afterwards the older man sentimentalized their friendship in a condescending account written when he stood at the height of his fame and Crane, a generation dead, was almost forgotten.* In 1897 critics were pointing out, justly enough, the influence of *The Red Badge of Courage* on *The Nigger of the Narcissus*, and Conrad was writing to Crane (December 1st): "I am envious of you—horribly. Confound you—you fill the blamed landscape—you—by all the devils—fill the sea-scape" and (December 24th): "Do you think I tried to imitate you? No Sir! I may be a little fool but I know better than to try to imitate the inimitable. But here it is. Courtney says it." Instead of Conrad's self-satisfied memory of "I—like—that—Joseph," we hear the great man writhing with envy and despair: "Dear Stephen I am like a damned paralyzed mud turtle—I can't move—I can't write— I can't do anything. But I can be wretched, and, by God! I am!"

We have not to do with reminiscent fancy but with an actual friendship between two poor and desperately serious men hard at work. For Crane it was the third such friendship with an older man, and he had none of the artistic reservations that had been unavoidable with Garland and Frederic: he admired Conrad fully. To Huneker later in New York he was to speak of him "as if he were the B. V. M." How far the two understood each other personally is another matter. Conrad oddly says that "no human being could be less abrupt than

---

* The Introduction to Beer's study (1923). Mr. Mencken's opinion—"a long, pointless, and wearying introduction by a literary big-wig"—is perhaps less damaging to it than the admiration of the *Boston Evening Transcript* for "Mr. Conrad's very lovely portrait of a shy, furtive, half-venturing wood-flower of American letters." This and his earlier note on Crane contain much of value, it goes without saying, and much affection, but their egotism is grievous. Nearly every writer on Crane, it may as well be added, has succeeded in exaggerating (following Conrad) Conrad's degree of fidelity to Crane's memory. To the half-century celebration in 1921, H. G. Wells for instance wrote as follows: "I do not think criticism has yet done justice to the unsurpassable beauty of Crane's best writing. And when I write these words, magnificent, unsurpassable, I mean them fully. . . . He was, beyond dispute, the best writer of his generation and his untimely death was an irreparable loss to our literature." Conrad just wrote of "my old and unforgotten friend . . . who did not live long enough to reap the reward of his honest toil in the field of letters."

Crane," and his testimony is often otherwise at variance with that of Crane's friends. "His phraseology [Conrad remembered] was generally of a very modest cast. That unique and exquisite faculty . . . found in his writing, 'of disclosing an individual scene by an odd simile,' was not apparent in his conversation. It was interesting, of course, but its charm consisted mainly in the freshness of his impressions set off by an acute simplicity of view and expressed with an amusing deliberation." Others found his talk very different. Linson, writing in 1903 about the stories Crane told him after the western trip, is the most intimate of various witnesses. The tales "held me breathless and intent. That his luminous phrasing was not a trick was never more evident than then. It was simply Crane. His speech was free from the danger that his writing ran, of weakening with repetition. Each scintillation eclipsed the last, but left a complete impression of delight." "The charm of his talk," said Huneker, "defies description. It was all adjectives and adverbs." Crane was perhaps in England generally more silent, but he never knew Conrad really, nor Conrad him. Though each had seen much more of life than most authors, their own lives they never discussed. Conrad was a really nervous, uncertain man, alternately groveling and Olympian, but both affectionate and penetrating. Their friendship was valuable to both. Crane went soon to dinner at Ivy Walls in Essex, where he sat telling stories gravely about his dawgs, fascinated by the baby that Conrad's young English wife was to have in two months. When the baby— Borys—came, a great box of flowers followed from Cora, with an invitation, and five weeks later the Conrads brought Borys to Ravensbrook, where the Cranes were absorbed in him, and where were also Frederic, Hueffer, and John Stokes, a cousin —Mrs. Conrad learned with interest—of the Duke of Norfolk.

Anyone might have been there. They came in hordes from London and America, to visit an old friend, to see the celebrity, to check up on the rumors, or to enjoy Cora's memo-

rable cooking. They brought each other, they brought notes
of introduction, they invited themselves and the Cranes invited
them. Both Stephen and Cora Crane were hospitable. Crane,
who had never had a house before, was probably "returning"
the hospitality he had received for years himself from brothers and friends. Both were long-suffering. But Crane was trying to work, and already by November they were talking of
moving somewhere less accessible to London; Edward Garnett suggested a vast house in Sussex—Brede Place, owned by
a friend of his and empty. Crane had come to hate their tidy
brick villa. But money was flowing out and not coming in.
The house was full of guests and fruit and flowers—they
would spend three or four pounds for flowers for a dinner. "In
one way," Cora told one of his friends, "Steve and I are the
same person. We have no sense about money at all." By the
end of November they were half-crazy with guests. "As Stephen is asleep," she wrote to Sanford Bennett on the 29th,
"I have taken the liberty of opening your telegram. Will you
do a distracted wife a favour? I know that Stephen wants to
see you as soon as possible. But we have been overwhelmed
with callers all week. He is desperately trying to finish a
story. Just this morning a literary boy who lives in the neigh-
bourhood imposed himself on us from 9 to 4! So I am *not*
going to tell Stephen that Mrs. Bennett and you have arrived
in London. Please telegraph or write again, day after tomorrow. I know this is rude. . . ." Next day, the 30th, an American lawyer turned up with a note from Stokes: Crane was very
pleasant to him in a "quiet, boyish way," Mrs. Crane asked
him to lunch, and in the middle of lunch Frederic came in
with five other men unexpectedly and stayed, Frederic im-
pressing the lawyer as "downright rude to Mr. Crane several
times. They made Mr. Crane shoot with his revolver after
lunch and he is a very fine shot. Some children came over
from the next house to watch and Mrs. Crane made biscuit
for tea. . . ." Then Crane fled. On December 3rd, from
Dover Street in London: "I have been staying at this hotel

two days so as to finish some work. Cora just now wires me that she has got rid of some people who have been boarding with us for three days, so I can go home." The story undergoing this nightmare was "Death and the Child." Posting it to Reynolds, " . . . For heaven's sake raise me all the money you can and *cable* it. Cable it sure between Christmas and New Year's. Sell 'The Monster'! Don't forget that. . . ." The *Century* had refused the long work, an editor exclaiming to Reynolds that they "couldn't publish that thing with half the expectant mothers in America" subscribing. Crane wrote to Acton Davies in New York to ask X and Y for what they'd borrowed in Greece: "I hate to press nice fellows but . . . some of these Comanche braves seem to think I am running a free lunch counter. Seven men have been staying over Sunday." On December 5th he was writing "lines," with more than his usual irony:

> The successful man has thrust himself
> Through the water of the years,
> Reeking wet with mistakes—
> Bloody mistakes;
> Slimed with victories over the lesser,
> A figure thankful on the shore of money.

With fools' bones he buys banners—

> With the skins of wise men
> He buys the trivial bows of all. . . .
> Complacent, smiling,
> He stands heavily on the dead.
> Erect on a pillar of skulls
> He declaims his trampling of babes;
> Smirking, fat, dripping,
> He makes speech in guiltless ignorance,
> Innocence.

It is not a good poem, and he was about to begin a masterpiece. One wonders where and how he wrote in that house.

When the Sanford Bennetts arrived, their hosts were swamped with seven or eight callers. Crane had been drawn strongly to this man of a life as luckless as in crucial ways his own was (it would continue a quarter-century past Crane's, heartbreaking, dreadful to the end). "Destiny sets an alarm clock," Crane wrote of him, "so as to be up early and strew banana peels in front of him. If he trusts a friend, he is betrayed. If he starts a journey, he breaks an ankle. If he loves, death comes to her without a smile." (Stephen Crane had himself, for Conrad, "a quiet smile that charmed and frightened one"; it was "not like a ray but like a shadow," and "Crane had not the face of a lucky man.") When the two got a morning to themselves with Frederic (Robert Barr was in Algeria and Frederic was using his house), Crane read *The Monster* aloud, and he and Frederic had a violent quarrel about it while they waited for lunch, Crane swarming up and down beating his revolver-butt on the furniture. When Frederic attacked Conrad's novel, his young friend smashed a plate, shouting: "You and I and Kipling couldn't have written *The Nigger!*" Frederic did not like Henry James either, and Crane's friendship for James belongs later, though they had presumably met in the fall, and they certainly talked style one weird evening in a young American's rooms in London early in February when some nobleman's drunken mistress (" half Greek, half French, the dragon fly") tried to make love to James and then poured champagne into his top hat. Her lover had passed out, Frederic had abandoned the piano and reeled away, Charles Griswold was helpless, so Crane got the woman out of the hotel and came back to help a valet with the hat. Frederic was amused by all this; Crane not.

His health was poor this winter, with colds, his spirits low, his nerves worse, and he was slaving at one of his greatest stories. Early in January (1898) Amy Leslie sued him in New York. On the 14th he wrote grimly to Reynolds: "In all the months I have been in England I have never received a cent from America which has not been borrowed. Just read that over twice! . . . My English expenses have chased me to the wall. . . ." But money came from *Harper's* for *The Monster*; other money came; he signed a contract with his London agent James Pinker for forty pounds per thousand words, and finding Hueffer at Ravensbrook when he came back— "nervous and distracted, truly, and very late—but extraordinarily glad"—he talked for hours in a high mood of the future: of travel, of work, of a great series of heroic poems in vers libre. One inquires in vain how far into illness he was by now. Authorities speak of *hopefulness* as a peculiarity, even "the one peculiarity," of the consumptive, and it was very uncommon with Crane, now or ever.

Then the *Maine* blew up, on February 15th, exciting everyone but Crane. Stokes reproached him for his coolness, and it was proved to him at the Savage that American troops "always run at the first shot and there is no such thing as the U.S. Navy. . . . I have vainly tried to tell some good men and true that Cuba is not on friendly terms with California geographically." He liked to get things straight, though he was ready with any fantasy in drawing-rooms when he thought people insolent. Well, his father was a Presbyterian Cardinal, he solemnly informed one lady—after another lady had quizzed him at John Hay's, had been told "a Methodist minister," and had laughed, offending Hay as well as Crane. He had fantasies for hurt feelings also, as when he found out from fifteen-year-old Vera in Oxted her secret sorrow. Her mother, a friend of Ouida's, had named her Vere after a heroine. Consoled with information that in the States almost every girl was called Sunset or Orange or Praline, she adored him. But he was not very subject now to war-fever, Crane, with his own war. "This war," he wrote contentedly, "will be fought in English. I can at least swear in Spanish and it will be more comfortable all around. But I have not decided on going yet."

He was not well, nor was Harold Frederic. After dinner at the Savage on March 19th, Crane talked long with Conrad, very eager, telling him—exceptionally—a subject for a story,

"The Predecessor." It was to be laid in the West and the hero was to impersonate his "predecessor" who had died, in the hope of winning a girl's heart. They developed this until Crane decided they should write it together but as a play—"a dead-sure thing." Conrad too came down to Ravensbrook that night convinced. "Mr. Conrad and I are writing a new kind of play"—but nothing came out of it except a queer tiny play very quickly by Crane, *The Blood of the Martyr*, and a remarkable story by him much later, "The Clan of No-Name", to both of which we shall return. The play perhaps occupied him on shipboard, for he gave it to Curtis Brown in New York for the *Press*, where it appeared on April 3rd, and it must have been very shortly indeed after their evening together that Crane was racing madly over London, white-faced with excitement, with Conrad, trying to raise sixty pounds to get immediately to war. They were refused everywhere until Conrad took him to the London office of *Blackwood's* and guaranteed the advance. He frightened Conrad this day: "Nothing could have held him back. He was ready to swim the ocean." Crane left a note at Sanford Bennett's—"Sorry· not to have seen you. I have raised the wind and sail tomorrow. Nothing I can do for Harold. Barr will look after him. Write me at Hartwood, N.Y., care of Edmund Crane. Shall get myself taken in the Navy if possible"—and was gone.

Let us trace the stages of development of Crane's feelings during these later months in England. One we have seen in the exquisite temper of "The Bride Comes to Yellow Sky," and we hear it with aggressive confidence in a passage of the late October letter to Will. After touching on the enmity in America toward him and urging Will not to be troubled by it, he goes on ungrammatically: "Your little brother is neither braggart or a silent egotist but he knows that he is going on steadily to make his simple little place and he cant be stopped, he cant even be retarded. He is coming. . . . I have managed my success like a fool and a child but then it is difficult to succeed gracefully at 23. However I am learning every day. I am slowly becoming a man. . . ." Pressure on him then of money, spongers, time, illness; other pressures not seen yet; and they all moved him to another stage. After his visit to Ivy Walls, Conrad wrote to Garnett (December 5th): "I had Crane here last Sunday. We talked and smoked half the night. He is strangely hopeless about himself. . . ." And then they moved him to a final stage, which we find in "The Blue Hotel."

This story, finished early in February 1898, is not much longer than "The Open Boat" and forms with it his master-work, though the advocacy of men like Hemingway and Mencken (who calls it "superlative among short stories" *tout court*) has not yet made it standard; like *The Monster* it was long inaccessible. Six men are concerned in a tragedy in Nebraska.* Pat Scully, a merry little Irishman with a son Johnnie, runs the Palace Hotel near Fort Romper. One day he snares from the train three passengers: a "shaky and quick-eyed Swede," a tall cowboy, "a little silent man from the East, who didn't look it, and didn't announce it." The Swede behaves oddly. He seems guilty, badly frightened, shows inexplicable excitement, laughs childishly. Nevertheless the others invite him to play High-Five, and on learning that it is a game he has played before under an alias, he agrees, approaching them "nervously, as if he expected to be assaulted." The four play (all but Scully). His conversation grows more disturbed and baffling, until he announces his conviction that he is going to be killed before he can leave the house. When Scully comes in on his tragic attitude, he is flat: "These men are going to kill me." Scully rounds on his son and the two guests, but of course they can make nothing of it. They say he's crazy. The Swede bursts out, "Yes, of course, I'm crazy—yes," is certain he will be killed, and says he'll leave. Scully assures him of

* Crane had seen in the West, Beer says, at some lonely junction a hotel of a dreadful blue. Another element in shaping the story was perhaps Chapter XXXI of *Roughing It*. When the would-be miners are isolated at an inn by flood, the two men most irritating are a little Swede and a stalwart bully who terrifies the landlord. A blizzard succeeds the flood.

protection under his roof; and, when the Swede goes to pack, takes him to his own room and gets out a bottle of whiskey to keep him. "The weak-kneed Swede was about to eagerly clutch this element of strength, but he suddenly jerked his hand away and cast a look of horror upon Scully. 'Drink,' said the old man affectionately. He had risen to his feet and now stood facing the Swede. . . . 'Drink!' The Swede laughed wildly. He grabbed the bottle, put it to his mouth; and as his lips curled absurdly around the opening and his throat worked, he kept his glance, burning with hatred, upon the old man's face."

Downstairs the astounded men are wondering whether the Swede is perhaps not a Swede but some kind of Dutchman, and what is wrong with him. "Why, he's frightened," the Easterner Mr. Blanc explains. It's the West, and dime novels: "he thinks he's right in the middle of hell." Then the Swede comes down laughing and bullying, with Scully. They play again, Scully sitting by reading a paper and looking "curiously like an old priest." A blizzard is happening outside. The Swede curses and accuses Johnnie of cheating. After furious raging back and forth about a fight, with deprecation by the Easterner, Scully changes: "I've stood this damned Swede till I'm sick. We'll let them fight." Outdoors, the Swede bawls that the whole gang will pitch on him. Scully reproaches him. "You are all a gang of——" booms the Swede but the storm seizes his words. "You'll not have to whip all of us," Scully says angrily. "You'll have to whip my son Johnnie. An' the man what troubles you durin' that time will have me to dale with." Blanc's mind takes lasting impressions of the men before they fight, and then as they fight: "To the Easterner there was a monotony of unchangeable fighting that was an abomination. This confused mingling was eternal to his sense, which was concentrated in a longing for the end, the priceless end." The cowboy howls: "Kill him, Johnnie! Kill him! Kill him! Kill him!" Scully tells him icily to keep still. The big mad Swede whips Johnnie. Inside again, a wife and daughters appear for an instant to cry shame on Scully and carry Johnnie away. The Swede packs, and on his way out mimics the cowboy's "Kill him! Kill him!" guffawing with victory. "But he might have been jeering the dead. The three men were immovable and silent, staring with glassy eyes at the stove." Only after he has passed into the storm do two of them break out. While the Swede was upstairs, Scully commanded the cowboy who wanted to fight him to sit still: "It wouldn't be right." Now he leads the cowboy in a fantastic chorus of what they would like to do to the Swede in the way of beating and hammering.

The Swede, blazing with victory, works through the blizzard to Romper. "He might have been in a deserted village. We picture the world as thick with conquering and elate humanity, but here, with the bugles of the tempest pealing, it was hard to imagine a peopled earth. One viewed the existence of man then as a marvel, and conceded a glamour of wonder to these lice which were caused to cling to a whirling, fire-smitten, ice-locked, disease-stricken, space-lost bulb. The conceit of man was explained by this storm to be the very engine of life. One was a coxcomb not to die in it." But he finds a saloon, with four men at a table, drinking. He drinks. Twice the bartender remarks that it's a bad night and thrice the Swede denies it. " ' . . . It's good enough for me.' . . . 'Yes I like this weather. I like it. It suits me.' It was apparently his design to impart a deep significance to these words." Asked how he hurt his face, he boasts loudly, then asks the men at the table to have a drink. Two prominent local businessmen, the district attorney and a professional gambler, they refuse. He keeps on drinking, babbling, then snarling, and finally insists that they drink *now*, going to the table and laying his hand by chance on the gambler's shoulder. The gambler advises him, kindly, to lift his hand off and go his way, but the Swede grasps him by the throat. "There was a great tumult, and then was seen a long blade in the hand of the gambler. It shot forward, and a human body, this citadel of virtue, wisdom, power, was pierced as easily as if it had been a melon. The Swede fell with a cry of supreme astonishment." The others have tumbled backward out. The gambler wipes his knife on a towel at the bar, tells the bartender he will be at home waiting for them, vanishes, and the bartender runs. "The corpse of the Swede, alone in the saloon, had its eyes fixed upon a dreadful legend that dwelt atop of the cash-machine: 'This registers the amount of your purchase.' "

Months later, on a ranch near the Dakota line, the Easterner brings news to the cowboy. The gambler got three years, a light sentence. "It's funny, ain't it? If he hadn't said Johnnie was cheatin' he'd be alive this minute," says the cowboy; "I believe he was crazy." "The Swede might not have been killed if everything had been square," the Easterner muses, and when the cowboy retorts full of contempt that the Swede invited it all he gets angry. "You're a fool!" the Easterner cries viciously. "Johnnie *was* cheating! . . . I saw him. And I refused to stand up and be a man . . . We are all in it! This poor gambler isn't even a noun. He is kind of an adverb. Every sin is the result of a collaboration. We, five of us, have collaborated in the murder of this Swede. Usually there are from a dozen to forty women really involved in every murder, but in this case it seems to be only five men— you, I, Johnnie, old Scully; and that fool of an unfortunate gambler came merely as a culmination, the apex of a human movement, and gets all the punishment." Injured, rebellious, the cowboy cries out blindly against "this fog of mysterious theory" and the story ends.

Crane's mind, again, is what concerns us—suspending judgment a little on Mr. Blanc's summation. The rescue theme has disappeared, but "The Blue Hotel" is *The Monster* in a more terrible form. That story, while recognizing the ruin of the family, embodies still the consolatory power of the father's protection to the monster. This story, while offering hostages in all directions, recognizes the raging power of the family, but combats it—winning an apparent victory—only to withdraw the monster (as will be clear presently) to self-destruction.

The priestlike old Scully, the head of the family, is evidently Dr. Trescott again, more fully disguised—as the scene too flies from Whilomville to Nebraska. He practically makes the guests "prisoners . . . each probably felt it would be the height of brutality to try to escape." He protects one prisoner, the Swede, and incurs in doing so punishment from the rest of his family, as Trescott incurred punishment from society. But how light the punishment, and how imperfect the protection: it is he who gets the Swede drunk (overcoming the timidity that might save him), and in the end he turns utterly against him in a fantasy of destruction. Crane's tortured mind relied on the support of his father's spirit no longer.

The Negro hostler, though a *debased* member of the household, was yet a sort of member of the family. The Swede is an outlander—of what sort they aren't sure. "Stranger," Scully says to him when he whips Johnnie, "it's all up with our side." The Crane-masks here are complex, and one of them is Johnnie, the reasonable, decent son. But the dominant one is the crazy Swede, and what he has whipped (in fantasy and despair) is the normal Crane in him, the proper son. Scully's speech comes to a disowning by Crane's father; there is a brief, *conventional* resurgence of protection after this, and then hatred. Stephen Crane had brought a Cora into the family. In Scully's room he shows the Swede two pictures, one of a little girl, graceful and of the (ominous) hue of *lead*: "There," he says tenderly, "that's the picter of my little girl that died. Her name was Carrie. She had the purtiest hair you ever saw! . . ." But the Swede *is not looking*—"not contemplating the picture at all, but, instead, was keeping keen watch on the gloom in the rear." The other photograph is of "my oldest boy, Michael. He's a lawyer in Lincoln, an' doin' well. . . . Ain't he bold as blazes, him there in Lincoln, an' honoured an' respicted gintleman! An honoured and respicted gintleman!" and he "smote the Swede jovially on the back. The Swede faintly smiled."

Now the Negro became crazy after the rescue, harmlessly crazy. The Swede (the rescue, say, is over) arrives dangerously crazy, and he *knows* it. Therefore the disguises of the story must be stronger: Crane himself has to be present, Crane perfectly obvious to himself and to everyone, as the Easterner "Blanc," disapproving of everything that takes place but not making a move and above all misinterpreting what happens.

The Swede is wild to die. This is obvious, and in a narrative sense he even kills himself, he invites his death, as the cowboy says. Not only in a narrative sense. For the gambler is an inverted Crane-mask: "it was popular that this gambler had a real wife and two real children in a neat cottage in a suburb, where he led an exemplary home-life. . . . However, when a restriction was placed upon him—as, for instance, when a strong clique of members of the new Pollywog Club refused to permit him, even as a spectator, to appear in the rooms of the organization—the candour and gentleness with which he accepted the judgment disarmed many of his foes. . . . He invariably distinguished between himself and a respectable Romper man so quickly and frankly that his manner appeared to be a continual broadcast compliment." Only the children of this strange passage are fantasied in *desire*. In Crane's mind he was leading a false life, the images of his family told him, and his imagination threw up this ironic opposite *identity*, "a professional gambler of the kind known as 'square.' " There are two lines of connection here. "Every sin is the result of a collaboration" recalls the fire in *The Monster* planned as if by "professional revolutionists" and even the happy guilty couple of "The Bride." And if everything had been "square," the Easterner observes, the Swede would not have died. But things *were* "square"—and the notion that Johnnie *was* cheating is a disguise that must be reserved till later. In the saloon in Romper, Crane murders himself. The fact is in some ways obvious but in other ways so heavily disguised that it seems clear that the desire was imperfectly conscious in Crane. The Swede, crazy, drunk—two stages of irresponsibility—fearful and arrogant, is a big man. The gambler is a gentle, "little, slim" man, and the Swede calls him a "dude." Now Henry Johnson, the Negro, was a dude. There is an operation of the mind known as displacement: something that belongs in a certain connection, censored from that connection, throws itself up anyway in another. We have met Henry Fleming and Henry Johnson, and we shall meet a Henry stranger still, later on. As the nameless gambler stands over his victim the nameless Swede, "The bartender found himself hanging limply to the arm of a chair and gazing into the eyes of a murderer. 'Henry,' said the latter, as he wiped his knife. . . ." It takes a moment's thought to see who Henry is—and then one is wrong, like the author.

But the thrust toward suicide is *localized* closely enough. In the magnificent passage of the Swede through the blizzard, a life in which "one was a coxcomb not to die," he hears the *bugles* of the tempest; and he *likes* this weather, "I like it. It suits me." Crane was going to war again.

Three ⁓ END

Cuba

From the confusion of Crane's nine months' absence from England in 1898 certain clusters of fact emerge, obscured for fifty years. Cuba, first, was not another Greece: the desires of the pilgrim and artist of war were satisfied. Then, on naval rejection as physically unfit, he signed as war correspondent for the New York *World*, and though he told a photographer (Jimmy Hare) that he did this only to get a military pass, in order to write a book about the war, though his old friend Scovel running the *World* correspondents found it hard to get copy out of him, though he was increasingly ill and luckless as usual, missing the fleet's bombardment of Matanzas in May and the destruction of Cervera's fleet in July—on the whole, brilliantly, he did his job. Between April 27th and July 9th, he sent the *World* some twenty dispatches, including the most celebrated one of the war. Then, back with Hearst, he sent the *Journal* some twenty dispatches, between August 5th and November 9th.* As in Greece, he was not the most dependable correspondent in Cuba, but he was an active one and (on the word of an author-itative contemporary, Davis) he was the best. Third, he re-

* The dates are those of dispatch, of course; some were much delayed in transit and publication. Ames W. Williams's list of their publication dates can be consulted now in *The New Colophon* for April 1948.

peatedly and openly ran senseless risk from enemy fire. And finally, he delayed, delayed to return to England; after the war and obscure weeks he tried in vain from New York to get his wife to come to America; it was only upon renewed police brutality and other hostilities in New York that he left his country for the last time.

It is almost certain that Crane tried to be killed, and it is probable that he consciously tried to. Beer supposed he came to the Spanish-American War out of "curiosity." His white-faced excitement in London, the subjects of his thought in "The Blue Hotel" and in work still unwritten, poorly suggest curiosity. The reason it is not certain that he tried deliberately to be killed is that his fatigue and illness were such that nothing can be certain about his conscious mind. The two chief witnesses to his two suicidal exposures both speak of his semi-automatic, dreamlike state during them.

But first he had to wait, with hundreds of other correspondents. He was in Key West, where he discussed B. Altman's Corset-Skirt with Frank Norris and leaned on a bar near a group of newsmen who were abusing the absent Richard Harding Davis. Davis had been offered a commission and on advice declined. "How many of you Indians," Crane asked quietly, "tried to enlist?" In Tampa he gave a discharged Wisconsin boy fifty dollars to get home. Mainly he lived on the *World's* tug *Triton*, and then an old acquaintance, the *Three Friends*, which was cruising uncertainly about in the blockade zone, crammed with poker and jawing. He had happened to replace the immensely popular and happy Ralph Paine, which was unlucky, but—old friends like Scovel, Acton Davies, Charles Michelson aside—most of the correspondents detested him on his own. There was his fame, and his incongruity with it—slovenly in a wretched outfit, taciturn, ironic, unwilling to talk about his books or pass gossip about his celebrated friends. He wrote, trying to get on with *Active Service*, sending dispatches, planning a novel to be called "The Merry-Go-Round" (or "Tramps and Saints" perhaps) about

a carnival wandering through the United States; and one letter plays with a plan of going around the world. He refused
invitations from army and navy officers, who were eager to
get at him, but he played poker with colleagues on the tug,
and in Key West with a gambler who fascinated him, "straight
out of a dime novel, moustache and all, with bunches of dia-
monds like cheap chandeliers on each hand,"—and straight,
later on, into a Bret Harte-ish story "Moonlight on the Snow."
Though friends observed that his luck at poker was bad, and
were of opinion also that his poker was bad, he won $300
from this man—the amount exactly that *Collier's* paid for
"The Blue Hotel," after *Scribner's* and the *Atlantic* had declined one of the most brilliant stories ever written by an
American.

The newspapers, Crane remarked later, should have sent
playwrights to the first part of the war. Playwrights can lower
the curtain now and then, while with nothing to report the
correspondents had to keep it up. Theatrical allusions and
imagery were increasing in his prose as the likelihood dimin-
ished of his ever being able to satisfy a hankering for dramatic authorship that he shared with poets from Keats to
Auden and fictionists from James to Hemingway. On the
Three Friends he tinkered with another playlet or so. But the
only thing he liked about these weeks of floating inactivity was
such experience as they gave him of the navy. A commodore
from Elizabeth, William Montgomery Crane, of Tripoli and
the Lakes, was an ancestor* and Crane's having been rejected

---

* He was chief of the Bureau of Ordnance at the time of the disaster on
the *Princeton*, February 28, 1844, when a new gun "Peacemaker" exploded,
killing the Secretaries of State and Navy. He had disapproved of the gun and
refused to attend the trials, but brooded, and cut his throat in the Navy
Department offices two years later. This tragedy may account for the obscure passion in Chapter III of *Active Service*. In a prolonged, irrelevant
episode, the editor-hero refuses to advertise the invention of a German: a
new gun "supposed to have a range of forty miles and to be able to penetrate
anything with equanimity and joy. The gun, as a matter of fact, had once
been induced to go off when it had hurled itself passionately upon its back,
incidentally breaking its inventor's leg. The projectile had wandered some

could not discourage his imagination. "The Revenge of the Adolphus," though it ranks far below his masterwork, was the most charming account of a tiny naval action that the war produced, or any of our wars. He animates the ships, which scarcely any writer has been able to do. At the perspective of a year, it was Admiral Sampson whom Crane thought the most interesting personality of the war: "it is his distinction not to resemble the preconceived type of his standing"—a manner "indifferent, even apathetic," nothing bluff—"men thought of glory and he considered the management of ships . . . Just plain, pure, unsauced accomplishment." This was Crane's distinction also, as a famous author pajama-clad and sardonic, and the one serious excellent dark story he wrote on the *Three Friends* grew from an incident, not altogether humorous, of the casual persecution he enjoyed on it. The story was "His New Mittens," in which a widow's boy of Whilomville, forbidden to snowball with his new red mittens, is tormented by the "cruel and monotonous music" of the other boys: "A-frayed of his mit-tens!" This refrain, so analyzed, is repeated not fewer than seven times, "A-fray-ed! A-fray-ed!"

One day off San Juan they came on the cruiser *Prairie* baffled by a Spanish destroyer strutting up and down under the guns of the shore batteries, trying to lure her in. The *Prairie* mentioned to the tug that perhaps if she went in close the Spaniard could be lured out. Presently the *Three Friends* did veer inshore. The man in charge of the correspondents left excitedly for the pilothouse to find out why. Crane was there, reckless and intense, baiting the captain to run in close. "You don't think," said the captain fervently, "You don't think I'm going to let this damned frayed tholepin think he's got more guts than me, do you?" A frayed tholepin: it was quite a phrase, and Crane, who was hated as the type of unsociable conceit, who had picked up some accent during his residence

---

four hundred yards seaward, where it dug a hole in the water which was really a menace to navigation. . . ."

in England, and who had unfortunately mentioned to some-body Brede Place, was Lord Tholepin till the gibe died.

Then Crane went ashore with the Marines at Guantanamo for his first American engagement. They fought along the coast, the *Dolphin* shelling, towards the guerrillas head-quartered on a well five miles away, just inland. Crane had four terrible days of almost constant fighting, June 11th to 14th. He prepared for them by spending the whole night of the 10th watching trenches being dug and discussing con-sumption with an assistant surgeon named Gibbs. Next morn-ing he was shivering, lugging canteens, and Gibbs gave him quinine, advising him to clear out; this was the first day of combat. Two nights later he had to listen to Gibbs die, for hours, seven feet away in the darkness in some depression.

"He breathed," Crane wrote, "as all noble machinery breathes when it is making its gallant strife against breaking, breaking. . . . Every wave, vibration, of his anguish beat upon my senses. . . . I thought this man would never die. I wanted him to die. Ultimately he died." Next day Crane was hallucinating. He thought Ralph Paine coming off the tug was Harold Frederic in a fur coat, thought so for hours, through whiskey and food. Richard Harding Davis was a corpse seen at Velestinos, Caspar Whitney was the Reverend Mr. Crane. His mind seethed with death. Next day, the last, running errands for a lieutenant in the energetic action at Cuzco, he was officially cited for coolness under fire though he was suffering hallucination (which "War Memories" a year later tamed to a verbal comparison): he and his brothers were shooting at Hartwood, and the shells were setters—dogs who went in and stirred out the game or Spaniards. His battle-report, filed on the 22nd (*World*, July 1st), contained the war's most famous image: "a spruce young sergeant of marines, erect, his back to the showering bullets, solemnly and intently wig-wagging to the distant Dolphin" under the fire of twenty rifles. "Coffee!"—it closes—"Hard-tack! Beans!

Rest! Sleep! Peace!" But a soldier (later a friend of Van Wyck Brooks, who reports the incident) was with him behind an earthwork on one of these four days at Guantanamo. "Suddenly Crane, who was incapable of bravado, let himself quietly over the redoubt, lighted a cigarette, stood for a few moments with his arms at his sides, while the bullets hissed past him into the mud, then as quietly climbed back over the redoubt and strolled away. It was impossible, H—— said, to question the insouciance of this act: Crane's bearing was that of a somnambulist."

Ten days later, June 24th, he was at the inland ambush called Las Guasimas, for which he had prepared meanwhile by an adventure with Scovel. They swam Jamaican horses ashore, found some insurgents and got scouts to take them, after a night's stop, carefully through a Spanish-held valley to a headland overlooking Santiago harbor, with Cervera's doomed ships riding tranquilly at anchor. A thirty-one-mile ride that day, and his spinal cord burned like a red-hot wire. Most of Las Guasimas Crane missed because Ed Marshall caught a bullet near his spine. Propped under a tree, between convulsions, he dictated his story to Crane, who then ran five miles to the coast for help from the *Journal's* staff, lay down and explained the need for a stretcher, rose and conducted the bearers back, then accompanied them once more to Siboney. That night, unable to eat, he shocked Acton Davies and Henry Carey by talking of places on his body for a bullet's entry, muttering that it must be interesting to be shot; they got the impression that he wanted to be. Treating Davies for sunburn, he imagined aloud how his plump old crony would look if a shell hit him: like a squashed peony. The dispatch written this night relied on style. After the Spaniards flee: "Then the heroic rumor arose, soared, screamed above the bush. Everybody was wounded. Everybody was dead. There was nobody. Gradually there was somebody. There was the wounded, the important wounded.

And the dead." (Pulitzer's impression of this coda has not been preserved, but the *World* never forgave Crane—though Scovel did—for sending Marshall's dispatch.)

A week later, July 1st, in the sharp attack before San Juan, there was an occasion that became famous. Crane stood conspicuous on a crest, drawing fire, in a coat that was either a light English waterproof or a gleaming white raincoat, and then strolled about, seeming abstracted. Soldiers called curses. Leonard Wood, crouching in a depression with Richard Harding Davis, shouted at him, and finally Davis—his nerves busy with sciatica—yelled. "Crane jumped," Davis says in one of several accounts he wrote of the incident, "as if he was waking from a nap and looked at me, astonished by my voice, perhaps. He flattened out on the grass and crawled back behind a small hillock. But pretty soon he rose on his knees and then stood up once more, absorbed in watching. I called out as sarcastically as I could that Colonel Wood and I were not impressed by his courage and he blushed scarlet before he lay down. . . ." Davis seems never to have reported what Thomas Beer found out—that a little later when Wood had moved away Crane got up again, and Davis then, pardonably exasperated, rose himself, stepped over some soldiers and took Crane by the shoulders, forcing him down. Two bullets actually hit Davis, knocking his hat off and chipping his binocular-case. So Crane limped back to El Paso that night alive—and quinine and whiskey gradually supervened, as the Santiago campaign drew to an end.

What are we to make of this history? Crane had walked once across in front of a train to see how it felt. Of his recruit, early in *The Red Badge of Courage*, he had observed that no amount of speculation would tell Henry Fleming whether he was a coward or not: "he must have blaze, blood, and danger, even as a chemist requires this, that and the other. So he fretted for an opportunity. . . ." Whatever Crane's mental state during three destroying weeks, it is impossible to ignore this quizzical and aesthetic motive. But one has certainly another impression also, of a young man very willing to be killed. He did not even fail.

It must have been inhibition over the publicity of this last day that afflicted the "War Memories" Crane wrote a year later with their intermittent falseness. His account shows him moving about "cautiously," "absolutely sheltered," he and Jimmy Hare exposing themselves only as much as they "dared"; and for the notion of exposing themselves he uses the nervous word "gallivanting." The long dispatch he sent on July 4th to the *World* (written on the *Three Friends* going to Jamaica, so that to his chagrin he missed the destruction of Cervera's fleet) is impersonal, circumstantial, a good piece of reporting—now very dull. He invokes historical parallels: the battle in the Cuban forest was "like Inkermann, where the English fought half leaderless all day in a fog," and the road, grim with wounded and dead, from El Paso to San Juan, "should have a tragic fame like the sunken road at Waterloo." One feels chiefly his passion for the private soldier. This had flared at the battle of Las Guasimas, where five correspondents were with the celebrated Rough Riders, none with the regular troops over on the right. Newspapers were in fact much overplaying the role of the volunteers. Crane's sense too of his family's military and naval record, as well as his training at Claverack, may have contributed to the establishment of the position. His last dispatch from Siboney (sent August 9th) is rarely irritable: "The main fact that has developed in this Santiago campaign is that the soldier of the regular army is the best man standing on two feet on God's green earth. This fact is put forth with no pretense whatever of interesting the American public in it. . . . Just plain Private Nolan, blast him—he is of no consequence." Lists of the regulars killed and wounded were left out of the papers to make room for life-sized oil-paintings of young society warriors, themselves "in this game honestly and . . . gallantly" —when they were made to look ridiculous, the fault was the public's. "We are as a people a great collection of the most arrant kids about anything that concerns war. . . ."

A photograph of Crane made now on the tug shows a man ten or even fifteen years older than the handsome youth posing in a Greek studio a year before. Unkempt, in hiked-up pajama-trousers and a loose open shirt sitting in a canvas chair at a desk, he looks like a beachcomber except that the whole figure is hard with purpose, the pencil only pausing in the hand, brows contracted, the eyes tense and straight. This will kept him going too long, through a week of wandering about among troops and refugees to ceremonies, still writing dispatches, chatting, mad for pickles, delirious, until July 8th when Scovel and George Rhea saw him aboard a transport, ordered to isolate himself with "yellow fever." The fever was defined "variously," but (as Beer says) it was presumably intestinal consumption. When on a hotel veranda in Old Point Comfort, Virginia, July 13th, he bowed to a lady who had dined at Oxted in March, she did not recognize him, and her grandson cried with fright. Then she did recognize him and tried to get him to bed, in vain. He sat talking and watching: the women, the officers, the troops, the stretchers. This was Mrs. Bolton Chaffee. Somebody saw them, made her the wife of the hero of El Caney, General A. R. Chaffee (unmarried), and sent them swiftly west. "You must be careful," Crane wrote presently, "about feeding runaway dogs. Mr. Bemis informs me that you and I are sinners and that we have flown to San Francisco. They have promoted you to the rank of Mrs. Brigadier General Chaffee. Perhaps it is not known to you—and it has not long been known to me—that my name in New York is synonymous with mud. Give my regards to your husband and tell him the cigars made many correspondents happier. My friends will pile a mountain of lies on me but they will smoke my cigars as freely as I smoke theirs. That is cynicism."

He had gone over to Fortress Monroe and outfitted himself for twenty-four dollars—discarding the clothes he had scarcely changed for three months—then appeared at the *World* offices in New York, bronzed and frail, for another advance. Marshall's book on the "Rough Riders" mentions with contempt the paper's refusal even to pay for Crane's new outfit, and a Pulitzer man long afterward wrote that the financial manager asked whether Crane did not think he had had enough of Mr. Pulitzer's money "without earning it." * Crane, who never defended himself, simply vanished with "By-by" and signed with the *Journal*, but his biographer had better dilate. Pulitzer's people had evidently not forgiven his sending a Hearst dispatch when his friend Marshall was wounded. As for "earning it," the handsome judgment in next May's *Harper's* of Richard Harding Davis deserves record: that if the best correspondent is properly defined as "the man who by his energy and resource sees more of the war, both afloat and ashore, than do his rivals, and who is able to make the public see what he saw," then "Stephen Crane would seem to have distinctly won the first place among correspondents in the late disturbance." In vividness of report, especially, "Mr. Crane easily led all the rest."

For the *Journal*, then, the sick man went back again to report the mild, brief Puerto Rican campaign. He watched a soldier's funeral where the chaplain's "I am the resurrection and the life" was swallowed up in the ejaculations, inquiries, comments which came over the wall from a crowd of eager natives. Just before peace was signed on August 12th, approaching a village with another *Journal* man (a business manager appointed by Hearst to ride herd on the star), he learned that there were Spaniards in it. Crane was riding a "long, low, rakish plug, with a maximum speed of 7 knots. We had no desire to win fame by any two-handed

* From Don C. Seitz' narrative in *The Bookman* (1934). Perhaps this question is the one true thing in the article, for Seitz remodeled Crane's whole reporting of the war to lead to it. His attribution to Crane of a *World* dispatch critical of the New York 71st has now been disposed of by Ames W. Williams (*The New Colophon*, April 1948); Scovel wrote it.

attack on the Spanish army, so, on receiving the peasant's information, we slowed down to a pace that was little more than a concession to one man's opinion of another." They came into Juana Diaz two and a half miles ahead of the American scouts, and the natives glowered for a little, then surrendered to Crane. He was sipping coffee when American troops cautiously advanced, and next morning he was drilling kids on the main street.

Somehow he slid into Havana this month without permission from anyone and established himself in the Hotel Pasaje while the authorities were imprisoning nine correspondents on a steamer in the harbor. He got first scowls, then toleration, then courtesy—and dodged them all. There were still only thirty Americans in the nervous city when his first dispatch was sent to the *Journal* on the 25th. He amused himself with Columbus's bones, which became an issue when some "high-priced dreamer" decided that the United States was going to seize them. The Duke of Veragua, lineal descendant of the discoverer, he announced a week later, "has decided that he and he alone shall have the bones." One Edwin Emerson, in an unbook of 1899, said Crane promised to go with him and look at them, didn't show up, and was found at the *Three Friars* "far gone in dalliance with two morena damsels"—one of them no doubt Mrs. General Chaffee in brownface. Somebody now befriended Cora Crane with word of this San Francisco adultery. Crane had evidently not written to her for weeks, perhaps since his illness, and one imagines her frantic equally about his illness and his health. Then a correspondent who did not know Crane, hearing in a Havana bar that he was lost, made this public in a dispatch. Cora wrote late in September to the Secretary of War, who communicated with Major General J. F. Wade, who inquired among newsmen and learned that Crane had not been out of Havana. Crane came by to apologize to Wade for all the trouble and still did not write to Cora.

What had happened was that he had gone underground, to recuperate, to work, and perhaps also to save money, moving from the Hotel Pasaje to a lodging-house described later in "His Majestic Lie" and there run by a motherly Irish widow named Martha Clancy—her actual name possibly Mary Horan. He was sending dispatches regularly to the *Journal*, but kept in personal touch only with William Crane (at intervals) and his agent in New York, Paul Reynolds.

Desperate for money, he was trying to finish *Active Service* and making stories that he enjoyed as intensely as he hated the novel. "Now this is IT," he crowed, or "I am sending you a *peach*. I love it devotedly." He wrote and wrote. Perhaps the tough, quiet, moving "Price of the Harness" was first. Dreaming of a young sailor's tale, shipwrecked off Cuba in mid-century to become a Spanish lady's lover in the tropical city, he wasted some energy on Spanish history and grammar. In October he sent Reynolds a set of harsh, awkward, jealous, impassioned, guilty, despairing love poems called "Intrigue"—some of which seem to have his wife in mind and others some vanished love.

Jealousy bulks in *Active Service*. The Sunday editor of the New York *Eclipse*, Rufus Coleman, in love with a professor's daughter Marjory, learns that her father is taking her and her mother with some students to Greece on an archeological expedition. Coleman feels jealous of all the students, but especially one named Coke, and takes a vacation: he becomes a war correspondent for the scrap coming in Greece in order to follow them. They get into difficulty, lost between the Greek and the Turkish lines; he finds them and rescues them. But an American theatrical star, Nora Black, described as tall, "with a pair of famous eyes, azure, perhaps—certainly purple at times—and it may be, black at odd moments," and "young," though a little reflection reveals that she has had a public career of at least twelve years—this woman is in love with Coleman and, dissatisfied with her London stage en-

gagement, takes an assignment as war correspondent to follow *him* to Greece. She turns up, not plausibly, between the
opposing lines, too, with an old lady companion, and she and
Marjory wage a war of jealousy, active on her part, passive on
the heroine's. Her "respectability" is the issue. Coleman and
Coke have a blazing scene when Coke declares that his own
"prehensile" qualities "had not led him to cart a notorious
woman about the world with him." Earlier, on Coleman's
telling her that she is raising the very devil, Nora Black herself is made to ask outright: "Rufus Coleman do you mean
that I am not a respectable woman?" and this "direct throt-
tling of a great question stupefied him utterly." They have just
one dinner together, in fact,—where the writing becomes
very odd. "He simply sat watching her with eyes in which
there were two little covetous steel-coloured flames. He was
thinking, 'To go to the devil—to go to the devil—to go to
the devil with this girl is not a bad fate—not a bad fate—not
a bad fate.' " Then she mentions Marjory, they quarrel, and
he goes. A few pages later, after Coke's insult, we are assured
that Coleman has upon his face "the curious look of temper-
ance and purity which has been noted in New York as a singular physicial characteristic. If he was guilty of anything in
this affair at all—in fact, if he had ever at any time been
guilty of anything—no mark had come to stain the bloom of
innocence." (Crane, as we know from Claverack on, *looked*
guilty of everything.) Of course he is innocent enough, and
gets Marjory, while Nora goes casually off with a noble and
rich little Greek.

It is a wonderfully bad, uncomfortable, stupid book, like
an elaborate, unnecessary, and superficial self-reassurance
rather than like a story or like one of Crane's lightning in-
vestigations. The coarsening of himself into Coleman (who
is perhaps based also on Edward Marshall or Sylvester
Scovel) lets him make nervous references to what he felt disreputable in his life after Florida, but it does not produce a
character. Neither of the women has life. Marjory, of whom

Coleman stands in terror, is blank; and Nora, who must be an uneasy amalgam of Crane's theatrical friend (and newspaperwoman) Amy Leslie and Cora Crane (a war correspondent in Greece, perhaps not respectable, and Nora's "me son" to Coleman recalls Lady Stewart's inscription of her photograph in Athens to "me old pal Stevie"), is little better. The professor and his wife are overdrawn, and the students, queerly, are farcical. The fine details are feardetails: Coleman keeps abreast of his dragoman on the road because he knows that the dragoman's heart "had for the tenth time turned to dog-biscuit," and in the pitch darkness they hear sudden volleys: "Coleman and the dragoman came close together and looked into the whites of each other's eyes." Of the very pleasant student Tounley, who defends Coleman, Crane created a lovely image for "his perfect willingness to fight on occasions with a singular desperation, which usually has a small stool in every mind where good nature has a throne." But in the book as a whole only his anxiety, not his imagination, is present. He finished it, then threw away the end and wrote it again. Did Coleman first succumb to Nora Black, and did Crane rewrite away from autobiography?

Calm and objective, "The Price of the Harness" hardly seems possible to that novelist. On November 3rd he was furious about a change of title: "Damn Walker . . . it *is* the price of the harness . . . paid for wearing the military harness . . . and they paid blood, hunger, and fever." But it appeared as "The Woof of Thin Red Threads"—a phrase in Chapter V—until he changed it back. There is a silly legend, which Frederick Palmer may have originated, that Crane wrote well about war only until he saw it. But this story and the later "Virtue in War" and several others ring as true as his first imaginative studies, though their merits are different. They are much more matter of fact, less brilliant, more humanly funny (extremely so), and affecting. Crane's imagery continues infallible: "with his heavy roll of blanket and the half of a shelter-tent crossing his right shoulder and under his left arm, each man presents the appearance of being clasped from behind, wrestler fashion, by a pair of thick white arms." Harness indeed. And the hoarse conversation of his friends with Nolan wounded moves awkwardly, inevitably, towards a little paragraph like the turn of a melody in Schubert: "He did not know he was dying. He thought he was holding an argument on the condition of the turf." Through the excruciation of Crane's mind one hears also something happy. Nolan, endlessly trained for the task he is now finally about, as the charge begins has his creator's thoughts in his own: "Something fine, soft, gentle, touched his heart as he ran. He had loved the regiment, the army, because the regiment, the army, was his life,—he had no other outlook; and now these men, his comrades, were performing his dream-scenes for him; they were doing as he had ordained in his visions. . . ." The author of *The Red Badge of Courage* had been disappointed in Thessaly; he was not disappointed in Cuba. And with imagination again freed, his studies of war had yet to move to a final stage.

Time was running. "I enclose a 'personal anecdote' thing for McClure," he had told Reynolds, October 20th: "Hit him hard. Hit him beastly hard. I have got to have at least $1500 this month." Cora Crane was also writing Reynolds desperately for money. Summonses had been served at Ravensbrook for debt, and she had not herself only to look after. Harold Frederic had had a stroke in August. A specialist diagnosed embolism of the brain and endocarditis at the same time that Kate got a Christian Scientist practitioner named Mrs. Mills from London. Frederic was not a Scientist himself but skeptical of doctors, and after a heart seizure he dismissed them, to return to whiskey—even a cigar until his heart fluttered. He would not stop work; he even drove over to Ravensbrook (October 11th) with Kate and Mrs. Mills, five hours out of the house. Cora urged doctors again on the 17th, they came, and on the 19th he died. Kate (with three children) took refuge with Cora. A manslaughter charge was brought against Mrs. Mills and her. It must have been news of all this, and an urgent letter from Conrad written at Cora's imploring, that early in November shook Crane out of his solitude. He does not, however, seem to have been prepared to return to England, as they wanted. His state of mind during the weeks to come is very obscure.

Going north in mid-November Crane stared at Congress again and was told by some senator that he had visited the War Department hourly on July 1st. "I asked him what good that did and he said it showed his interest in the campaign. Nobody would believe in him. I can't believe in him but it is true that I saw him." He had all but Mark Twain's ferocity upon this subject. "In our next war," he had cabled from Havana, "our first bit of strategy should be to have the Army and the Navy combine in an assault on Washington. If we could once take and sack Washington, the rest of the conflict would be simple." Yet in "The Second Generation" Crane's irony is chiefly for a senator's worthless son, not for the senator—whose "mind moved like the wind, but practice had placed a Mexican bit in the mouth of his judgment. This old man of light quick thought had taught himself to move like an oxcart."

Crane's month or six weeks in New York is mysterious, except for loafing and chatting with James Huneker. Thomas Beer has him visiting Hartwood and Port Jervis, as one might expect, but a careful niece was repeatedly certain he did not. Ravensbrook was seized, and Cora prepared to move somehow to Brede. On November 28th he wrote to an old friend Mrs. William Sonntag: "How do you persuade anybody to do anything by cables and letters? I am very anxious to have Mrs. Crane come to this country. Mrs. Crane is very anxious to have me come back to England. We are carrying on a duel at long range, with ink." Circumstances changed his mind with great rapidity.

He was hunting a house in New York, thinking of one in the country, even a ranch in Texas. Probably his finances had improved—Stokes took his poems *War Is Kind* and wanted a novel, and Bacheller was going to syndicate *Active Service*. But he struck old friends in New York (those not, like Linson, abroad or scattered here) as listless and very low. At a luncheon Howells gave him he sat silent, and after it fell asleep on the critic's couch. Garland, in McClure's office, thought he looked ghastly and offered some well-meant, hearty, useless advice. Stiff work all fall, after the campaign, had worn him out. In short he was in no state to defend himself against enemies or even editors. Two destroyed stories relate to this time. The first was "Vashti in the Dark," believed to have been written in February 1895 in the South, which he revised on the correspondents' tug off Cuba; Acton Davies who typed it for him then thought it marvelous, but *Harper's* is said to have rejected it, and Crane burnt it. It was about a young Methodist preacher from the South who finds his wife has been raped by a Negro in a forest at night, and kills himself. The second was "The Cat's March": the artist's model of *The Third Violet* (in love there with the hero Hawker, who is in love with a respectable girl) marries the novel's Pennoyer, settles in a small town, and becomes the victim of its respectable women. Huneker liked its humor. This is said to have been written in Cuba, typed by Davies, rejected by an editor or so, and destroyed.

On November 23rd he and Huneker were in Delmonico's for cocktails, Crane was observed, and when they left some men at the bar went over him. He had tried to get himself killed in Cuba, hadn't he? Somebody was incredulous. A famous young writer? *why?* The tall McCumber, whom we have met before, insisted: Crane was dying of syphilis, everyone knew it. Richard Harding Davis, ordering dinner in the corner, came through the group and required him to be silent. McCumber repeated and added, drunk. Two dozen men watched Davis, blushing, throw the giant out. Coming back, he asked the men he knew not to speak of the matter; and it went everywhere. Crane was peculiarly vulnerable just now because slander had Frederic a suicide. After a December trial the Crown relinquished its case against Kate, and Mrs. Mills was acquitted, but Crane had to hear all this continually in New York versions. And the usual talk went forward: "Three or four times," said Huneker, "when he had been spending the whole evening with Ryder and myself I would be told in the morning how drunk and disorderly he had been the night before by men who had not seen him. For a mild and melancholy kid he certainly had fallen completely into the garbage can of gossip. . . ."*

Then in the first week of December he was leaving a theater with Mrs. Sonntag, her son, and her cousin the Reverend Patrick Hart. Mrs. Sonntag, white-haired now at forty-three, was ill and used crutches; she had a lisp. She and Crane came into the lobby first, talking. Somebody said, "Oh, there's Stephen Crane!" and several men spoke to him, Acton Davies perhaps one. Suddenly a policeman shoved through, asked if he was Stephen Crane, and said: "Come round to the station, you drunken bum!" When Mrs. Sonntag cried out, the fellow turned on her, yelling: "That will be enough from you, you goddam French whore!" Some men intervened, Crane standing absolutely still and silent. Then the priest came forward. At sight of him the policeman mumbled an apology and fled. The newspapers missed the affair, but young Sonntag was asked about it at school. The same thing was tried by another policeman when Crane was with James Laurens Ford on Madison Avenue, and again. He cabled his wife on December 20th and sailed on the *Manitou* early in January.

* Reluctantly, the record must be set straight about the final passage in this rivalry-chivalry, a caricature of Crane by Davis in "The Derelict," published after Crane's death. Beer denied the fact: "Illustrations of the story happened to resemble Crane somewhat and Mr. Davis suffered a deal of comment for which he was not responsible." "Channing," a correspondent at the Spanish War, is a "genius," a borrower, indolent, ill-dressed, praised by English reviewers, author of "Tales of the Tenderloin," looks like an opium-eater, indifferent to his work after writing it, self-pitying, and "ought to brace up." He talks Crane's style. The illustrations do not resemble Crane.

Brede

Few places could have suited his state so little as this immense, unrestored manor-house near Rye in Sussex. Brede Place had been in the Frewen family for two hundred years, but Moreton Frewen—"the bimetallist, as kind a man [said Robert Barr] as steps on leather"—had only just bought it from his brother when he gave it to Crane for a few pounds' rent or for nothing, with an ancient butler, Heather. Crane saw it first on January 16, 1899, driving from Hastings in the twilight with Cora between high hedges and oaks, across Groaning Bridge, and up through the vast unkempt park to the great house. A noseless bishop looked down on the courtyard, there was a stand for falcons in the outer entrance hall, an owl's nest inside, and they wandered with lamps through the high, bare, stone-vaulted rooms. "It is a pretty fine affair," he admitted, returning ten pounds to Sanford Bennett, "and Cora believes that Sir Walter Scott designed it for her. They began one wing in 1378 and somebody kidded it with artillery in Cromwell's time." Ghosts walked, parts of the house were in ruins. It was a residence for a healthy poet. As recently as twenty-five years before, the lessee had bricked up underground passages which flooded enough on occasion to float a boat dark distances. Not even servants would sleep in, disliking ghosts.

But there was peace as well as excitement in settling again. Collecting furniture for a few rooms and arranging for Crane's things to be shipped from Hartwood, they moved in, with entourage: Mrs. Ruedy, Harold Frederic's orphans, canine retainers. Crane bought a horse. Callers at first were few, and though the chronology of his final work is uncertain he seems to have written little this winter—another Spanish War account or so. He was resting. Whether he had energy yet for another long story is doubtful, and there was a second obstacle. Crane apparently knew where his genius lay: in formidable longish tales and very brief ones. Yet the collection of his greatest power had brought him chiefly gall. *The Open Boat*, the year before, had gone almost unnoticed. *The Athenæum* which gave *The Little Regiment* four sentences gave this book three: so much for Stephen Crane as a story-writer. There were standard admirers: Frederic in the *New York Times* (May 1st), Talcott Williams in *Book News*, a dozen casual reviews; to the *Academy*, if he was still "the analytical chemist of the subconscious," this was "a volume made up of odds and ends," for the *Literary World* it was a "livid blur" except for the brilliant "Bride Comes to Yellow Sky." Some mentioned "The Open Boat" itself, which had received extraordinary attention when it appeared in *Scribner's*, and that was all. Several friends heard Crane upon this subject. He was specially keen toward neglect of "The Bride"—in fact the finest work (after the title-story) in the book, which included "One Dash—Horses," "The Five White Mice," "Death and the Child," others; and the English edition had added nine Midnight Sketches, of which at least two are tiny masterworks, "An Experiment in Misery" and "An Ominous Baby." Crane had sufficiently proved his ability to go his own way against indifference, but now in the wrecked body all that was changing. "His greatest difficulty," Mrs. Crane had written to Garnett on January 10th, "is a lack of that machine-like application which makes a man work steadily. I hope that the perfect quiet of Brede Place and the freedom from a lot of dear good people, who take his mind from his work, will let him show the world a book that will live." Mechanical industry was perhaps what he least needed. Crane was at twenty-seven the author of seven books besides three or four others written but unpublished, several of which would live—at this age Chekhov was just emerging from humorous journalism, and Maupassant was still a poet.

Crane though had no future. Did he know it? He did not act as if he knew it. He began to *read*, for the first time in years of scrambling about the world. Beer recovered some reading of a week in March: Turgenev's *Smoke*, Henry James's new *In the Cage*, Shaw's *Cashel Byron's Profession*, and some books less likely, *Literature and Dogma* and one on Greek vases. He also read history, military of course and even constitutional (May's on England). Norris's *McTeague*—of which *The Outlook* sighed on the 18th that it was "a misfortune that he should have devoted so much skill and virility to a life so essentially without spiritual significance, and so repulsive in its habit and quality"—Crane exactly thought "too *moral*," but besides admiring it he begged Heinemann to take on Norris in England. *In the Cage*, a gift from James elaborately inscribed in French, he "got horribly tired [of] half through and just reeled along through the rest," he confessed on lending it. "Women think more directly than he lets this girl think. But notice the writing in the fourth and fifth chapters when he has really got started. . . ."

Henry James had Lamb House in Rye and during one period came visiting two to four times a week. They regarded each other inevitably with a certain irony, but apparently the ceremonial Master loved and admired his dry junior "so truly gifted," "of the most charming sensitiveness," "so very lovable," with "the mannerisms of a Mile-End Roader." Crane honored him, resented his withdrawal from the scandal over Harold Frederic's death ("He professed to be er, er, er much attached to H. and now he has shut up like a clam"), and found him thoroughly odd. "I agree with you," he had written to somebody after the debacle of the top hat, "that Mr. James has ridiculous traits and lately I have seen him make a holy show of himself in a situation that—on my honour—would have been simple to an ordinary man. But it seems impossible to dislike him. He is so kind to everybody." Thomas Beer in a well-written passage mysteriously assaults James with this kindness, but it was a fact and Crane was to feel it, before he could not feel it. On the day this man died in Germany, James wrote to his wife wishing her courage and hope, and venturing to enclose a cheque for fifty pounds—"I've money, moreover I care. . . ." It is in this absolute context of humanity that James's dislike of Cora Crane, familiar to his friends, should be recorded. Blunt and sometimes careless, she ground his nerves on occasion; and no doubt he had listened to gossip about her past, which would matter to James, who though ruthless and shockproof in his art at its heights was conventional and nervous in social life. A schoolmate of Crane's who visited Brede in June and August, however, and heard from English friends much about what James had to endure from Mrs. Crane, describes a converse occasion when James bowled over from Rye with a carriageful of people one day, announcing that he had brought them to lunch. "Mrs. Crane was mad as a hornet, but did not show it. She vanished into the kitchen and concocted a lot of extra lunch in a chafing dish. . . ." Not very important, this, but pro and con of a difficult relation ought to be indicated. At fifty-six James was just on the verge of his greatest works, and Beer astonishingly tells us that he sent the Bohemian, who at twenty-seven was not on the verge of his greatest works but was dying, five manuscripts for criticism. Crane had no critical language whatever and the insight of a master; one wonders what he said.

With warmer weather guests began to swarm, but they got away for a little themselves to the Conrads' (Pent Farm now) where they so took Borys's heart that for nights after they left—Conrad pretended—the boy had insomnia chatting about the "nice man" and "Ann-Anns" (Aunties). Crane would lie at full-length on the grass for hours, gazing gravely into the eyes of the baby propped up on a rug. Sometimes they laughed, and Conrad never heard Stephen Crane laugh otherwise than at "The Boy." Early in June the Conrads came to Brede. Crane rode down to the park gate to meet their landau at noon and trotted back beside it smiling—perhaps his morning's work had gone well—perfectly happy, Conrad thought: "it had really been given to me to see Crane perfectly happy for a couple of hours."

He wrote slowly in his long old upstairs study facing down the park. Frederic's orphans, whom he and Cora Crane loved, chattered in the great rooms and on the lawn. With a mind relaxed and a longing near the surface he went to Whilomville for a third time, not so much to the Trescotts themselves as to their visitors one summer: Mrs. Trescott's cousin —a nationally known painter, unnamed, "quiet, slow, and misty," "of a most brittle constitution"—with his nameless, beautiful, healthy, imperious wife, and their little girl, who is named Cora. "They had one child. Perhaps it would be better to say that they had one CHILD." She takes after her mother. Jimmie Trescott falls in love with her and she rules all the Whilomville children like a Begum. When the painter dreamily gives her a five-dollar bill the children stuff themselves but there is money left, so she decides that they must all have their hair cut; chaos that evening in a dozen houses, fury over the golden lost curls of the Margate twins. "The Angel Child" charmed *Harper's* which wanted others, and a celebrated professor has declared that "The 'angel child' is as unscrupulous a tyrant as can be found in the annals of irresponsible monarchy"; but actually the story is a bore.

Old persecutions imaged in *The Monster* and "The Blue Hotel" survive, worth notice. There is even a Swede or a "sort of Dutchman." Crane whose brother freed him from his curls, and who gave the Albany children money to have their curls cut, imaged himself evidently not only as the painter. Along with his anonymity and use of common names, Stephen Crane was alive to weird names, names that invite query and ridicule. On the night of the action at San Juan he met a Claverack friend among the wounded, Reuben McNab. "Perhaps" (he reflects in "War Memories") "there is a good deal in that name. Reuben McNab. You can't fling that name carelessly over your shoulder and lose it. It follows you like the haunting memory of a sin." Now the heinous barber of "The Angel Child" has a name worse than McNab. New to the town, he would have attracted no attention except for his name; but shortly "the best minds of the town were splintering their lances against William Neeltje's signboard" trying to pronounce him. The twins' grandfather is besieged by the Margate women in passionate terms: "He must destroy the utter Neeltje. He must midnightly massacre the angel child and her mother." Then the mask turns back. "The rains came and the winds blew in the most biblical way" when the real criminal is discovered, he who financed the murder of the curls; and the story ends at the railway station as the visitors fly, the painter bewildered but even more "vexed, as if he would be saying: 'Damn 'em! Why can't they leave me alone?' "

Even at Brede he was not immune. It was less remote from London than they had thought, fine weather taught them. Friends old and new (A. E. W. Mason, H. G. Wells, Mark Barr) were well enough, but strangers were subject to audible distress at the incongruity between the "Indian" and the manor, poker games in the great hall, Crane's muddy boots perhaps and pistol, diction, dice, Mrs. Crane's informality. Sanford Bennett called him "Baron Brede" one day when James was by; perhaps Cora's calling him "Duke", and her bed on a dais in the ballroom, were disapproved. Heather was stern about coatlessness, but the cook drank, while dinner waited hours. Already in April there is a flicker of helplessness under the master's humor, when he came on some new housemaids washing the dogs, and wrote: "My man can hire me a pair of maids while I ride to Rye and back. If I went to Russia I should come home and find Parliament in buttons and Marie Corelli in the kitchen." These dogs vied with young people noisy at Animal Grab and Blindman's Buff, and a second horse—Hengist and Horsa he named them—aroused his remnant of delight. There was Sponge, the King, the terrier bitch Flannel, their complex offspring, including a wicked tiny fluffy lady Powder Puff (the favorite), and two Russian poodles without souls.

Crane showed young people now a paternal air—feeling, with some reason, a hundred years old—and enjoyed entertaining them. His brother Wilbur turned up at Brede in May bringing William Howe Crane's eldest daughter Helen, on her way to school in Switzerland. On the same train was a young friend of Robert Barr, Karl Harriman. Crane met them driving the brake himself, coatless and quiet, in riding-breeches and puttees, a flannel shirt. Wilbur, an asthmatic and (so Harriman thought) "indifferent" man, was startled by Mrs. Crane in a blue mandarin smock, plaid skirt, strapped sandals. Stephen and Cora Crane should have been born later. A whole party crossed to Paris and waited while Crane took Helen on to Lausanne—having to borrow in order to get back. Brede's living space was bursting—friends, children, strangers mostly journalists—and though Crane seldom protested in personal matters, he blazed to James Pinker in July: "If you don't tell some of these lice that Cora and I aren't running a hotel I'll have to advertise the fact in the *Times!*"

War Is Kind emerged, with one of the decade's major poems and several of its most acute moments of thought.

> The wayfarer,
> Perceiving the pathway to truth,

Was struck with astonishment.
It was thickly grown with weeds.
"Ha," he said,
"I see that none has passed here
In a long time."
Later he saw that each weed
Was a singular knife.
"Well," he mumbled at last,
"Doubtless there are other roads."

The speculation is quite different in tone from poems about God in his earlier book:

A man said to the universe:
"Sir, I exist!"
"However," replied the universe,
"The fact has not created in me
A sense of obligation."

There swelled also—if anyone had listened—a strange singing:

I explain the silvered passing of a ship at night,
The sweep of each sad lost wave,
The dwindling boom of the steel thing's striving,
The little cry of a man to a man,

* * *

And the soft lashing of black waves
For long and in loneliness.

"Prithee, Mr. Crane . . . quit fooling," wrote the *Criterion*. Crane would die a month too soon to hear the *Bookman* stating that a dozen poems in this second book "cannot be matched in individuality and force of impact by more than one or two of the gentlemen now writing poetry in English. Mr. Kipling would come nearest"—and fifty years later the perception was not yet standard. Will Bradley's physical production of the poems was one of the most fanciful, unluckily, of that tasty period.

The poet was being urged again by his wife and others to undertake the political novel McClure had once suggested, and refused, but he began work this summer on a "satiric romance," for the advance he had evidently got from Stokes. Between taking some young people to the Henley Regatta and a flower show in Rye ("Jesus! What a diversion!") he was going on with stories about Whilomville. These never again touched the level of *The Monster* or "His New Mittens" except the third short one, "Lynx-Hunting"; but after three then that were negligible he hit the stride of what he wanted, clearly, in "Shame," a story genial, charming, and natural; "The Carriage-Lamps," which followed, is nearly as good. Then they slumped, progressively weaker except for "The Fight." He must have been busy with them into the fall or even later: *Harper's* had one in every issue for thirteen months from August. These tales established a mode that has had various dilution since in Booth Tarkington, Thomas Beer, others.

But he began his "War Memories" of Cuba for Lady Randolph Churchill's magnificent *Anglo-Saxon Review* in the full summer, and his table was littered with papers one day when a young editor who had been admiring him for the *Academy* cycled over from Winchelsea to look at him. Crane read aloud in his "precise, remote voice" ("soft, velvety tones" had been the description of a friend in Syracuse) what he had written that afternoon: the second paragraph, about a bunch of bananas hung like a chandelier in the correspondents' cabin. To Lewis Hind he seemed "over-anxious about the right description of that huddle of bananas; and it seemed strange to find this fair, slight, sensitive youth sitting in the quiet of Brede Place writing about wild deeds in outlandish places." Hind says nothing of the Mexican blanket on the wall, the pistol, the swords, or the first paragraph, which begins: " 'But to get the real thing!' cried Vernall, the war-correspondent. 'It seems impossible! It is because war is neither magnificent nor squalid; it is simply life, and an expression of life can always evade us.' "

He was not going again, though. "I shall never see another war. I don't care if Buller drives all the Boers up Egypt's fattest pyramid," he wrote to somebody. But as a minoritarian he composed presently a circumstantial sympathetic account of "The Great Boer Trek". Africa had engaged him always, and then Miss Schreiner, and now history, though British overconfidence in the Guards regiments annoyed him. "When a Yankee says such things he is bragging but I guess an Englishman is just lugging the truth from some dark cave." By now he had certainly contracted to write a series of accounts of "Great Battles" for *Lippincott's*, and he began —moved no doubt by the ambiguity of sentiment that attacks intermittently all Americans living in England and Englishmen living here—with a resounding British defeat, that at New Orleans. Bits were lively: of the first disciplined troops to engage molasses—"bedraggled, sticky, and astonished"; of Pakenham's final plan, which "was surprisingly simple, and perhaps it was surprisingly bad," when he "might have eaten them at leisure"; of Andrew Jackson, "one of the most irascible figures in history" who yet "knew how to speak straight as a stick to the common man,"—who "sallow, gnarled, crusty . . . came ill to his great work; he should have been in bed." Then he wearied, and ground out eight more, without interest. "Bunker Hill" has been praised but the good Lossing's account of the battle is better. His nerves were bad; not his nerves only. He tore up a Cromwellian tale called "Siege," then a Mexican "Tarantula." Early in September a fistula was driving him mad because he couldn't ride, and he was writing George Wyndham that he was thinking of another journey. "What do you know about the Black Forest . . . ? I mean as a health resort? The truth is that Cuba Libre just about liberated me from this base blue world. The clockwork is juggling badly. I have had a lot of idiotic company all summer."

Unable to ride or use the boat he and Conrad meant to share in Rye, Crane amused himself with ironies in Whilomville. The painter turns up once more in "The Stove" and there is a tea party to which "A few came to see if they could not find out the faults of the painter's wife." To Elbert Hubbard: "I must have Egyptian blood in me. Mummies rise from the tomb and come to pay me calls that last for days." To Conrad, infuriated at their parasites' gossip about the Cranes, all the host said was, after some mob had ultimately retired, and after a silence, "I'm glad those Indians are gone." Even to Sanford Bennett Crane only complained that men wandering in uninvited should "patronize my wife's housekeeping." Of course this was too formal for some, informal for others.

Resentment rarely flared in Stephen or Cora Crane except at some sham, as when Hubbard had set up a fake hero with fifteen hundred words of "A Message to Garcia" in the March *Philistine*. (The New York Central Railroad, enchanted with it, reprinted a million copies to teach employees everywhere how to be selfless and dutiful—at last the piece had a circulation of 40,000,000, mostly among the armies in the Russo-Japanese War, on both sides). "I object strongly," Crane wrote, "to your paragraphs about Rowan. You are more wrong than is even common on our humble incompetent globe. He didn't do anything worthy at all. He received the praise of the general of the army and got to be made a lieutenant col. for a feat which about forty newspaper correspondents had already performed at the usual price of fifty dollars a week and expenses. Besides he is personally a chump and in Porto Rico where I met him he wore a yachting cap as part of his uniform which was damnable. When you want to monkey with some of our national heroes you had better ask me, because I know and your perspective is almost out of sight. . . ." The only time one intimate saw

Mrs. Crane angry was at another charlatan, during her collection of a subscription for Frederic's children Heloise and Barry, to which James gave fifty pounds and everyone what he could except the well-heeled author of *The Christian* who gave nothing with a righteous letter.

It was with similar feeling, wrongly, and in his poverty, that Crane was indifferent on August 29th to another subscription. "About Wilde and his troubles a mere stranger and runaway dog like myself can't be supposed to care. I met him once. We stood and looked at each other and he bleated like a sheep. With those bad manners that are so awfully much mine I laughed in his face. He tried to borrow money from Dick Davis when he was being tried after insulting Davis all across London. Something pretty poor in him. And I owe my brothers too much money to bother about helping with subscriptions for a mildewed chump like Wilde. . . . All I ought to do right now is pay some of my debts. My charities begin in the right pants pocket." A comment of two years before balances this bitterness. Crane thought Wilde a sentimental neurotic wanting treatment by some doctor who "knows all about that kind of thing." "He has a disease and they all gas about him as though there was a hell and he came up out of it. . . . Mr. Yeats is the only man I have met who talks of Wilde with any sense." Posturing was the infallible switch to his circuit of the sardonic. Emerging from a London club where Mark Twain had brandished himself all evening, Crane's drawl defined an author as "a man licensed by public opinion to act like a chorus girl at supper." In Cuba, when Acton Davies was hamming up a Broadway dream—certain dishes and wines in a certain place, a lady wonderful across the table—Crane asked, "Why don't you just say you want a good meal and a girl and be done with it?"

This habit of mind was one not for a romance, even "satiric," and the tired young man, restless to pay debts, anxious now about Cora's future, must have felt wryness within wryness, planning *The O'Ruddy*. But he struck his tone at once and probably enjoyed it. "My ancestors lived in castles which were like churches stuck on end, and they drank the best of everything amid the joyous cries of a devoted peasantry. But the good time passed away soon enough, and when I had reached the age of eighteen we had nobody on the land but . . . people who were almost law-abiding, and my father came to die more from disappointment than from any other cause." On his deathbed he explains to his son that "there is only enough money to last a gentleman five more years," and two swords, and some important papers given him once by an Englishman now an earl: "I don't know what they are, having had very little time for reading during my life, but do you return them to him . . . he may reward you, but do not you depend on it, for you may get the back of his hand. I have not seen him for years. I am glad I had you taught to read. They read considerably in England, I hear. . . . I have said everything. Push the bottle near me." The O'Ruddy, then, passes to England, where he encounters everywhere the opinion that the Irish run naked through their native forests, counters the Earl's arrogance and trickery, loves his daughter ("a pair of bright liquid eyes"), outduels all (notably his rival Mr. Forister, a "little black man"), takes into service a highwayman and an Irish peasant with an unspeakable head of red hair that gave A. E. Housman later, perhaps, a savage poem ("Oh who is that young sinner"— Housman, weeding his library, kept Crane), and so on. The Lady Mary, he considers, regards him as a "spud," and he has no technical luck. By chance half-hidden near a conversation she holds with her mother, he not only is not undetected but cannot hear a word: "It seemed unfair that I, of all men in literature, should be denied this casual and usual privilege." For the third time this year, in short, Crane was at a work extended, necessary, and unimportant.

This year he made to some visitor a remark behind which one hears with pain the lifelong conscience of an artist dying: "I get a little tired of saying, Is this true?"

On November 1st he was twenty-eight, and his mind was blazing with death. Next month appeared "Twelve O'Clock," a Western nightmare of spreeing cowboys waiting in Placer's Hotel for a cuckoo-clock to strike and the bird to come out that one has seen. Nobody believes him about the bird. Placer writes in his ledger. Big Watson a drunk comes in, quarrels, laughing shoots Placer in the throat, is killed, another is killed, and "Placer, in some dying whim, had made his way out from behind the pink counter, and, leaving a horrible trail, had travelled to the centre of the room, where he had pitched headlong over the body of Big Watson." The wooden bird comes out. His imagination one feels as parodying itself, without meaning now. One November night he drove to meet a guest—a famous cricketer—and frightened him sleepless by galloping full-tilt through the narrow blackness to Brede.

Crane ate less, smoked less, was more still. Somebody frightened his wife one day, and there is a note: "Please have the kindness to keep your mouth shut about my health in front of Mrs. Crane hereafter. She can do nothing for me and I am too old to be nursed. It is all up with me but I will not have her scared. For some funny woman's reason, she likes me. Mind this." His friends worried. Come stay as long as you want, he told Edwin Pugh, "Eternity's an entr'acte." He refused to see doctors, but wrote hard on, reading the Whilomville episodes to the children, excited rarely by something new like "The Procurator of Judaea", sometimes answering letters. "I am not carnivorous [he confessed to a stranger] about living writers. I have not read any of the books that you ask me to criticize except that of Mr. Howells, and it has disappointed me. My tastes? I do not know of any living author whose works I have wholly read. I like what I know of Anatole France, Henry James, George Moore, and several others. I deeply admire some short stories by Mr. Bierce, Mr. Kipling and Mr. White. Mr. Hardy, since you especially inquire about his work, impresses me as a gigantic writer who 'overtreats' his subjects. I do not care for the long novels of Mr. Clemens, for the same reason. Four hundred pages of humour is a little bit too much for me. My judgment in the case is not worth burning straw, but I give it as portentously as if kingdoms toppled while awaiting it under anxious skies." Tolstoy, Miss Schreiner, Conrad—odd omissions even as careless. He talked slowly to a young man turned up from America late in the fall, Willis Clarke, of his parents, his childhood, *Maggie*, while Clarke took his talk down in shorthand. He wandered off about Texas then, and baseball teams, till his admirer tried to bring him back to literature with a remark about his hard luck in beginning at the same time as Kipling.

"Yes," Crane said, "I'm just a dry twig on the edge of the bonfire."

Brede was cold. Throughout the immense party over Christmas a guest remembered him sitting in a corner of the great fireplace, not unamused but very silent. There were thirty or forty people romping, dancing on waxy floors under candles dripping over the sconces Cora and a blacksmith had improvised on the beams. American girls charmed English men. Crane had helped James, H. G. Wells, Conrad, George Gissing, A. E. W. Mason, others, put together *The Ghost*, which was rehearsed uproariously and given at Brede schoolhouse the stormy second night. Bedding and plumbing were primitive, husbands and wives separated into dormitories, some in the turret, and Robert Barr was alarmed one night by the main Brede ghost. This was a giant's ghost, sawn in two parts, of which Crane was fond. It rattled from the priest-hole off Barr's room and the Canadian piled everything movable against the door. Late one night the host tried to teach the men poker, without success. He growled, but smiled then at Wells, to whom he'd given months before some kernels of corn for planting. How had it made out, Crane asked, and on hearing they'd enjoyed it, asked how they cooked it. "Cook it!" cried the Englishman. "We didn't cook it. We cut it when it was six inches high and ate it for salad. Wasn't that right?" The company wandered down to midday breakfasts of bacon and eggs, sweet potatoes (from America), and beer. Stephen and Cora Crane were homesick. When Wells asked whether he was writing anything Crane's response was joyless: Pinker had *fixed* some stories for him. "I got to do them," he said, "I got to do them." On New Year's Eve he drank to the Twentieth Century despite a scientific objection (Mark Barr's) that this was not beginning yet. It was late this last night that a guest came on him alone at a peculiarity—humming with his face near the strings of a violin. The man approached and Crane fainted against his shoulder.

He had had a hemorrhage, which his wife discovered, and Wells cycled off in the dawn for a doctor. The crisis passed, but now friends were sure he should be out of England—in the south of France, or even to South Africa for the journey. He himself thought of Texas and as scandal rattled back to the Cranes over their "orgy" he decided. "Mrs. Crane [Robert Barr wrote on January 24th] is so incensed by the nonsense talked about the New Year Party at Brede that Stevie is taking her home. England has been kind to Stevie in many ways, but some of his cherished friends have said things too carelessly about his most generous but not too formal hospitality and I have heard some gossip that must wound him deeply. His skin is very thin and he is subject to a kind of jealousy that knows how to hurt him worst . . . between ourselves, it is all over with the boy. He may last two years." Friends heard even that Brede had been shut, but this mood too fled and they stayed. Perhaps Crane was too weak to travel. "A socialist cannot be sure what is best for the world at the moment," he remarked in the New York *Journal* on the 25th, "as a paregoric, as a sleeping powder or as a disinfectant. . . ." Even for the birth of a new Stephen Crane he could only cable, as the month closed: "You and I will struggle on with the name together and do as best we may. . . ." Unable to defend himself, he still roused for a friend. "You are wrong," he wrote to Sanford Bennett, "about Hueffer. I admit he is patronizing. He patronized his family. He patronizes Conrad. He will end up by patronizing God who will have to get used to it and they will be friends. . . ."

Nothing worse is known of Cora as Crane's wife than that her cook drank and she herself was given sometimes to telling long true sentimental stories during which her husband sat wooden and unhappy. "Somewhere in him"—as in Johnnie of the late weak story ("His Majestic Lie") based on his experiences in Havana—"there was a sentimental tenderness, but it was like a light seen afar at night; it came, went, appeared again in a new place, flickered, flared, went out, left you in a void and angry. And if his sentimental tenderness was a light, the darkness in which it puzzled you was his irony of soul. This irony was directed first at himself; then at you; then at the nation and the flag; then at God. It was a midnight in which you searched. . . ." Hard for such a man to protect himself, insulted, but indeed no satisfactory way of responding to malice or insult in overcivilized life has yet been evolved. As one of the persons then living most thoroughly insulted, Crane had given the matter thought, and his imagination had fixed on dueling. The O'Ruddy, who supposed dueling an artificial affair, finds it very quickly in England the practice of honorable and thoughtful men and spends much of his time at it with a good conscience and perfect success. For little insolences it might rise to Crane's tongue, as in a tavern of Rye one afternoon when lounging with a party of unshaven friends (poker had spoiled the night before) he remembered his errand, to return a manuscript to Henry James, and an outraged, cultivated voice explained from a corner that Mr. James saw strangers only on appointment. "Oh, sir," said Crane, "I know that the duel is not practiced in this country but I am prepared to waive that for your benefit."

At dinner this evening James—who also had, he once con-

fessed, "the imagination of atrocity" and saw life as ferocious and sinister—dropped his mask long enough to hor-
rify a matron with careful details of a prizefight he had seen
in a motion picture. These men were not understood. James
trivial and squeamish, Crane vulgar and arrogant—so for
years the legends ran, and after a generation "wistful" was
still Beer's word for James that night. Somehow they invited
patronizingness, being in their superiority of intellect, passion, concern, unapproachable on terms of equality. Nothing
could be stranger than this close relation, within a few Sussex
miles of each other, of the two Americans who were making
ready Twentieth Century prose in English, with nearby in
Essex a Pole the friend of both, who learned from both, their
solitary peer in art though not in originality. Art likes these
junctures, as when fifty years before, a few miles apart in
Massachusetts, were simultaneously in composition the two
American novels accepted as supreme so far—one intense as
an ordeal by Crane, the other billowing like James. Conrad's
howls of fury and impotence mean less, after all, than his
friend's silence. "Hope," Crane wrote to Wyndham, "is the
most vacuous emotion of mankind." Down into the details
of living, it was not possible to act in such a way as to forbid
misjudgment even by people acute and sympathetic. "He
was profoundly ill and weary, if I had been wise enough to
see it," Wells recognizes speaking of New Year's in his autobiography, "but I thought him sulky and reserved. He was
essentially the helpless artist; he wasn't the master of his
party, he wasn't the master of his home; his life was altogether out of control; he was being carried along. What he
was still clinging to, but with a dwindling zest, was artistry."

Artistry? Anything of that left? Through all the down-
hill trash of the year 1899, exception made for some child-
tales and parts of "War Memories," perhaps only "Virtue in
War" shows undiminished power of conception and execution. It studies a West Pointer who having left the service
goes back on the outbreak of war to become a major in a vol-

unteer regiment, detested for his professional manner by one of his casual democratic privates. The two pages of their first interview, outrageous and effortless, suggest how far Crane had got even beyond Chapter XXI of *The Monster* toward a laconic perfection of mannerless phrasing which is one ideal of our prose since Crane but which scarcely existed even in conception until upon a hint or so from Mark Twain he invented it. In style, point, value, the story resembles "The Price of the Harness." Both insist a little too much, as the titles insist: the price is death, the virtue, doing one's duty and in silence, the duty being courage. At this point Stephen Crane might have been supposed through, paralyzed by disease, except for remnants of phrasing. Even the toneless Revolutionary episodes (assembled as "Ol' Bennet and the Indians") that grew out of his study of Lossing for the *Great Battles* have a phrase or two—"I gave my rifle to the grass" as the hero flees. Not even a father-son theme similar to *The O'Ruddy's* gives these interest. But perhaps Crane knew that—they were printed after his death by his widow, who printed everything, whereas on January 20th Crane retrieved two stories from Pinker as not good enough. He knew about the novel too: he hoped in February that it would be "good enough to get me to Colorado. It will not be good for much more than that. . . ." He knew where he was, and at some time very late indeed he moved his art again.

Mr. Smith is in love with Margharita of Tampa, so that her mother is "commercially excited"; but Margharita, in love with a Cuban soldier, makes Mr. Smith wait. Then the soldier is killed. She receives Mr. Smith. He trembles—"It was part of his love to believe in the absolute treachery of his adored one"—but proposes and is accepted, and that night she burns the soldier's photograph. But we have resumed the opening and last chapter only. The story is that of the soldier, the predecessor: a young lieutenant named Manolo Prat, with a stunning new machete. Early in his initial action he is running forward when a voice tells him to "Drop! Drop!" It is Bas—an officer known for his courage—who calls him a desperate and careless officer. Manolo is hugely delighted: he has "early achieved a part of his ambition—to be called a brave man by established brave men." Later, lying wounded, helpless, he sees an insurgent coming: "His negro face was not an eminently ferocious one in its lines, but now it was lit with an illimitable blood-greed. He and the young lieutenant exchanged a singular glance; then he came stepping eagerly down. The young lieutenant closed his eyes, for he did not want to see the flash of the machete." Between these moments is the battle. "Men could have been drunken in all this flashing and flying and snarling and din, but at this time he was very deliberate. He knew that he was thrusting himself into a trap whose door, once closed, opened only when the black hand knocked and every part of him seemed to be in panic-stricken revolt. But something controlled him; something moved him inexorably in one direction; he perfectly understood but he was only sad. . . . He was of a kind —that seemed to be it—and the men of his kind, on peak or plain, from the dark northern ice-fields to the hot wet jungles, through all wine and want, through all lies and forgotten truth, dark or light, the men of his kind were governed by their gods, and each man knew the law and yet could not give tongue to it, but it was the law . . . always with the law there is only one way. But from peak and plain, from dark northern icefields and hot wet jungles, through wine and want, through all lies and unfamiliar truth, dark or light, he heard breathed to him the approval and the benediction of his brethren."

"The Clan of No-Name" they are called, and the story is, asserting Stephen Crane's community, casting accounts. The success of Mr. Smith—an ironical one—is based on the Cuban's failure—an ironical one. Remembering Crane's first nom-de-plume, Johnston Smith, and "A Man by the Name of Mud" (because he has let himself fall in love), we may see a Crane-mask in the contemptible lover; there is profound rejection in the story as well as high claim. It differs from the two other Spanish War stories, than which it is much more ambitious, in important ways. And first in narrative style: "The block-house stood always for some big, clumsy and rather incompetent animal, while the insurgents, scattered on two sides of it, were little enterprising creatures of another species, too wise to come too near, but joyously raging at its easiest flanks and dirling the lead into its sides in a way to make it fume, and spit and rave like the tom-cat when the glad, free-band fox-hound pups catch him in the lane." Together with familiar elements there is an interest here in prose-movement and syntax which is new. So with the structure, the weakling enclosing the soldier. A "frame" in fiction is a simple device enough, but Crane had never used it before, he characteristically avoided all device, and the change of mind implied is remarkable. So with the "blowing" style of the climax quoted: new. None of these developments had another chance. Then "The Clan of No Name" returns to the sense of the *atrocious*, the affront, that ruled "The Blue Hotel"—a universe such that "One was a coxcomb not to die in it." Only, in this universe now lives "law": the obligation to courage whether resisting or submitting. As far back as 1895 in Crane occurs the expression, the stranger for its trivial context, of "man lawing away at nature"; and now this has its meaning. Certainly life is painful, faithless, horrible. Still, there are men who are brave. If one can be brave oneself, one joins them. To be brave is all that one can do, but then it is all that one is required to do. And for the last moment it is permitted to shut one's eyes.

But the essential difference between this story and the others is that it was written for himself and so marks a turn back to pure art. And then—no more wind, coughing—some little stories. A fantasy-murder, "An Illusion in Red and White," to which its humanness gives the sense of reality and increased strangeness denied "A Tale of Mere Chance" or the persecution-fantasy "Manacled." Six pages for the last time about the Civil War: a lieutenant's wound, "An Episode of War." Eight pages, and then six pages, of an imaginary war finally—Spitzbergen infantry campaigning in Rostina: the attempt to hold a house, and a burial.

Composer of these twenty pages, if not a word ever else, Stephen Crane might claim rank as a master. They are like confrontations. But writing nothing else, of course he would not have had these either: behind them, for their magic and wisdom, lay the galled decade of observation, feeling, reflection, labor. Crane still grinned at the priestlike view taken of art by most modern masters and nearly all aspirants; half-grinned. To a youth hesitating between sculpture and fiction: "You might be one of the people who have picked on a defenceless art as a means of telling how much certain things have meant, or mean to you, but did you ever think that this world is full of artists in alligator growing and the promulgation of mixed vegetables? Mr. James was recently quoting a piece from some French poet [André Gide] who shows Narcissus seeing in himself the motion of all time. An artist, I think, is nothing but a powerful memory that can move itself at will through certain experiences sideways and every artist must be in some things powerless as a dead snake." As this sick man with a bottomless mind moved once again through war and death, in the fulness of power, he cannot have been unhappy and such a man cannot seem wholly pathetic. How to act, wounded, is his Lieutenant's problem—under the strange new dignity but also lack of consequence; and this is described with such deliberation and force as to make one feel that no wounded man has ever been correctly described before. But the triumph of "An Episode of War" is the sense it conveys of the man's change of vision and thus of its objects, the whole context (in six pages) of battle and field hospital—near which, while drivers quarrel and crowds of bandaged men come and go, "Sitting with his back against a tree a man with a face as grey as a new army blanket was serenely smoking a corn-cob pipe. The lieutenant wished to rush forward and inform him that he was dying."

The first two sketches in "The Kicking Twelfth," about Crane's imaginary war, little matter, though one bears a suggestive title—"The Shrapnel of Their Friends." But the third, called "The End of the Battle" ("And If He Wills, We Must Die,") is an affair of fantastic energy and range. Sergeant Morton and fifteen men occupy a house, are attacked, outnumbered, and overcome; just a job, and bad luck; an enemy subaltern bursts in, halts, turns with a shrug: "God, I should have estimated them at least one hundred strong." The story swings all round the reader as the men fire from the windows: Odor, sound, light, pace, emotion, so draw him in that he scarcely knows at any moment whether he is with the sergeant or one of the others. Sense of confusion, curiosity, irritation, delight, weakness, reproach, irrelevance, vigor, hysteria, anger, loss, and—the sergeant is the last defender to speak, "thickly," and drops on his face—sense of *pride*.

"The Upturned Face" is unlike this and all Crane's other stories. No amount of reading will convince one that it does not occur at night; though perfectly naturalistic in technique, it affects one as pure symbol, senseless and ghastly, like one of Goya's last etchings, and has the posthuman quality of certain late art by other masters. As the Rostina sharpshooters fire briskly, Timothy Lean and the adjutant are burying their comrade Bill. Two privates dig, Lean with horror searches the corpse's clothes. When the wretched shallow grave is ready, the adjutant laughs—"a terrible laugh, which had its origin in that part of the mind which is first moved by the singing of the nerves"—and they tumble the corpse in by its clothing, being particular not to feel the body. The bullets spit overhead. They try to remember some sort of service, while the aggrieved privates are ordered to attention, but break down, both of them forgetful and shamed, into the word "Mercy." " 'Mercy,' said Lean. And then he was moved by some violence of feeling, for he turned suddenly upon his two men and tigerishly said, 'Throw the dirt in.' " Now the ordeal begins. The chalk-blue face looks keenly out from the grave, and the private empties his shovel on—on the feet. "Timothy Lean felt as if tons had been swiftly lifted from his forehead. He had felt that perhaps the private might empty the shovel on—on the face. It had been emptied on the feet. There was a great point gained there—ha! ha!—the first shovelful had been emptied on the feet. How satisfactory!" The adjutant babbles, and a private is hit; Lean sends the privates off to fill the grave himself. Plop! He works frantically—plop!—until nothing is visible but the chalk-blue face. The two men are at the edge of hysteria, Lean stuttering, the adjutant crying out, pale, to go on. "When the earth landed it made a sound—plop!"

His mouth filled with blood at the end of March, when Mrs. Crane was in Paris to meet Helen from Switzerland, and doctors came. James rushed to London for a great specialist wrongly reported there. Crane lay dreaming and reading at his father's sermons. No change of mind that we know: "Men have never much deserved Christ and Buddha," he wrote, "because they went to work and changed the teaching of generosity into a teaching of roars and threats. I can not be shown that God bends on us any definable stare, like a sergeant at muster, and his laughter would be bully to hear out in nothingness." People still came, advised, pretended to hope. He sent his publisher a dedication of *Wounds in the Rain* to Moreton Frewen. He even began a tale, about the master of Oldrestham Hall, who knocked into posts at a gate because he "dreamed almost always," who flared out on a stupidity or double-dealing but: "His feeling was suddenly ashes at the moment when one was certain it would lick the sky." The villagers think him mad, then reluctantly his wife does—and Cora would have to finish this.* That perfection of double-sense, "lick," was the last. In the unimaginable loneliness of the soul as it hovers towards death, what is occurring that we can know but usual things? Frewen had given the pathetic wife money for Germany, and the day before she got him, "sunken and stoical," to Dover, he dictated a last note to Bennett: ". . . My condition is probably known to you. . . . I have Conrad on my mind very much just now. Garnett does not think it likely that his writing will ever be popular outside the ring of men who write. He is poor and a gentleman and proud. His wife is not strong and they have a kid. If Garnett should ask you to help pull wires for a place on the Civil List for Conrad please do me the last favor. . . . I am sure you will."

A sinking fortnight of May at the Lord Warden in Dover. Conrad came a day, ill too, and to Robert Barr who had promised to take over *The O'Ruddy* the dying man whispered the dry gay situations still to come—the hero was to rescue the girl and seize and barricade Brede Place against her father. . . . Barr said something about plans, and Crane winked. "Robert—when you come to the hedge—that we must all go over" (he gasped slowly) "—it isn't bad. You feel

* She did, concluding with, not the Squire mad, but his wife. Once Cora understood Crane was doomed she must have been desperate; for devotion, and then her own fate too was at stake. A word about it. After taking her husband's body back to the States she stayed a time with his brother Will's family, then returned to England; to be an author. She did not succeed, but the sale of Crane's unpublished stuff helped; she held Sunday afternoons, everyone was pleasant to a distinguished widow, and in the winter she was full of projects: a volume of Crane's sketches (*Last Words*, 1902), completion of half a dozen stories he had left unfinished, forwarding of a novel of her own on the Revolution and a short biography of her husband. Only the first emerged. In August (1901?) she was facing eviction, after a serious struggle to keep her head up. She packed, invited Crane's friends to a last "at home" to test their loyalty to his memory, and went with Mrs. Ruedy back to Jacksonville. She married again, and was divorced. Her effects included Crane's papers, carefully preserved by her. Upon the headstone in Evergreen Cemetery, Jacksonville, was cut, by her wish: "Cora Crane/1868–1910."

sleepy—and—you don't care. Just a little dreamy anxiety—which world you're really in—that's all."

That was all. She took him to Badenweiler, where his niece Helen came and he rallied a little, and early on the 5th of June his anxiety left him.

The body was on London view in a stall between champing horses, off a littered stableyard, where it looked to an old friend as if its tenant had suffered horribly. Taken by Cora Crane home to New Jersey, it was followed on a blustery day in Elizabeth by brothers and others to the Crane plot in Evergreen Cemetery, and dropped into the fifth position front. The name stands on the left side of the family monument. There is no separate marker.

Four — CRANE'S ART

Crane's Art

ince Dr. Johnson observed that a century was the term
commonly fixed as the test of literary merit, authors
have crowded each other out of sight more and more
rapidly. The term cannot be now so long. An English critic
says the present point is to write a book that will last just ten
years; but a decade must be too short—fashion can catch up
older trash than that. For Johnson, remember, the "effects
of favour" must have ended. Under our industry of literary
scholarship, having to be kept supplied with subjects, "sur-
vival" is a more ambiguous condition than it used to be: one
may stand to gain by overvaluing his author however meager,
or his author's toe. Other conditions make a term difficult to
fix. But Crane has been dead half a century, academic interest has avoided him as both peculiar and undocumented, and
some of his work is still decidedly alive. This is long enough.
We are not dealing with absolutes: the questions of interest
with regard to an author remembered at all are how, and
what part, and why, and whether justly. Perhaps a question
more general arises too in connection with Crane. American
genius has not been literary. The executive idealism of a few
men like Washington represents our spirit at a higher level,
probably, than can any of our literary masters. It may be
merely our failure so far to have produced a national author

that creates this impression, though we have to reckon also with a kind of national commitment as different as possible from, say, French cultural commitment. At any rate the fact is certain: we have had little genius in literature. The question is this: whether we have not in Stephen Crane a genius very formidable indeed, an artist of absolute and high vision —the sort of writer before whom most of our imposing earlier authors utterly shrivel away—a national glory, if the nation cared.

Let us lay aside at the outset matters of influence. Enough has been mentioned in passing, of influences felt by Crane (Tolstoy, Mark Twain, Goethe, Emerson, Whitman, Olive Schreiner, others), to rescue him from the status of a "sport." He concentrates tendencies and powers already tentatively in play. At the same time these influences certainly tell us very little about him; Crane was perhaps as original as an author can be, and be valuable. We shall have to study him by himself. More interesting by a good deal is the influence he exerted, great and distinct upon Conrad, Willa Cather, Ernest Hemingway, very decided upon others of his contemporaries and then upon Theodore Dreiser, Sherwood Anderson, Carl Sandburg, even Sinclair Lewis, as well as T. E. Lawrence, F. Scott Fitzgerald, more recent figures. Strong and lasting despite interruptions in his fame and availability, this influence is part of his importance. "The stones he put in the wall"—as Anderson said it—"are still there. . . ." But critics have read him so little that the source of this whole aspect of recent English and American literary art has gone mainly unrecognized and must remain matter for special study. Crane's influence will be found no simple affair, traced through these authors: it affected vision, technique, material. Whether, however, it has ever been commensurate with the degree of revolution Crane effected is doubtful. I think it has not, and look for an explanation to the fact that his work of characteristic power has not yet been isolated from his inferior, ugly, and trivial work.

I ought to say where this power is. It is in "The Open Boat" above all, and "The Blue Hotel"; in the single long work *The Red Badge of Courage* and short war-studies from "A Mystery of Heroism" through "Death and the Child," "The Price of the Harness," "Virtue in War," to "The Clan of No Name," "An Episode of War," "The End of the Battle," "The Upturned Face"; in the early and late companion studies of society's ferocity, *Maggie* and *The Monster*; in two singular visions of happiness, "The Pace of Youth" and "The Bride Comes to Yellow Sky"; in other prose constructions delicate, dreadful and humorous, from "A Dark Brown Dog," "The Reluctant Voyagers," "An Experiment in Misery," through "The Veteran" to "Shame" and "An Illusion in Red and White"; in two dozen poems from "Once I Saw Mountains Angry" through the title-poem of *War Is Kind* to the posthumous marvelous "A Man Adrift on a Slim Spar." The list by no means exhausts Crane's excellence—very little behind some of this work come a number of other stories, such as "The Little Regiment" and "Three Miraculous Soldiers," the three Mexican stories, chapters even in *George's Mother* and "War Memories," passages scattered everywhere. But at any rate not much less than this list will do in instance of where this author remains vivid, living.

You need very little to live. With *Wuthering Heights* and some verses one woman is with us always. But my display of Crane's work will certainly surprise both in bulk and variety most readers and critics. The truth is that Crane sprang into fame amid a storm of excited bewilderment and has passed into permanence in almost perfect silence. The occasional critic or historian who looks at him is just puzzled. A few are not comfortable yet about his being here at all, and among the majority who accept him there is no agreement about what kind of author he is. The most considerable attempts to account for him are still those by two of his English friends: first the very able ten pages written by H. G. Wells for the *North American Review* just after Crane's death in 1900. Wells spoke of his "persistent selection of the elements of an impression," of his ruthless exclusion of mere information, of the direct vigor with which the selected points are made; distinguished calmly the perfect restraint of "The Open Boat" from overinsistence in "Death and the Child" (then the critical favorite in England among Crane's stories); and concluded with a prophecy brilliantly fortunate: "It seems to me that, when at last the true proportions can be seen, Crane will be found to occupy a position singularly cardinal. . . . In style, in method and in all that is distinctively *not* found in his books, he is sharply defined, the expression in literary art of certain enormous repudiations. . . . It is as if the racial thought had been razed from his mind and its site ploughed and salted. He is more than himself in this; he is the first expression of the opening mind of a new period, or, at least, the early emphatic phase of a new initiative—beginning, as a growing mind must needs begin, with the record of impressions, a record of a vigour and intensity beyond all precedent." Crane's position sank for a generation nearly to zero, and for forty years Wells's essay was never reprinted. Meanwhile Edward Garnett, whose "Appreciation" in *The Academy* (December 17, 1898) was the most acute view taken during Crane's lifetime, added some remarkable sentences when he extended it in 1921 for *Friday Nights*. Two qualities in especial, he said, combined to form what is unique in Crane, "viz., his wonderful insight into and mastery of the primary passions, and his irony deriding the swelling emotions of the self. It is his irony that checks the emotional intensity of his delineation, and suddenly reveals passion at high tension in the clutch of the implacable tides of life. It is the perfect fusion of these two forces of passion and irony that creates Crane's spiritual background, and raises his work, at its finest, into the higher zone of man's tragic conflict with the universe." I do not feel sure of the meaning of the impressive middle sentence here, but the other two show that Garnett understood Crane better than everyone since taken together and would form a happy point of critical departure for us if we had not some elementary difficulties to encounter.

There is first the question, baffling to most of his friends, his critics, and his age, of whether Stephen Crane did not write almost entirely from *inspiration*. His work seemed to come from nowhere, prose and poetry alike. The word "dream" is recurrent in comment on him—even Hemingway, vouching for the authority of *The Red Badge*, uses it when he calls that book "a boy's long dream of war." When Crane told an interviewer that it was a product of labor, the man was not less but more astonished, that Crane should have "kept this story in hand for nearly a year, polishing and bettering it. Perhaps this is the most amazing thing about a thoroughly amazing book. If he had said he wrote it in three days (as he wrote the 'Black Riders') one might understand such a *tour de force*." Crane's rejection of the notion of "inspiration" is irrelevant. Of course he *did* write from inspiration, and of course he wrote also from close long observation, inquiry, study, and then he rewrote. He was like other men of genius, in short, often inspired and immensely deliberate. Yet this double explanation does not really account for the impression his work has always given, which might be put as follows: one is surprised that it exists at all—and one's surprise, if it diminishes, does not disappear with familiarity. Hamlin Garland tells us indeed that Crane just "tapped" his brain for his poems. He certainly went through no apprenticeship in poetry; he just began—began, we shall see, at a very high level—and if *The Black Riders* was not, evidently, written in three days, it was written abruptly and with effortless rapidity. As for prose, we have discovered an early development there, but so early and masterly that the prodigy remains. All this is thoroughly exceptional.

At the same time, Crane looks like a polar type of modern self-consciousness. He copied into his notebook—whether as program or as confirmation is unknown—a sentence from Emerson which comprehensively defines one effect of this art which lighted the 'nineties: "Congratulate yourselves if you have done something strange and extravagant and have broken the monotony of a decorous age." Literary ambition unusually deliberate and powerful is manifest all through his early life. "I began the war with no talent but an ardent admiration and desire. I had to build up." Readers and critics have recognized an effort in his work, and it forms a large basis for critical objection. They see affectation, strain. A word applied nearly as frequently as "dream" is its converse: "trick." Just before his death, a feminine critic put the objection as established: "Men of intelligence yawn. The trick is too easily seen through."

Impressions more contradictory are hard to imagine, and a third must be mentioned. Crane's work ever since it appeared has struck readers as "barbaric." His poems were "crazy," and they still—in standard anthologies—look very weird. The ferocity of his prose, whether intended or casual, seems primitive. His animism is like nothing else in civilized literature. Mountains, trees, dogs, men, horses, and boats flash in and out of each other's identities. The sun "had its hat over one eye" and one man's voice makes another man "wish that he was a horse, so that he could spring upon the bed and trample him to death." This is characteristic and frequent. A disappointed boatman has a "face like a floor." If Crane lulls you into safety for a minute, wait only. He is examining the electric chair in Sing Sing: "the comfortable and shining chair . . . waits and waits and waits" for "its next stained and sallow prince . . . an odor of oiled wood, a keeper's tranquil, unemotional voice, a broom stood in a corner near the door, a blue sky and a bit of moving green tree at a window so small that it might have been made by a canister shot." The sentence concludes like an electrocution, and when the keeper is quoted he might be a friendly aesthetician describing Crane's effect on the reader: "We calculate that the whole business takes about a minute from the time we go after him." These images come all from early, negligible, unreprinted newspaper stories; assaults in his important work may be more violent still. Crane's humor, finally, and his irony are felt as weird or incomprehensible. When he began a book of poems with the line,

> Do not weep, maiden, for war is kind,

the reviewers treated him, reasonably, as an *idiot*.

A dream, a trick, a savage or imbecile attack: any account of his work which hopes for assent will have to try to reconcile these views with each other, and with still other views. All we need agree yet is that it seems to display an essential, *obvious* coherence, originality, and authority, such as will justify any care we may take to appreciate it.

2

Let us begin with his poetry. The poetry and the prose show difference as well as unity, but an understanding of the poetry, if we can arrive at one, will help us with the prose. Since Crane is the important American poet between Walt Whitman and Emily Dickinson on one side, and his tardy-developing contemporaries Edwin Arlington Robinson and Robert Frost with Ezra Pound on the other, it has interest that he perhaps drew on both of his predecessors. He does not sound much like them.

> I saw a man pursuing the horizon;
> Round and round they sped.
> I was disturbed at this;
> I accosted the man.
> "It is futile," I said,
> "You can never—"
>
> "You lie," he cried,
> And ran on.

This does not sound much like a poem either. Here is another one:

> On the horizon the peaks assembled;
> And as I looked,
> The march of the mountains began.
> As they marched, they sang,
> "Ay! we come! we come!"

A conflict here between the sense of terror communicated and a suggestion of desire ("Ay!" answers as it were a question or entreaty) produces more appearance of a poem. But both look rather like *impressions of fatal relation* than poems. They are a world away from Whitman, an includer, an accumulator; these pieces would plainly do with even less if they could, though less is inconceivable. They differ too from Emily Dickinson, who as R. P. Blackmur has shown *tried* always to write regular verse, in that there is obviously no attempt to write regular verse, or even, perhaps, verse at all. On the other hand, no immaturity can be heard in them. Whatever it is they try to do they do; they are perfectly self-possessed. Very odd is the fact that in the first piece, despite its smallness, the rhymes are almost inaudible. There they are: sped-said-cried, horizon-man-on. Quite a set of rhymes for eight lines; yet even after you know they are there, you can scarcely hear them. It opens indeed with a regular heroic, but this effect is destroyed so rapidly that it scarcely affects the ear as regular. Now it does not appear to be deliberately destroyed, just as it does not appear to have been deliberately arrived at. So with the rhymes: the writer does not appear to fight their effect but seems to have come into the rhymes themselves by accident, and simultaneously, by instinct, arranged for their muting. The famous color and style of Crane's prose are absent, blankly absent.

All this is peculiar. Let us try a technical approach to two other pieces, which stand at opposite limits of Crane's poetry. The first is tiny:

A man feared that he might find an assassin;
Another that he might find a victim.
One was more wise than the other.

The other is one of the major lyrics of the century in America and I must quote it all.

Do not weep, maiden, for war is kind.
Because your lover threw wild hands toward the sky
And the affrighted steed ran on alone,
Do not weep.
War is kind.

Hoarse, booming drums of the regiment,
Little souls who thirst for fight,
These men were born to drill and die.
The unexplained glory flies above them,
Great is the battle-god, great, and his kingdom—
A field where a thousand corpses lie.

Do not weep, babe, for war is kind.
Because your father tumbled in the yellow trenches,
Raged at his breast, gulped and died,
Do not weep.
War is kind.

Swift blazing flag of the regiment,
Eagle with crest of red and gold,
These men were born to drill and die.
Point for them the virtue of slaughter,
Make plain to them the excellence of killing
And a field where a thousand corpses lie.

Mother whose heart hung humble as a button
On the bright splendid shroud of your son,
Do not weep.
War is kind.

There is nothing to approach in the first piece, though, technically. For a moment you don't hear it, then you do, with a little fear, as if a man had put his face suddenly near your face; and that's all. The indifference to craft, to *how* the thing is said, is lunar.

The second poem is based on the letter *i* in the word "kind." There are rhymes "die" and "lie" in the set-in stanzas; wild, sky, affrighted, flies, bright; just these, and they ought to make a high lament. But of course they do nothing of the sort. The author is standing *close* to one, not off on some platform, and the poem takes place in the successful war of the *prose* ("unexplained," "gulped," and so on) *against* the poetic appearance of lament. It takes some readers a while to hear this poem. Once heard, it is passionately moving; and it is moving then exactly in the lines where ordinarily a poet would not be moving,—not at all in the "bright splendid shroud" line, but in the beautiful and *i*-less line before it. A domestic, terrible poem, what it whispers is: "I would console you, how I would console you! *If I honestly could.*" In all its color and splendor, this is really not much more like an ordinary poem than the other three; its method is theirs. The four pieces have in common also cruelty and pity, their nakedness, a kind of awful bluntness; and contemptuous indifference to everything that makes up "poetry" for other people. What shall we do with them?

The poems have an enigmatic air and yet they are desperately personal. The absence of the panoply of the Poet is striking. We remember that their author did not like to be called a poet nor did he call them poetry himself. How unusual this is, my readers will recognize: most writers of verse are merely dying to be called poets, tremblingly hopeful that what they write is real "poetry." There was no pose here in Crane. His reluctance was an inarticulate recognition of something strange in the pieces. They are not like literary compositions. They are like things just seen and said,

said for use. The handwriting of doctors is not beautiful; the point of their prescriptions is just to be made out. (It is very remarkable, I have noticed since the present chapter was written, that Crane used the peculiar word "pills" for his poems. He had often a mysterious and even dreadful exactness of terminology. "Some of the pills," he said in New York when *The Black Riders* was under attack, "are pretty darned dumb, anyhow. But I meant what I said." He had in mind no doubt their lack of sugar-coating.) Robert Graves, one of the shrewdest, craziest, and most neglected students of poetry living, laid out a theory of the origin of poetry once. A savage dreams, is frightened by the dream, and goes to the medicine man to have it explained. The medicine man can make up anything, anything will reassure the savage, so long as the manner of its delivery is impressive; so he chants, perhaps he stamps his foot, people like rhythm, what he says becomes rhythmical, people like to hear things *again*, and what he says begins to rhyme. Poetry begins—as a practical matter, for *use*. It reassures the savage. Perhaps he only hears back again, chanted, the dream he just told the medicine man, but he is reassured; it is like a spell. And medicine men are shrewd: interpretation enters the chanting, symbols are developed and connected, the gods are invoked, poetry booms. Now Crane's poetry is like a series of primitive anti-spells. Sometimes he chants, but for the most part on principle he refuses to (no coating). He has truths to tell. Everybody else in the 'nineties is chanting and reassuring and invoking the gods. So Crane just says, like a medicine man *before* chanting or poetry began. And what he says is savage: unprotected, forestlike. Man's vanity and cruelty, hypocrisy and cowardice, stupidity and pretension, hopelessness and fear, glitter through the early poems. God may exist; if so, He rolls down and crushes you. Part of the irony in Crane's poetry results from the imposition of his complex modern doubt upon a much stronger primeval set of his mind.

A man saw a ball of gold in the sky;
He climbed for it,
And eventually he achieved it—
It was clay.

Now this is the strange part:
When the man went to the earth
And looked again,
Lo, there was the ball of gold.
Now this is the strange part:
It was a ball of gold.
Ay, by the heavens, it was a ball of gold.

The first four lines were written by a minister's son and intellectual of the 'nineties, the rest by a bushman.

Now I wish to be more serious and explode some errors. Crane has a textbook fame for his "experimentation" and for his "anticipation" of the free-verse movement. The notion of writing irregularly Crane probably got from Whitman; possibly the notion of very short short-line poems came to him after hearing Howells read Emily Dickinson; W. E. Henley's free verse may have affected him, the English Bible certainly did. There is no evidence in the poetry or outside it that he ever experimented in verse. Instinct told him to throw over metrical form, visions were in his head, and he wrote them down. Some of the poems were no doubt more consciously composed than others, and he revised some of them; their parable and proverbial form they owe in part to the Bible and to Olive Schreiner's *Dreams*; but "experiment" is not the word. As for "anticipation": some of the later people probably learned from him (Pound mentioned him early, and it was Sandburg who introduced Sherwood Anderson to his verse), and more would have if his books had been more available; but his work is quite different from theirs. A comparison of any of the short poems of Pound or H. D. with the piece of Crane last quoted will make this clear. The later poets are deeply interested in manner; Crane is deeply uninterested in manner. In order to appreciate Crane's poetry, you must understand that it differs in intention and mode from the poetry both of his period and of ours. It is primitive; not designedly so, but naturally primitive.

Some assistance for this view, which may perhaps need it, turned up recently. T. S. Eliot in his paper on Poe and Valéry distinguishes three stages in the development of poetry: a middle stage in which the auditor or reader is interested in both the subject and the way it is handled (the style), an earlier stage in which attention is directed entirely upon the subject, and our stage, in which the subject has become "simply a necessary means for the realization of the poem. At this stage [Mr. Eliot goes on] the reader or listener may become as nearly indifferent to the subject matter as the primitive listener was to the style." This account is less incompatible with Mr. Graves's than it may appear, for the savage is not aware that he is worked upon by the chanting: he thinks he is attending wholly to the matter. So Crane's phrasing and pausation affect us insensibly, and the subject appears naked. One conclusive aspect of this whole analysis will be considered fully when we come to the prose, but the curious ground of Crane's personal preference of *The Black Riders* to *The Red Badge* (expressed in a letter to Hilliard) must have a word. Though absolutely opposed to "preaching" in literature, he nevertheless preferred his poetry as "the more ambitious effort," attempting "to give my ideas of life as a whole, so far as I know it," while the novel was "a mere episode."

Crane as a poet, in fine—a poet is the only thing we can call him—I take to represent an unexampled reversion. I take the steady drift of our period toward greater and greater self-consciousness, an increasing absorption in style, to be what has obscured the nature of his work and delayed its appreciation. How far its point of view really is from ours can be seen as well in a comparatively conventional, gentle piece as in the others:

> Ay, workman, make me a dream,
> A dream for my love.
> Cunningly weave sunlight,
> Breezes, and flowers.
> Let it be of the cloth of meadows.
> And—good workman—
> And let there be a man walking thereon.

He writes as if this presence of the man were inconceivable. "War is kind" is perhaps his finest poem. The phrase is so repeated and with such pity that in the face of reason one cannot learn to believe he does not mean it; the poem may be compared to Webster's great dirge in *The White Devil*, actually a nightmare of horror behind the consolation, and contrasted with Hart Crane's *Voyages (II)*, a serious beautiful desperate poem less mature than these others. But a considerable number of Stephen Crane's poems, once their range is found, will be remembered. They do not wear out and there is nothing else like them. It is said by Thomas Beer and others that Crane lost his poetic faculty several years before his death; but not all the poems have been collected, and the dating is very uncertain. Fewer, certainly, of the more personal poems in the second book (1899) are valuable. One first printed long after his death, and presumably late, is one of his best, "A man adrift on a slim spar"—

> . . . A pale hand sliding from a polished spar.
>   God is cold.

> The puff of a coat imprisoning air:
> A face kissing the water-death,
> A weary slow sway of a lost hand
> And the sea, the moving sea, the sea.
>   God is cold.

The poetry, then, *has* the character of a "dream," something seen naively, in a new relation. It *is* barbaric, and so primitively blunt that one sees without difficulty how it can be thought a trick. But tricks are not this simple. And tricks can be learned; whereas none of his innumerable parodists could simulate either the gleam or the weight of his true work—they hang out at the edges of Crane's tone. Neither

> The sea was blue meadow,
> Alive with little froth-people
> Singing

nor

> A horse,
> Blowing, staggering, bloody thing
> Forgotten at foot of castle wall

would ever be seen again. Crane was not only a man with truths to tell, but an interested listener to this man. His poetry has the inimitable sincerity of a frightened savage anxious to learn what his dream means.

3

Moving from Crane's poetry to his prose, we recognize the same sincerity, the same bluntness, the same hallucinatory effect, the same enigmatic character, the same barbarity. There is a formal difference, however; and before taking it up, I want to say something of an aspect of his art Garnett correctly thought fundamental, namely, his irony.

This word has spread and weakened until it scarcely means anything, or it means whatever we like in the general direction of difference-from-appearance. Accepting it seriously so, as *abdita vis quaedam* or "a certain hidden force"—the phrase quoted by Saintsbury from Montaigne who quoted it from Lucretius—Crane's work is a riot of irony of nearly every kind. A baby, consumed with grief for the killing of his dog (Crane does not say so), is so small that he can go downstairs toward its body only very slowly, backwards. Henry Fleming hands back the packet to his shamefaced friend (who has *not* run away the day before) with sentiments equally generous and self-congratulatory. A Swede, crazy with fear of Western aggression, gets drunk and stirs it to life. Examples plunge for citation and classification. But Crane is strong enough, as will appear, to bear any weight; we want the force of a concept.

Suppose we take two modern impressions of irony: as a comment downward, the expression, that is, of a superior man, antisocial; and as a refuge of a weak man. Both are trivial, but the first is more debased than the second. A refuge is a serious matter, and no human is very strong. The careful student J. A. K. Thomson observes that, tracing the Ironical Man to his beginnings, we "find him, not the remote and fastidious Intellectual, but someone far more elemental, simple, grotesque, and pitiful." This habit of mind —which one possesses by nature or not at all; it cannot be learned—is a form of *lying low* before the Divine Jealousy. Thomson associates it with man's development away from animism. Under the gradual growth of the recognition that Nature is inanimate, man learns to distrust the universe and pretends that he is nothing so as not to be an object of destruction. So long as trees and brooks were like him, he could understand them; once he cannot, the way is open to general fear: he had better hide. Thrusting back through this recognition, as Wordsworth had to and Crane, the exceptional modern man—animistic—is opened to both the primitive and the ironic.

Specifically, early Greek comedy presented a contest between the *Alazon* (Impostor) and the *Eiron* or Ironical Man: after vauntings and pretensions, the *Alazon* is routed by the man who affects to be a fool. The Impostor pretends to be more than he is, the Ironist pretends to be less. Now in most of the criticism of Stephen Crane that displays any sensitivity, whether outraged or not, one nearly makes out a nervous understanding that this author is simultaneously *at war with* the people he creates and *on their side*—and displays each of these attitudes so forcibly that the reader feels he is himself being made a fool of; so that Crane's position is still disproportionate with his achievement, and people after his death were so eager to forget him that it took a World War, and later another World War, to recall him generally to attention. I wonder whether explanation will ease this feeling; for the truth is that, in a special and definite sense, the reader *is* being made a fool of. Who are the creations Crane is most at war with? His complex ones, his "heroes"? or his simplest ones, his babies, horses, dogs, and brooks? With the first class his art is a Greek comedy, a contest with the impostor. Not even Maggie escapes this: "At times Maggie told Pete long confidential tales of her former home life, dwelling upon the escapades of the other members of the family and the difficulties she had had to combat in order to obtain a degree of comfort." God knows these distresses are real enough; one feels them, and at the same time one is made to feel even more strongly that the character has to run a gauntlet to the author's sympathy. So far as his creations of the first class are striving to become members of the second class, they become candidates for pathos or tragedy; so far as they fail, they remain figures of (this deadly-in-earnest) comedy. Crane never rests. He is always fighting the thing out with himself, for he contains both *Alazon* and *Eiron*; and so, of course, does the reader; and only dull readers escape. As comedy, his work is a continual examination of pretension—an attempt to cast overboard, as it were, impediments to our salvation. With creations of the second class, his work is much more simply an irony of talisman, a prayer to Heaven for pity; and it *technically* resembles Greek tragedy, in which the theme is the Jealousy of Heaven.

There is regularly an element of pathos, therefore, in his

ironic (oppositional) inspection, and an element of irony regularly in his pathos. A Crane creation, or character, normally is *pretentious* and *scared*—the human condition; fitted by the second for pathos, by the first for irony. If the second feeling can save the first, as in Henry Fleming, the first can doom the second, as in the Swede. This pattern in his work seems hardly to have been perceived at all and is worth some insistence. The received account of Crane depends heavily upon the Gratuitous. He was bored by "plots," he drew "maps of accident," he emphasizes and ends in the "senseless," or he just brutalizes both his characters and the reader. The gratuitous is certainly very prominent, *outside* the central fate by which either one is lost or one is saved. Everything else—but only everything else—spins in irrelation; why pretend otherwise? in effect he says. And when he pretended himself, as he did sometimes, he was craftless as a sore thumb.

Let us look at this "fate" a little. It is against it that Crane's irony is most complex and energetic, and yet there is always one standpoint from which the product of this irony is not ironic at all. The Gordian example in his work would be the dreadful legend upon which the Swede's dead eyes rest, over the cash-machine: "This registers the amount of your purchase." But this death does. The Swede begged for it, *bought* it with his excess of fear and then his pretentiousness and even his over-protest against a boy's cheating in a game where no money was at stake. There is nothing accidental in the murder of this Swede except that it was the gambler who committed it and he gets a light sentence. Collins, in "A Mystery of Heroism," pretentiously gets himself into the position of taking an extreme risk to get a drink of water; he takes it, and finds out that this is what heroism is—not so much; but then the water is spilt. But that the water is spilt is the point, one way. He pretended that he could be a hero, he found that he could, and he found that it got him nothing, that nothing was changed; or, that everything was changed.

The elimination of the water sends our eyes straight to the mysterious fate. In "The Open Boat" the community of the four men is insisted on, and Higgins is given special attention throughout, so that he is specially fit to be the price the others pay for their rescue: a sacrifice. Nothing of Crane's seems more gratuitous than the chapters devoted to the self-pity of her persecutors after Maggie's death. But besides serving as ironical distribution of the remorse that society ought to feel, this self-pity *is* suffering. Pete suffers agonies of drunken self-abasement and is fleeced. The mother's final scream is one of "pain"—she invents it, as we know, revels in it, but then she actually suffers it. If the author's tacit contempt here is intense, so is a (carefully guarded from pretentiousness) passion for retribution.

Carefully guarded—and the pattern of justice in his art has to manifest itself as best it can under the dreadful recognitions of honesty. Life is what it is. The consequences of these recognitions, bitterness and horror, disguise themselves in his grotesquerie of concept and style, his velocity, his displacements of rage. Open, they would be insupportable; and this will bring us in a moment to the difference between Crane's prose and his poetry. But I am afraid his use of grotesquerie will not be clear without illustration. I take two of its great strokes, one verging towards this author's wonderful humor, the other towards horror. "Many a man ought to have a bathtub larger than the boat which here rode upon the sea." This dry, gay, senseless remark enables him to contrast like lightning, with the sinister wilderness of water, isolation, and danger where the men toil, the most domestic, sheltered, comfortable home-situation imaginable: with the painfully moving, the stationary; with the effort for salvation, the pleasant duty of washing oneself. Note the mock-heroic outset— "Many a man . . . "—at once abandoned. Many a man is to *own* a bathtub—these men own nothing but, precariously, their lives. Instead, the boat is alive, it "rides," running the risks of a rider. And then the point of a bathtub is to have water in it, water rising in it—and with this ominous flash of the tiny dinghy shipping water, the little sentence has done its work and is superseded by: "These waves were most wrongfully and barbarously abrupt and tall. . . ." Clearly, an artist able to give such compact expression to such complexly bitter alternative reflection, with an air of perfect good nature, will not easily be found at the mercy of bitterness. My other illustration is the famous ninth chapter of *The Red Badge*, where the death of the tall soldier occurs in a prolonged uncanny ecstasy. Several million readers have been appalled by this and perhaps no reader has ever explained to himself what Crane was doing, as perhaps Crane never to himself named it: the Dance of Death.

Between the verse and the prose of an author who has written both successfully we expect to find a relation of a certain kind. Poetry, as the more highly organized form of communication, requires and evinces more art. The interminable verse of various Nineteenth Century novelists (Dickens, Thackeray, George Eliot) is indeed artless but this is not successful verse. The relation I am speaking of appears clearly in Keats, in Gray, even in Swift, even in Shakespeare. The greater nervousness of Meredith in his prose, for instance, is not the nervousness of art but the nervousness of temperament; his poetry is more artful. Hardy is a better craftsman in prose than critics allow. When young Jude is described as walking carefully over plowed fields lest he tread on earthworms and not liking to see trees lopped from a fancy that it hurt them: "This weakness of character, as it may be called, suggests that he was the sort of man who was born to ache a good deal before the fall of the curtain upon his unnecessary life should signify that all was well with him again." The Shakespearian stress upon this "well" is a product of style; the sentence stays in the mind. But the art of his poetry has been usually slighted also, and is much greater. Crane, so far as I am aware, is singular in this regard. Crane's poetry is characteristically and recognizably by the author of his prose;

it shows the style of a master—as the soldier "raging at his breast," the horse a "Blowing, staggering, bloody thing"—and this is almost his prose-style. But it shows *less* style, less of devoted *art*. The prose looks often crafty, the poetry scarcely ever. We shall come back to this.

Crane I daresay is one of the great stylists of the language. These words "master" and "great" will trouble some readers, as they trouble me. But they seem unavoidable. The trouble we feel arises from several causes, which are worth examination. Crane's works that matter are all short. We don't see how works so little can be with any decency called great. Greatness of prose-style, however, does not require length for display. We hear Dryden in his *Essay of Dramatic Poesy*, Johnson in the letter to Chesterfield, fully. Another trouble is that Crane was writing greatly, if he ever did, in his early twenties. We are told that prose-writers mature slowly; scarcely anyone writes prose worth reading under thirty. There are exceptions. Congreve is a large one, Miss Austen is, there are others; and Crane anyway, as I have been trying and shall try more exactly to show, is in several respects a case unique. We wish if we can to avoid preconceptions. A third trouble is just that he is comparatively recent; this matters less. Then there are the words themselves, grandiose. We have no objection to calling the boy Keats a master, Rimbaud a master, but the word "great" sticks a little. It looks like a catchword. Our major troubles, though, I think are two, both of them proceeding from the nature of his work and of its historical situation. There is first the relation of his style to prose style in English and American before him, and second the relation of his general art-form, the story, to Western fiction before him. (The term Western is unsatisfactory because it must include Russian fiction, but no other seems better.) Though these troubles are closely related, we must take them separately.

Nothing very like Crane's prose style is to be found earlier; so much will probably be granted at once by an experienced reader. Here I must observe that Crane wrote several styles. He had even an epistolary style—extended, slow, uninflected, during most of his life, curter and jotty towards the end—but we are interested in his narrative styles. He began with the somber-jocular, sable, fantastic prose of the "Sullivan County Sketches" and the jagged, colored, awkward, brilliant *Maggie*. *Maggie* he probably revised much barbarousness out of before anyone except brothers and friends saw it, and he abandoned deliberately the method of the sketches—though fantasy, and fantasy in the quality of the prose, remained intermittently an element in his work to the end. A movement towards fluidity increases in *The Red Badge* and the "Baby Sketches" he was writing at the same time and produces a Crane norm: flexible, swift, abrupt, and nervous—swift, but with an unexampled capacity for stasis also. Color is high, but we observe the blank absence of the orotund, the moulded, which is Crane's most powerful response to the prose tradition he declined to inherit. In the fusion of the impassive and the intense peculiar to this author, he kept on drawing the rein. "Horses—One Dash" and "The Five White Mice" lead to the supple majesty of "The Open Boat," a second norm. *The Monster*, much more closed, circumstantial, "normal" in feeling and syntax, is a third. Then he opened his style again back towards the second norm in the great Western stories, "The Bride Comes to Yellow Sky" and "The Blue Hotel," and thereafter (for his two years) he used the second and the third styles at will, sometimes in combination, and the third usually relaxed as his health failed but peculiarly tense and astonishing in "The Kicking Twelfth." In certain late work also, notably in "The Clan of No Name," a development toward complexity of structure is evident, which death broke off. Nevertheless we may speak of "Crane's style" so long as we have these variations in mind, and my point is that it differs *radically* both from the tradition of English prose and from its modifications in American prose. Shakespeare, Dryden, Defoe, Johnson, Dickens, Arnold, Kipling, as these develop into Edwards, Jefferson, Hawthorne, Melville, James—Crane writes on the whole, a definite and absolute *stylist*, as if none of these people had ever existed. His animation is not Kipling's, his deadpan flatness is not Mark Twain's. He is more like Tacitus, or Stendhal in his autobiography, say, than like any of the few writers of narrative English who actually affected his development. He was a rhetorician who refused to be one. In Crane for the first time the resources of American spareness, exaggeration, volcanic impatience, American humor, came into the hands of a narrative author serious and thoughtful as an artist as Hawthorne or James, and *more* serious than any others of the New England-New York hegemony. Thus he made possible—whether by way of particular influence or as a symbolic feat in the development of the language—one whole side of Twentieth Century prose. It is hard to decide that a boy, that anyone, did this, and so we feel uncomfortable about the word that characterizes the achievement with great justice.

The second difficulty with "great" is the newness of his form. I am not referring to the immense burst of talented story-writing in England and America during the 'nineties, though this is relevant; the short story had scarcely any status in English earlier, and we are less eager, naturally, to concede greatness to its artist than to crown a novelist. Poe is an exception, absolutely genuine, very seldom good, more limited than Crane, superbly overvalued. Any sort of standard has hardly been in force for a generation. As late as 1923, in a survey not exceptionally stupid (Pattee's *Development of the American Short Story*), Crane existed merely at the head of thirteen nonentities (all save O. Henry and Harold Frederic) of whom Jack London was the one perhaps "most sure of literary permanence." The intensive literary criticism of the last twenty years has devoted itself largely to poetry and literary criticism, less to the novel, less still to the short story and the nearly extinct drama. If we are in a more enlightened state than Pattee was, we still owe it mostly to Mencken's generation. But I was referring to an operation that Crane performed. As he stripped down and galvanized prose, so he gutted the story of practically everything that had made it a story. "One fact is certain," Hardy decided in 1888: "in fiction there can be no intrinsically new thing at this stage of the world's history." This was one of the major blunders of all time, as James was then demonstrating, Crane would in a moment, and Joyce would presently. Hardy's novels can now be seen as really traditional and conservative when they are compared with something revolutionary, when *Tess* for instance is compared with *The Ambassadors*. Kipling, a story-writer neglected just now except by several of the best critics on both sides of the Atlantic, is less conservative and profounder than Hardy. But both Englishmen keep to the range. By setting a sentence characteristic of Crane against the sentence by Hardy quoted some pages ago, one learns. It is the two Americans who make formal war. James warred in the direction: elaboration of sensibility, consistency of point of view, qualification of style. The campaign cost him, progressively in his work, narrative in the old sense, even though he goes to every *length*. But his stories are still recognizably stories. Idiosyncratic and extended though they are, they are essentially far more like Kipling's* than the stories of either are like Stephen Crane's.

Crane's stories are as unlike earlier stories as his poems are unlike poems. He threw away, thoughtfully, plot; outlawed juggling and arrangement of material (Poe, Bierce, O. Henry); excluded the whole usual mechanism of society; banished equally sex (Maupassant) and romantic love (Chekhov—unknown to him); decided not to develop his characters; decided not to have any conflicts between them as characters; resolved not to have any characters at all in the

* It has interest that James was repeatedly prostrated by Kipling, as his letters show, and, though very generous, looked hard for holes; the persistent exaggeration of his letters everywhere does not conceal his eagerness, his particular eagerness, about "the infant monster," "the absolutely uncanny talent," the talent "diabolically great."

usual sense; simplified everything that remained, and, watching intently, tenderly, and hopelessly, blew Fate through it—saying with inconceivable rapidity and an air of immense deliberation what he saw. What he saw, "apparently." The result is a series of extremely formidable, *new*, compact, finished, and distressing works of art. Mencken dated modern American literature from *The Red Badge of Courage*. The new *Literary History of the United States*, coming to hand as I write, dates it from the reissue of *Maggie* in 1896. It must come from about there, apparently.

Of course Crane did nothing such as I have just described. He was interested, only, in certain things, and kept the rest out. It is the ability to keep the rest out that is astounding. But the character of the deliberate in his prose too is conspicuous. We saw that this was absent from his poetry, and it is time to come to the difference. The difference is that between presentation (in the poetry) and apparent presentation (in the prose); in the figure of the savage's dream that we were employing, between *rehearsal* and *investigation*. The poem can simply say what the dream (nightmare) was; at once it gets rid of the dream, and is solaced in hearing it said. An effect of style is undesirable. To *study* the dream, to embody it, as in a story—this is another matter. One needs a suit, a style, of chain armor to protect the subject from everything that would like to get into the story with it: the other impressions of life, one's private prejudices, a florid and hypocritical society, existing literature. The style of the prose aims at the same thing as the unstyle of the poetry, namely, naked presentment, but its method is ironic. Other authors are saying what things "are," with supreme falsity. Crane therefore will only say what they *seem* to be. "The youth turned, with sudden, livid rage, toward the battlefield. He shook his fist. He seemed about to deliver a philippic.

" 'Hell——'

"The red sun was pasted in the sky like a wafer."

Half of Crane's celebrated "coldness" is an effect of this *re-*

fusal to guarantee. "He seemed about to deliver a philippic." It sounds as if he weren't going to; but he is; but he isn't; but—one does not know exactly where one is. The style is merely honest, but it disturbs one, it is even menacing. If this extremely intelligent writer will not go further than that insistent "seemed," says the reader nervously to himself, should *I*? The style has the effect of obliterating with silent contempt half of what one thinks one knows. And then: a policeman begins "frenziedly to seize bridles and beat the soft noses of the responsible horses." In the next sentence the noses are forgotten. But to tell us about the horses if the author is not going to commiserate with them seems brutal. It makes the reader do the feeling if he wants to; Crane, who cared more for horses than any reader, is on his way. Again the reader is as it were rebuked, for of course he *doesn't* feel very strongly about horses—he would never have put in that "soft" himself, much less clubbed it in with "responsible." Or: "A saloon stood with a voracious air on a corner." This is either funny, a little, or an affront: it might be after the reader. One is not enough guided. Just: there it is, hungry, very hungry.

This is supposed, by the way, to be Realism or Naturalism. Frank Norris, who was a romantic moralist, with a style like a great wet dog, and Stephen Crane, an impressionist and a superlative stylist, are Naturalists. These terms are very boring, but let us agree at least to mean by them *method* (as Howells did) rather than *material* (as Norris, who called his serious works "Romance," did). "Tell your yarn and let your style go to the devil," Norris wrote to somebody. The Naturalists, if there are any, all *accumulate*, laborious, insistent, endless; Dreiser might be one. Crane selected and was gone. "He knew when to shut up," as Norris put it. "He is *the only* impressionist," said Conrad in italics to Garnett, "and *only* an impressionist." This is not quite right either: Crane's method shows realistic and also fantastic elements. But it would be better, as a label for what has after all got to be understood anyway in itself, than the categorical whim established now in the literary histories. Crane was an impressionist.

His color tells us so at once. This famous color of his plays a part in his work that has been exaggerated, but it is important. Gifted plainly with a powerful and probably very odd sense of color, fortified then by Goethe, he did not refuse to use it; sometimes he abused it, and he increasingly abandoned it. Most authors use color. "The sun emerges from behind the gray clouds that covered the sky and suddenly lights up with its bright red glow the purple clouds, the greenish sea . . . the white buildings." So Tolstoy at the end of *Sevastopol*, and it bears no relation whatever to Crane's use of color. "At this time Hollanden wore an unmistakable air of having a desire to turn up his coat collar." This is more like one of Crane's colors than Tolstoy's actual colors are. Color is imposed, from an angle, like this apparently physical and actually psychological detail. Crane was interested in what Goethe called the "moral-sensual effect of color." He owes nothing whatever, apparently, to painting.* The blue hotel "screaming and howling"—"some red years"—"fell with a yellow crash." The color is primitive. So with adverbs, metaphors. A man leans on a bar listening to others "terribly discuss a question that was not plain." "There was a general movement in the compact column. The long animal-like thing moved slightly. Its four hundred eyes were turned upon the figure of Collins." Here there is none of Crane's frequent, vivid condensation; and yet the eyes are not human eyes. It is primitive, an impression. A psychologist lately called red the most panicky and explosive of colors, the most primitive, as well as the most ambivalent, related equally to rage and

* This is an opinion. Wells disagreed, relying on very late passages like this in "War Memories": "I bring this to you merely as . . . something done in thought similar to that which the French impressionists do in color . . ." But all such allusions are metaphorical in Crane, who does not use color in the least like a painter. He knew, by the way, few real painters —Linson, Jerome Myers, later Ryder; mostly illustrators.

love, battle and fire, joy and destruction. Everywhere then, in style, a mind at stretch.

We may reach toward the subject of all this remorseless animation through his characters. They are very odd. To call them types is a major critical error, long exposed, ever-recurrent. The new *Literary History* describes the hero of *The Red Badge* as "impersonal and typical," for which read: intensely personal and individual. George Wyndham (and Wells after him) fifty years ago showed the boy an idealist and dreamer brought to the test. Pete in *Maggie* is not a bartender, but Pete. Billy Higgins in "The Open Boat" is not an oiler, but the oiler. Crane scarcely made a type in all his work. At the same time, he scarcely made any characters. His people, *in* their stories, stay in your mind; but they have no existence outside. No life is strongly imaginable for them save what he lets you see. This seems to me to be singular, to want explanation. I think he is interested in them individually, but only as a crisis reaches them. The "shaky and quick-eyed" Swede of "The Blue Hotel" is certainly an *individual* mad with fear, one of Crane's most memorable people, but it is as an individual *mad with fear* that he grimly matters. "Stanley pawed gently at the moss, and then thrust his head forward to see what the ants did under the circumstance." When this delightful thing happens, a love-scene is taking place two feet away, one of the most inhibited and perfunctory ever written. It is only or chiefly in animals that Crane can be interested when a *fate* is not in question. Once it is, he is acutely and utterly present with the sufferer, attending however to the fate.

"Apparently" the state of the soul in crisis: this is his subject. The society against the person will do; he uses the term "environment" in regard to *Maggie*, and this is more generally dramatized in *The Monster*, more particularly dramatized in "The Bride Comes to Yellow Sky." But one has less feeling in these works, and in a number of others like them, that the men are themselves against each other, than that they have been set simply facing each other—not by Crane—by a fate. War is the social situation that does this most naturally and continually, so he possesses himself of it; in imagination first, again and again, and then in fact. "The Open Boat" is his most perfect story partly because here for once the fate is in the open: one is *fully justified* in being afraid, one can feel with confidence that one is absolutely tested. The antagonist will not fail one, as another man might, as even society might. The extraordinary mind that *had* to feel this we shall look at in the next chapter; here we are concerned with the art. Now these states of crisis, by their nature, cannot persist; so Crane succeeded only in short work. *The Red Badge of Courage*, as most critics have noticed, is not really a novel at all, but a story, and it is a little too long, as Crane thought it was. His imagination was resolute in presenting him with conditions for fear; so that he works with equal brilliance from invention and from fact. To take "The Open Boat," however, as a *report* is to misunderstand the nature of his work: it is an action of his art upon the remembered possibility of death. The death is so close that the story is warm. A coldness of which I was speaking earlier in Crane is absent here. Half of this I attributed to the stylistic refusal to guarantee. The other half is an effect from far in the mind that made the art, where there was a passion for life half-strangled by a need for death and made cold. Life thaws under the need when the death nears. In the eggshell boat, the correspondent knew even at the time, under dreadful hardship, that this was "the best experience of his life"—the comradeship, he says this is, but it was really something else: "There was a terrible grace in the move of the waves, and they came in silence, save for the snarling of the crests. . . ."

The immense power of the tacit, felt in Crane's accounts of Maggie's brother's nihilism, her mother's self-pity, Henry Fleming's self-pride, George's dreams, gives his work kinship rather with Chekhov and Maupassant than Poe. "I like my art"—said Crane—"straight"; and he misquoted Emerson, "There should be a long logic beneath the story, but it should be carefully kept out of sight." How far Crane's effect of inevitability depends upon this *silence* it would be hard to say. Nowhere in "The Open Boat" is it mentioned that the situation of the men is symbolic, clear and awful though it is that this story opens into the universe. Poe in several great stories opens man's soul downwards, but his work has no relation with the natural and American world at all. If Crane's has, and is irreplaceable on this score, it is for an ironic inward and tragic vision outward that we value it most, when we can bear it. At the end of the story a word occurs that will do for Crane. "When it came night, the white waves paced to and fro in the moonlight, and the wind brought the sound of the great sea's voice to the men on the shore, and they felt that they could then be interpreters." Crane does really stand between us and something that we could not otherwise understand. It is not human; it is not either the waves and mountains who are among his major characters, but it acts in them, it acts in children and sometimes even in men, upon animals, upon boys above all, and men. Crane does not understand it fully. But he has been driven and has dragged himself nearer by much to it than we have, and he interprets for us.

For this reason, as well as for his technical revolution, he is indispensable. By a margin he is probably the greatest American story-writer, he stands as an artist not far below Hawthorne and James, he is one of our few poets, and one of the few manifest geniuses the country has produced. For a large sane art we will not go to Crane of course, nor to any other American so far. We do not go to Dostoievsky either. For a *normal* art you have to go to artists much greater still: Shakespeare, Mozart, Tolstoy; and not alone to their greatest works, where the range of experience dealt with is utterly beyond any range yet dealt with by an American, but to their small works also, like "Master and Man." Whether Tolstoy's is a *better* story than Crane's fantastic *The Blue Hotel* it is less easy to decide. *The Red Badge of Courage* is much better than *Sevastopol*.

Five — THE COLOR OF
THIS SOUL

The Color of This Soul

His friends while he was alive and his critics since have found Stephen Crane mysterious, inscrutable. Every reader has observed the ghastly reign in his work of the color Red and the emotion Fear. I once tried to puzzle out the relation between them, and coming back to Thomas Beer's book after a long time I was electrified: "Let it be stated that the mistress of this boy's mind was fear. His search in aesthetic was governed by terror as that of tamer men is governed by the desire of women." The first sentence seems now to be famous. It is cited by the account of Crane in the recent *Literary History of the United States*, which then goes on, implausibly enough, to speak of the "simple facts" of Crane's life, "the familiar story of romantic youth," "an almost classic formula," but is presently confessing that "the sources of Crane's philosophy and art are as yet undeciphered." "Simple" and "familiar" are not the words that would have occurred to one, though there may indeed turn out to be something classic in this life. It is better to recognize an enigma, as the author of this very fair new account then does.

The nature of the enigma was declared with precision by Mark Van Doren, twenty-five years ago, when he remarked that the compliment that would eventually be paid Crane "will take the form of an analysis of his need to live, at least as an artist, in the midst of all but unbearable excitement." We have now seen this excitement also in Crane's life, a fury of writing and action, coupled with an extraordinary personal silence, a mystery of inertia and sudden rebellious movement, hopeless tentative loves, a discontinuous kindness of life and wild cruelty of art, obsession with dogs and horses, with babies, with older women, with whores, obsession with death. Our impression is undoubtedly chaotic. Still, certain elements emerge distinct and strange, among them perhaps above all those associated with prostitutes and with war. Why was Stephen Crane obliged to champion prostitutes? Why was he obliged to spend his life imagining and seeking war? Perhaps no answers to these questions are to be had, but there seems no reason to suppose so until we have tried to answer them—as warily and also as boldly as need be. Let me say at this point that we are not in quest of *reasons* for Crane's greatness as an artist. I suspect that no explanation is available for greatness. All we can hope to see, with luck, care, time, labor and devotion, is *where it comes from. Why* it comes is another matter. Taking as a starting point the first of the two crucial questions just posed, what can we learn?

Ten years after Crane's death a Viennese student of the human mind published a dozen pages on "A Special Type of Choice of Object made by Men," attempting to account for an anomaly encountered repeatedly by him in psychiatric practice. Therapy was not an issue; the paper sought a general psychological explanation of certain very curious observed facts. The problem Freud set himself was to account for the juxtaposition in certain men of a disconcerting series of "conditions of love." He found four conditions. The woman loved must involve, first, an "injured third party"—some other man, that is, who has a right of possession, as husband or betrothed or near friend. She must be, second, "more or less sexually discredited"—"within the limits of a significant series" from a married woman known to be flirtatious up to an actual harlot; "love for a harlot" Freud called this condition. Third, this highly compulsive situation is repeated, with sincerity and intensity repeated; even, in consequence of external conditions (such as changes of residence and environment), to a long chain of such experiences. Fourth: "The trait in this type of lover that is most astonishing to the observer is the desire they express to 'rescue' the beloved."

Now though our knowledge of Stephen Crane's life is incomplete and in part uncertain, one or two of these "conditions" are immediately striking as characteristic of it: the "love for a harlot," and the "injured third party" (Cora Stewart's husband). It ought to be worth while to investigate the extent to which they are characteristic, and whether Freud's other conditions are present also. I must emphasize at once the fact that we are dealing mainly with *unconscious* compulsion. Depending upon temperament, strength of personal character, and circumstances, such compulsion issues or does not issue into consciousness or into action. We are interested not only in what Stephen Crane *did* but in what we find there is evidence that he was compelled toward. It is not here suggested that Crane knew his compulsions or felt, for instance, any conscious wish to "injure" a "third party."

The condition of an "injured third party" is certain in his common-law marriage. Mrs. Munroe or "L.B.", earlier, although unhappy with her husband, was married. Writing to a friend about Miss Crouse, Crane mentions someone's "rivals" for her; of whom he became tentatively one. Helen Trent was engaged to be married, but Crane (according to Beer) did not know this and withdrew immediately he learned it; the elderly lady she companioned falls within Freud's ground. Of Amy Leslie's situation, apart from the fact that her first husband had died, we know nothing, nor of early loves except that the Canadian lady with seven children was no doubt married.

His relation with Cora, and an exceptional concern with

299

prostitutes, must probably establish the second condition; but within the "discredited" range falls also Amy Leslie, as ex-actress.

The recurrences with which we have been dealing go far to establish the third condition also—including one to come. For a life so absorbed and short, one certainly hears of many loves. It must be mentioned as significant—dealing, I repeat, with unconscious compulsion—that with Crane's only change of environment after he married, the journey to Cuba, we hear of a widow in whose lodging-house he stayed, writing, long after even Beer remarks that he should have returned to England; she is said to have mothered him, insisting on his eating reasonably and taking a walk at night; her portrait in "His Majestic Lie" is devoted. But if the three long letters written to Cora and now announced for early publication are genuine, the slight doubt attaching to this third "condition" disappears: they are said, weirdly enough, to describe to her "his European amatory adventures."

Of the desire to "rescue" the beloved, enough has been said in earlier chapters. His appearance in court and Cora's prose-poem alone would do. But it has great interest that this last condition of the four appears to stand, Freud wrote, "merely in a loose and superficial relation, founded entirely on conscious grounds, to these phantasies that have gained control of the love-experiences of real life." The rescue theme, therefore, in life (Dora Clark, Doris Watts, Cora Taylor) was able *consciously*, no doubt, to imitate the rescue-action of his mother in regard to the fallen woman which he consciously remembered; and this theme is often, as we have seen, undisguised in his writing. This is the first time we have had occasion to allude to Crane's mother and almost the only time she will occur in a context *conscious* to Crane.

The life thus seems to display with perfect distinctness all four of the conditions that puzzled Freud. This great scientist observed carefully at the close of his paper that his aim in it had been simply "first of all to single out extreme types in sharp outline . . . there is a far greater number of persons in whom only one or two of the typical features, and even these but indistinctly traced, are recognizable." Crane strikes one then as decidedly "an extreme type in sharp outline." The paper reads indeed, upon sufficient exploration, like a study of Crane, and its immense insight receives from Crane's life and work decisive confirmation. But one major point remains to be noticed. It is required, in elaboration of the second condition, that jealousy accompany the valuing of the love-object—not jealousy of the "injured third party," strangely, but jealousy of new acquaintances or friends in regard to whom the woman may be brought under suspicion. Now we know little enough about Crane's relations with his wife (or any other woman), but one friend who did and whom the record has let speak is definite. On gossip concerning Mrs. Crane early in 1900, Robert Barr wrote that Crane "is subject to a kind of jealousy that knows how to hurt him worst." In the absence of any but this witness, evidence from Crane's writing may be given weight. In his three long novels jealousy as we have seen is dominant, not only of the heroes' chief rivals (Oglethorpe, Coke, Forister) but of others. In "The Clan of No Name," Mr. Smith sits waiting with a dull fear of the girl's having gone off with one of his "dream-rivals. . . . It was part of his love to believe in the absolute treachery of his adored one." In the third story dealing with two Kids, "A Man by the Name of Mud," one Kid is infatuated, again with a light woman (chorus girl) and behaves with brilliant indifference until, at the very end: "Wants to be dead sure there are no others. Once suspects it, and immediately makes the colossal mistake of his life. Takes the girl to task. Girl won't stand it for a minute. Harangues him. Kid surrenders and pleads with her—pleads with her. Kid's name is mud." * The exact coincidence, finally, of parts of "Intrigue" with Freud's formula may be taken as conclusive.

* Posthumously published, feeble, probably very late: the style is that of his curt, dying letters from Brede.

> Beware of my friends,
> Be not in speech too civil,
> For in all courtesy
> My weak heart sees spectres,
> Mists of desire
> Arising from the lips of my chosen;
> Be not civil.

The whole case, in fine, displays itself as classical, and the peculiar urgency of certain of these "conditions" for Stephen Crane is realized when we recall emotions out of his life: his startling excitement, for instance, over the necessity of *rescuing* Helen Trent from a rather abstract association which to her was nothing, to us seems nothing, and to Crane was all-important because it was capable of being regarded as *discreditable*.

The explanation of the type at which Freud arrived will perhaps, after forty years, surprise few of my readers, so familiar has time made us with two or three of his basic concepts. But this familiarity, fortunate so far as it has weakened our denying sense of shock, is very unfortunate so far as it can make us glib. It might be better to attend as to a matter wholly new, profoundly incongruous and difficult. The type, Freud said, is that in which "the libido has dwelt so long in its attachment to the mother, even after puberty, that the maternal characteristics remain stamped on the love-objects chosen later—so long that they all become easily recognizable mother surrogates." Following the revelation to a boy of the secret of sexual life, especially and incredibly as he applies it to his parents, and the further revelation of women who are said to be for hire and are despised (and now shudderingly longed for), the boy performs the cynical identification of mother and harlot: "they both do the same thing." Much earlier desires are re-activated, and he "comes, as we say, under the sway of the Oedipus complex": he begins to desire the mother, hates the father for standing in his way, and regards the mother as unfaithful to him with the father. Fantasies of the mother's infidelity, in which the lover bears his image, serve to gratify both desire and revenge; and fixation upon these fantasies produces the "harlot" as a surrogate. Thus the second "condition." In the first, the "injured third party" is simply the father himself. The repetition or series —Freud's third condition—resolves the pressing desire in the unconscious for what is irreplaceable, the "one" mother: she must be sought again and again (though in a fidelity each time sincere) since the satisfaction longed for is never found. "Rescue" is complex. Her propensity to infidelity means that the loved one must be watched and protected. But the "saving" of the mother, who gave the boy life, is by a shift to give her back another life, that is, a child, a child as like himself as possible—and this involves an identification of himself with the father. Fantasies of rescuing the father are usually defiant ("I want nothing from him; I repay him all I have cost him"). In rescue of the mother, however, "All the instincts, the loving, the grateful, the sensual, the defiant, the self-assertive and independent—all are gratified in the wish to be the father of himself." A fixation upon this fantasy, in the compulsive "rescue" of (degraded) mother-surrogates, then gratifies, obviously, powerful instincts; and one of Stephen Crane's most puzzling habits begins to make sense.

What have we learned? Something: that although Crane's situation in the type is special—a genius, bearing an historic name, the last child of a large family and a minister's, with a dominant mother, a widow's son early "deserted" by his father and left poor, dependent upon his brothers, and so on— there exists all the same a definite type of psychic life in which he is a case. He becomes *less* mysterious, at any rate; and certain things large and small in his life we can understand. We understand better, for instance, why he married a woman in the situation of Cora Taylor. It was a chance for rescue. The conversation Robert Davis witnessed with the girl on Broadway in 1897, related by Davis nearly thirty years later,

is now really guaranteed: "I can show you the way out. . . ."
The choice of the subject of *Maggie*, his first work, following
immediately upon his mother's death, is less mysterious: it
gave him a chance for rescue, he could show Maggie the way
out. (The way out was death, and we shall return to this.)
Light is thrown on the ambivalence of Crane's attitude toward women—on the one hand, his special attentiveness to
older women (Helen Trent and earlier the Canadian woman, Mrs. Munroe, Mrs. Chaffee and Mrs. Sonntag, Amy
Leslie, Cora Taylor, Mary Horan), and on the other hand
his obvious misogyny, expressed in the Claverack society
S(ic) S(emper) T(yrannis) Girlum, in hatred of society matrons and women on porches, in the extreme fear his heroes
show of the girls they love, in wild aggression against one
mother (made drunken and cruel) in *Maggie* and the over-
solicitous, virtuous *George's Mother*, the first shown driving her daughter into the street, the second shown driven
by her son to death. The pattern of simultaneous desire,
nervous loathing, and resentment described by Freud is recognizable again and again. When in *Maggie* Mrs. Johnson
whirls her great fist in grown Jimmie's face: "He threw out
his left hand and writhed his fingers about her middle arm.
The mother and the son began to sway and struggle. . . ."
But the general war upon Authority in Crane's life and art
we can look to find rooted rather in jealousy and hatred of
the father, when we have come finally round to that.

Let us begin as simply as possible with the notion of a
mind at formidable tension, in an acute form of the human
predicament with regard to parents. We have called a major
aspect of this tension Fear. Fear, I suppose, is a response to
danger. Now it is a singular fact that there is not very much
danger in Crane's work. There is a great deal of something
else, which let us call menace: an abstract form of danger,
the possibility of fatal intervention. Menace is everywhere at
all times in life, only most of us do not feel it, luckily. Crane
felt it. With what sort of fear did he respond? He has

reckoned certainly with every stage of this emotion, but few readers will doubt that at his most characteristic it is Panic. In "An Illusion in Red and White," for instance, the boy's mind "began to work like ketchup" under his terrible vision of his mother's murderer. The word is itself rather frequent in Crane,—at the outset of *The Red Badge*, "A little panic-fear grew" in the hero's mind wondering whether he will run away. But panic is not so directly a form of fear as it is an overwhelming form of anxiety, where control has failed and a regression occurs, driving the emotion back behind the point at which particular danger is occurring, toward an earlier general terror: toward what is called a trauma. As a response, that is, it exceeds any possible fear that can be felt for any conceivable particular danger, because it opens again some ancient vista.

Though panic has various situations in Crane, its situation as a rule is War. What can we make of this? Crane had never seen any war, and was only in the ordinary way familiar with the notion of war, when his feeling about it *possessed* him forever. Now in men whose Oedipus complex has persisted, the love-object is valued (unconsciously) because it can stand for the mother. So with other valued objects and activities: they may be representatives of dominating earlier objects and activities. Perhaps war is a representative. If so, it will represent a conflict of some kind. But let us put his situation (or subject) and his emotion together, or, more precisely, his obsession and his anxiety together. What early conflict is it that will produce a panic which, apparently forgotten, can rule a life?

I am thinking not so much of the so-called "primal scene" itself just here, as of what are known as primal-scene substitutes. These are observations of animals or adults, or of scenes even that may not objectively be sexual at all but that are experienced as sexual by the child—transferring themselves, under circumstantial similarities, and with powerful effect, to the unconscious memory of the "primal scene" proper. At the age of twelve, he "saw a white girl stabbed by her Negro lover" (I am quoting Beer, whose source I have not found—probably Willis Clarke's interview with Crane) "on the edge of a roadmaker's camp. He galloped the pony home and said nothing to Mrs. Crane although he was sweating with fright." It is a remarkable scene, and so is the silence, even though his mother had taught him to be "brave." If the incident can really show a relation with themes in Crane's art, perhaps we have found what we were looking for.

Examples of Negroes or Africa as a symbol—a natural one—for "darkness" and "sex" and "sin" come readily to mind. Crane's earliest signed sketch eulogizes an *explorer* of Africa. The destroyed story "Vashti in the Dark" told, we recall, "how a young *Methodist preacher* from the South killed himself after discovering that his wife had been ravished by a Negro in a *forest* at *night*"; and we have seen a Crane-mask in the Negro rescuer who becomes a "monster." But let us examine in detail his first published story, "The King's Favor." A promising New York tenor sings before an African king, is acclaimed a great warrior and is offered the honor of one of the king's wives, who stands six feet two; frightened, he offers the king, in order to propitiate him for not accepting her, a most suspicious collection of objects: an umbrella, suspenders, playing cards, a pistol, a knife, and so on. These are familiar, in fact, as phallic symbols and taken together with the other materials of this curious story make it hard to suppose that we have not here a sort of telescoping of the primal-scene substitute and the persisting Oedipal situation. The libido, wanting the mother, actually arranges for the father to offer her; but fantasy renders the acceptance as a rejection, the offering of symbols as "propitiation." The wife is made immense partly to satisfy the mother-image and partly to supply a ground for refusing her. But even more striking than the fact that the father is here imagined as an inhabitant of the attractive Dark Continent is the means employed by the intruder to win his favor and thus the offer of his wife. The tenor sings a *war*-song.

Little as we are yet equipped to assemble all these themes, let us see where this sudden, crucial introduction of War leads. Crane's original artistic interest was not just in war but intensely in the *Civil War*. He had already written *Maggie*, the subject of which is civil war in a slum family: parents against children and against each other, son striking daughter, son and mother wrestling, mother cursing and ruining daughter—the room is a scene of continual riot, blows, destruction, and Crane's language is *military*. Jimmie hiding on the stairway "heard howls and curses, groans and shrieks —a confused chorus as if a battle were raging." Even the public fight between Jimmie with his friend and Pete is civil, since these two have been comrades in thuggery, and their faces too "now began to fade to the pallor of warriors in the blood and heat of a battle." A predisposition toward war plainly was strong. The Civil War was the last war, the one heard about and mimicked; we have seen the child Stephen playing war games. But we lack still a direct connection backward with the Negro stabbing or the story of the African's "favor." Perhaps this is to be found in the fact that the Civil War was precisely *about the Negro*—about the object, that is, of Crane's own (fantasied) horror, envy, fascination, and inquiry. Driven to imagine repeatedly the feelings of boys and men panic-stricken, he took the natural line to the Civil War; but the point is that he seems to have taken it *compulsively*, obeying a bond, and once he had fastened upon the Civil War he left it chiefly to find representatives of it in other wars visited and imagined. It was no casual or accidental absorption that produced the greatest American novel about that war.

But the nexus Negro-War is wholly censored in *The Red Badge of Courage*, and so the present account had better be regarded as provisional until we come to further evidence of a different kind. Only two confirmations may be touched, one outside the novel and one in it. At the moments in Crane's work, first, where stabbing is in question, a Negro is always suggested with less or more distinctness in the context, and his latest one was openly of war. Reserving two examples, I shall give only that now with one introductory to it pitched very high indeed in tone.

When the New York Kid is confronted in a Mexican street, "fascinated, stupefied, he actually watched the progress of the man's thought toward the point where a knife would be wrenched from its sheath. . . . The emotion, a sort of mechanical fury . . . smote the *dark* countenance in wave after wave"; and "dark countenance" is more explicit at the death of the Cuban lieutenant with his stunning new machete in "The Clan of No Name": he lies wounded, a man comes to kill him having a "*negro* face," they exchange a "singular" glance, and the lieutenant "closed his eyes, for he did not want to see the flash of the machete."

Then as to the mother and *The Red Badge of Courage*. To make the mother sorry is a form of punishment; it leads also to renewed favor. The hero's leaving his mother is detailed with care, and even though it falls below his expectations—"He had privately primed himself for a beautiful scene"—her face at last is stained with tears (so that he goes off "suddenly ashamed"). This ambivalent theme is more undisguised still in "His New Mittens": "He would run away. In a remote corner of the world he would become some sort of bloody-handed person driven to a life of crime by the barbarity of his mother. . . . He would torture her for years with doubts and doubts, and drive her implacably to a repentant grave." This boy, whose sins against his mother began in a "delirium of snow-battle," does not get far before he is taken home by the butcher (an intimate friend of his dead father's) and "Upon a couch Horace saw his mother lying limp, pale as death, her eyes gleaming with pain. . . ." It can scarcely be coincidence that Kelcey of *George's Mother* is summoned home from a fight to witness his mother's death (for which his degradation is responsible). The impression one receives from these works is that in *The Red Badge* too the unconscious motive is to disquiet and woo—as with a war-song—the mother-image. All three appear to display, in their degrees, the Oedipal resentment-and-craving thrown into fantastic activity.

The father is dead in them, as in *Maggie* drinking and swearing he dies early, George's "fell off a scaffoldin'," Henry Fleming's "never drunk a drop of licker in his life, and seldom swore a cross oath," and this is all we know of them. But it is time to come directly to the father-image, against whom aggression is as remarkable in all this work as the author's reverence for his father was in life, and we can best approach this crucial, difficult subject through a consideration of some of the ways in which Stephen Crane represented himself in his art.

The *names* authors give their characters have seldom received sufficient attention unless the significance of a name is immediately striking, as in certain thousands from Marina and Perdita down to Princess Volupine (a syncopation of "voluptuous, lupine"). These are deliberate, conscious. So as a rule are Henry James's: everyone has noticed Mrs. Grose, whose perceptions are less "fine" than those of the nameless governess in "The Turn of the Screw," but it was pointed out only last year that the children's names are symbolic (Flora and Miles, for flower and soldier), and perhaps other names are, like Bly and Quint. Often the naming is less clearly conscious, though strongly patterned. Frank Norris's biographer notices, without attempting to explain it, his habit of giving masculine names to his women characters: Lloyd, Turner, Sidney, Page, Travis; his daughter Jeannette he called only Billy. Now Crane could be adroit on occasion with names. *Corwin Linson* he made into "Corinson," *Acton Davies* into "Shackles." But beyond these definite instances I shall not attempt to judge how far the habits of naming we are to study were *conscious* in Crane. In all likelihood many were partly so, but since the drives they illustrate in the personality were mainly unconscious speculation is futile.

And the first great fact we come on is the *absence* of names —a compulsive namelessness. Transposing the Crane family, fantasied and altered, into an Irish slum-family, he refuses to give the characters any names, and he will not give his name as the author. As the "little man" of the "Sullivan County Sketches," he usually has no name. Two of his main heroes have no name, the correspondent in "The Open Boat" and the Swede in "The Blue Hotel." When for three stories he apparently split himself into the New York Kid and the San Francisco Kid, both are nameless. Even after he taught himself to use names, his reluctance to divulge them is very great: we learn the surname of the hero of *The Red Badge* first on page 116, the Christian names of the heroine and second male lead of *The Third Violet* first on page 59, and so on. He loved to confuse names. The two Colonel Butlers opposing each other in "Ol' Bennet" are historical but he clearly enjoys them, and in one of the later, careful pieces about Timothy Lean ("The Upturned Face") we read: "Lean looked at his two men. 'Attention,' he barked. The privates came to attention with a click, looking much aggrieved. The adjutant lowered his helmet to his knee. *Lean*, bareheaded, he stood over the grave." Another instance of confusion more startling we saw long ago in "The Blue Hotel."

Some inhibition affecting the name "Crane" and then names in general must be at work, and we may suppose it a consequence of the Oedipal guilt-sense toward the father, whose place he wishes to take with the mother. But there is probably some self-consolation present also ("If I am not a Crane, my desire is not forbidden"), and some *defiance* (obliteration of the father's sign in him, the patronym). It is relevant that Crane fantasied a daughter for himself, "little Cora," not a son who would continue to bear the name, and fantasied a daughter so strongly that he can remark casually in

"War Memories," "If I had been the father of a hundred suffering daughters . . ." The defiance is more evident still in his insisting, when he has to take names, on taking *common* names, the commonest possible. For the historic name Stephen Crane, he takes "Johnson Smith"—which an error altered to "Johnston Smith"—and all three of these names recur, because Crane learned to use names for his purpose. He thought no doubt that he was picking names at random, but I am speaking of what his imagination learned and did.

The first hero of this antiheroic author was the African explorer Henry Stanley. Henry is the name of the hero of *The Red Badge of Courage*, the name of *The Monster*, and the name displaced at the catastrophe of "The Blue Hotel," and we shall come shortly to a Prince Henry. It is time to mention that Stephen Crane seems to have had a middle name beginning with "H" which he dropped after 1893,* and perhaps it was "Henry"—a name very common in the family. Not even the name Stanley disappears.

The second hero of this antiheroic author was the tenor Albert G. Thies. This man sang at Claverack the year before he was put in a story; I do not suppose he had been to Africa, but Crane sent him there to sing a war-song. How conscious Crane was of being a tenor we discover from allusions in the *Pike County Puzzle*, *The Black Riders* (II), *War Is Kind* (XVI)—all ironic.

> There was a man with tongue of wood
> Who essayed to sing,
> And in truth it was lamentable.

In the last chapter of *The Third Violet*, the hero says to the girl, "I didn't mean to act like a tenor," and later, "I suppose, after all, I did feel a trifle like a tenor when I first came here, but you have chilled it all out of me." We recall Crane's curious habit of humming with his face close to the strings of

---

* The New York City Directory for this year gives it:
    "—— [Crane] Stephen H. Author, h[ouse] 1064 Av A."

a violin; he liked to strum on a guitar, and no doubt he plucked the strings óf the violin, and it is time to say what he seems to have been thinking of: he seems to have been thinking of war. A number of passages about the sound of bullets suggest this odd conclusion, but one in "The Price of the Harness" seems to enforce it: "as these were mainly high shots it was usual for them to make the faint note of a vibrant string, touched elusively, half-dreamily." He was dreaming of war, or dreaming of love, a war-song. But what are we to make now of this tangle of music and war, desire, this tenor and Africa? It is hard to suppose that Albert G. Thies seized the boy's imagination just as a tenor sufficiently to be dispatched as a Crane-representative to the strange land where the father-image is king. Certainly this may have occurred but we shall need to know why in order to believe it.

Thies is an odd name. In various spellings it occurs in all of the Scandinavian countries, Holland, Germany. Perhaps Crane fixed it as Swedish, though doubtfully, but at any rate this cluster of associations must have stirred him considerably, for it seems to explain a succession of allusions in his work otherwise absolutely mystifying. *Fleming* as a name for the hero of *The Red Badge* is not mystifying, but *Hollanden* for the young writer (the secondary Crane-representative) in *The Third Violet* a little is, as it is that one of Crane's major heroes should be a nameless Swede. We recall suddenly a mysterious conversation downstairs in the Blue Hotel about whether this Swede is a Swede after all or "some kind of a Dutchman"—Mr. Blanc the Easterner refusing to decide. But this conversation is no longer mysterious: the characters are arguing out some problem of Crane's. When to "Fleming" we add "Hollander" (made Hollanden), this uncertain talk of a Swede or "Dutchman," an imaginary "Prince Henry of Prussia" whom we shall shortly see treating the father-image very differently from Thies, yet another fear-crazed Swede we will encounter at the end, and other evidence to be dealt with at once, the conclusion is inescapable that Thies cannot have set off in Crane's mind this complicated train. Instead he must be simply its first embodiment, and its origin we must seek earlier, in some connection made by Crane (unconsciously) between the Negro with his knife or razor and the Swede or German invading Zululand with his war-song.

These things are difficult. Perhaps the village barber was the link. Whilomville's is called "Reifsnyder" in *The Monster* and "Neeltje" in "The Angel Child," names suggestive indeed, in this context and in view of (1) Reifsnyder's almost unique opinion that Henry Johnson ought *not* to be let die, and (2) the coöperation with the dreamy painter of "the utter Neeltje." Whom for that matter except a barber would the boy, terrified by the Negro's stabbing, normally see with a knife or razor? His father shaving (in memory)— and the father-image of "Four Men in a Cave" terrifies the little man by drawing a long thin knife, Trescott in *The Monster* "was shaving this lawn as if it were a priest's chin." The town butcher—and it was actually the butcher, with knife poised and named Stickney, identified as an intimate friend of the dead father, whom we saw conducting home the runaway boy. But some Swedish, Dutch, or German barber seems alone to account for the series of dramatizations beginning with Thies. To the boy acted on by the fantasy of stabbing as a sexual act, all the associations forward to fighting and battle, Negroes and Swedes, backward to the Oedipal fantasies and inhibitions, start alive then with excited relation. A great body of his most powerful and casual-looking metaphor depends upon these. "The song of the razor is seldom heard," he will lament in a vivacious, nostalgic article on Negro killers in Minetta Lane of old. Or the body of the crazy Swede is "pierced as easily as if it had been a melon"—and only at the climax of "The Knife" can we guess what Crane's association was: there come on one another suddenly in a melon patch at night, each with knife ready for theft, two Negroes.

Passing to the grotesque aggression against the father-image of Prince Henry which initiates our final cluster of themes, a word of limitation. Just as very little of the complicated supporting evidence (positive and negative) for even the leading themes of Crane's unconscious thought which I have been following can be given, so a treatise elaborate indeed would be required to distinguish from the Oedipal elements in this aggression against the father, first, the sense of desertion and impoverishment (with the consequent resentments) arising from his death when Crane was a boy,* and second, the intellectual rebellion consciously waged by Crane against him. Thus in poems the father-image (sage or seer) is generally on a high place and hypocrisy is the usual charge, suggesting that the original incredulous revulsion on learning that the parent who preaches on Sunday "does it too" is still governing the poet's fantasies. It is remarkable how often *sight* is associated with these poems.

> You say you are holy,
> And that
> Because I have not seen you sin.
> Ay, but there are those
> Who see you sin, my friend.

Sometimes the "I" seems to be identified with the father, the Crane-mask being another, even a devil.

> I stood upon a high place,
> And saw, below, many devils
> Running, leaping,
> And carousing in sin.

* The story "A Desertion" contemporary with *Maggie* must be mentioned, even if briefly, as explicit. A girl much like Maggie but called "Nell" (the loose woman's name in the novel) comes home from work to find her father dead. Her shriek of agony is like "the first word of a tragic conversation with the dead." Neighbors hear and understand: "he's drivin' her inteh the street." In the veracious Cuban narrative "God Rest Ye, Merry Gentlemen," Crane's name for the correspondent who is himself is "Little Nell."

> One looked up, grinning,
> And said, "Comrade! Brother!"

But this is very uncertain, whereas from the hermit of "Four
Men in a Cave" (who took to drink and ruined his family) to
The O'Ruddy's father (who did not leave him any money)
there can be no doubt that in many dramatizations the unconscious reproach upon at least one subject is non-Oedipal.
So probably with family degradation. For the 'nineties the
Irish stood as—what by another delightful turn of democratic opinion the Jews stand as now—a popular type of social squalor; so that the Johnsons, the Scullys, the Kelceys,
and the other Irish into which Crane turned his family are
aggressive symbols. His light women are Irish: Florinda
O'Connor of *The Third Violet*, Nora Black of *Active Service*. The Irish are looked on of course by the English in *The
O'Ruddy* as barbarians. But an ambivalence is certain here.
The O'Ruddy, though eloquent about his father's lying and
drinking, is jealous of his father's honor, and the family
though penniless and Irish is noble. Perhaps, so mixed are
all these feelings, it is only with one or more of three symbols
present that we can be confident of Oedipal aggression:
knives, rivals, death.

Crane's little fantastic play "The Blood of the Martyr"
has three tiny acts, the scene laid in China. Prince Henry of
Prussia is extorting railway commissions from the Mandarins
by sending missionaries everywhere in the land to be mar-
tyred, and he is running out of them. In the first act he tells
an aide to get more from Berlin, drill them, "feed them up
for a time on broken glass, copies of Xenophon's 'Anabasis'
and blood," then turn them loose. The aide reports that the
missionary at Yen Hock has appealed for assistance, and
Prince Henry orders him sent a box of cigars and his com-
pliments: "Tell him he is the right man in the right place."
In Act Two the Mandarins are pondering the question of
what a railway concession *is*, when Prince Henry enters to

announce that the missionary at Yen Hock has been foully murdered: what about a railway concession? The Mandarins are "very tired" and agree to anything—"We wish to slumber, for all the towers are nodding. . . ." In Act Three unfortunately the missionary turns up from Yen Hock—on crutches, minus an ear, foot, and lung, garroted and flayed, but alive. Prince Henry, furious, declares him an unworthy son of Germany and deprives him of the cigars, but sends him to the kitchen for beer. This is the entire action of the play.

This skit on imperialism is not of course what it appears, so far as it appears anything. If the father was once an African King, the son is now a German Prince. In the missionary of "Yen Hock," however, we could not be certain of a father-image if it were not the nature of a railway concession. When one mandarin suggests that this is like a tea-junk, another says: "No. It looks more like a horse, only that it is a pale purple in color, and has red eyes." Now Crane had already written the story of a dying dope-fiend named "Yen-Nock Bill" with a voice such that his young friend used to wish "that he was a *horse*, so that he could spring upon the bed and trample him to death." A fantasy-horse, then, to murder in the most violent way possible Yen-Nock Bill and the missionary at Yen Hock. Nothing just like these names have I found; Crane evidently invented them. "Yen" is a passionate craving, associated first with the general aggressive word "knock," then particularly with a horse's ankle, both *striking* words. And Prince Henry, in his moment of triumph when he imagines the missionary dead at Yen Hock, cries out: "Thus do the glorious eagles of Germany soar above their rivals. . . ." *

* It is impossible to enter here on Crane's extraordinary Fables or a hundred other matters, but I may observe that the "little eagle" in one of them is a Crane-mask. The eagle, briefly, promises help to the mountain Popocatepetl, who is hungry: he will be given wings and can fly for food; but the help is not forthcoming. In "Popocatepetl" is telescoped, apparently, not only "Pop" but "Pope"—when Mr. Smith proposes to Margharita in

Stephen Crane as a horse:—a singular image; and intent ferociously upon his father's death. Both men were specially fond and solicitous of horses. Crane remembered his father's unwillingness even to hurry a horse, and Charles Michelson tells us that though other correspondents changed mounts whenever they could get a better one, Crane "took his for better or worse, until the campaign was over." Horses are above all *kindly* throughout Crane's work, they are continually *being* hurt to his silent agony. Identification and ferocity alike are strange; stranger still as they will relate presently to the death of the mother.

Dreams of the parent's death vision as a rule the death of the parent of the same sex; they represent survivals of very early feelings of rivalry, the girl of the mother, the boy of the father. These feelings were fixated in Crane and are certainly present in fantasies of the father's death—Prince Henry's (displaced) word "rivals" is crucial. Whether they entirely account for them is less clear. Sadism grinds strong in Crane's work, and its counterpart masochism does.

"The Clan of No Name," "it was like asking to be pope" and this is one of Crane's innumerable father-references to priests and monks, even (in life) to his father as a "Cardinal" (depriving the father of the sexual permission, or degrading the mother to a parnel). The point about various bird-symbols, and especially the eagle in the fable and in "The Blood of the Martyr," is not so much simply a crane-continuation as the fact that the eagle *can* fly. Flying is regularly a symbol of sexual activity in male dreams—"we should not be surprised to hear," Freud adds, "that this or that dreamer is always very proud of his ability to fly." The mountain is immovable, and it is worth notice that the fable is called "The *Voice* of the Mountain," as it is Yen-Nock Bill's *voice* that infuriates Swift Doyer (a swift is a bird). The two chief images of his father that appear in Crane's work are his voice (the long sermons the child listened to) and his sitting reading a newspaper, as in Old Scully during the game and *Black Riders* (XI). At the same time, not to mislead readers courteous enough to take my investigation seriously, it must be added that this use of the mountain-symbol is exceptional, for a reason I cannot now examine; the mountain is normally, as one would expect, a symbol for the mother. We have had a glimpse of this, in fact, in the "Sullivan County Sketches." Perhaps a death-wish, finally, is not far hidden in the recurrent priest-symbol ("If my father had been a priest, I would never have been born").

Torn, miserable, and ashamed of my open sorrow,
I thought of the thunders that lived in my head,
And I wished to be an ogre,
And hale and haul my beloved to a castle,
And there use the happy cruel one cruelly,
And make her mourn with my mourning.

We can guess at masochism also in the life, cultivating hardship, collecting and preserving all attacks on his poems, mounting all the premature obituaries in a book which he "greatly treasures." Now the last form of this is suicide-fantasy, as the last form of sadism is the parents' death, both parents'. Death ends the terrible excitement under which he is bound to live, death resolves panic, death is "a way out," a rescue. Perhaps the fantasy of rescue is *not* by any means always concealed under the imaged deaths of both father and mother.

Recalling that it was as a mother-surrogate that Maggie took her author's imagination, at the same time that aggressions against both parents are being discharged in her parents the Johnsons, we shall not be surprised if unconscious identification in Crane's work was often much more complex than a summary study like this one can take explicitly into account. The mother is present twice, that is, in *Maggie*—under Mrs. Crane's name Mary as Mary Johnson, and as the girl who becomes a prostitute. Whether the name Maggie is related to Crane's sister Aggie, or (as Margaret) to the light beloved (Margharita) of "The Clan of No Name" and perhaps the heroine of *Active Service* (Marjorie) whose mother is also named Mary, or even to the name Mary itself (as especially in the Lady Mary whom The O'Ruddy adores), is doubtful. But it is very remarkable that the hero of *George's Mother* loves—vainly—"Maggie Johnson" and imagines "scenes in which he rescued the girl." Equally remarkable is the use of her *mother's* name for the fallen girl in the first novel. During Maggie's march to death in the river, which is telescoped as one walk wherein she meets men progressively more terrible, two of them address her: "Hi, there, Mary. . . . Brace up, old girl," one says, and another, "Come, now, old lady. . . ." This connection of the "rescue" fantasy with *water*, in the type of fixation to which Crane belongs, Freud thought especially significant. Water is a birth-symbol: "When in a dream a man rescues a woman from the water, it means that he makes her a mother," which in view of the father-identification analyzed early in this chapter "means that he makes her his own mother." Now Maggie is not being rescued *from* the water but *to* it—exactly as we are about to see George's mother being. By some frightening twist, Crane's fantasy had to secure father-identification by drowning the actual mother-representative.

If the act is clear and the person disguised in *Maggie*, the act is disguised and the person clear in its companion-work *George's Mother*. George drives his mother to her death by drinking. This is the whole open plot of the short novel, though nothing could be more emphatic than George's fantasy about Maggie Johnson: "He reflected that if he could only get a chance to rescue her from something, the whole tragedy would speedily unwind." We never learn the mother's first name. Their Irish name "Kelcey" will be enough for us shortly. The story is flooded with water-images about her: cleaning the room, she "came from the sink streaming and bedraggled as if she had crossed a flooded river," and instead of a representation of her death (in bed) our last view of her is this: "The little old woman lay still with her eyes closed. On the table at the head of the bed was a glass containing a water-like medicine. The reflected lights made a silver star on its side." It is significant perhaps that her son kills her by *drinking*. But these signs would hardly convince if it were not for one astounding fact and the astounding passage in which Kelcey receives on the street from a little boy word that she is "awful sick" (in fact, dying). Here the actual word occurs, displaced like the murderer's "Henry!"

in "The Blue Hotel." His gang are howling derision at him for attending to the boy's news, and he mutters: " 'I can't— I don't wanta—I don't *wanta leave me mother be*—she—' His words were *drowned* in the chorus of their derision." The fact is, that behind "Kelcey" seems to stand, incredibly enough, the familiar *Irish water-spirit* in the form of a *horse* who warns of drowning or *helps to drown:* the kelpy.

The reader's head will not improbably be swimming at this point, but is our alternative explanation for these phenomena (coincidence) really plausible of a mind with the habits of naming and symbolization we have seen in Crane's, dealing entirely now in operations that were unconscious? Skepticism would seem to require us to fall back here and elsewhere on the assumption of a series of coincidences more fantastic even than the operations of the human mind, since we are dealing, not with points selected (to prove some thesis) from a large random body of work, but with themes mysterious and dominant in the most imposing products, as well as some of the most puzzling products, of Crane's art. I have been trying simply to isolate the themes, to display them at crisis, and to trace their sources. We are ready, now that we have seen the horse-symbol associated with both the father's and the mother's death, to move toward its origin. Just one poem in *The Black Riders* involves horses; Crane so valued it that he put it first and called the book after it.

> Black riders came from the sea.
> There was clang and clang of spear and shield,
> And clash and clash of hoof and heel,
> Wild shouts and the wave of hair
> In the rush upon the wind:
> Thus the ride of Sin.

It is a queer little poem and a rather famous one. One wonders what thousands of readers have made of it. The riders seem to be enjoying themselves, the "wave of hair" especially has a sensual look, but the poem is madly warlike, and our passage recently with "Hock" tilts "hoof and heel" into prominence. The second and third lines seem to suggest with great force that *the same kind of things* are clashing with each other. "Riding" is a sensual concept, as well as here an aggressive one, and the whole action is described as "sinful." Beyond these considerations I do not know how much further we could get, except that luckily we know the poem's source. At the age of about four Stephen Crane had a recurrent, terrifying dream of black riders charging up at him from the surf. This dream the poem seems faithfully to represent, with adult addition of the last line. The horses themselves are *suppressed in the poem* as perhaps they were also in the dream. We have black riders on horses, but we do not see the horses. What color, I wonder, were the horses? Combers are *white.* And suddenly we remember that just before the summer of this dream "Stephen was held on a white horse which he remembered twenty years later as a savage beast. But it was no part of Mrs. Crane's theory that a child of hers should be afraid of anything. He was told to stay on the horse and not to be scared."

Just possibly we have reached here the bottom of Crane's mind. To ride the white horse is to gratify the mother, to win her favor. The childish dream of fright persisted, at both conscious and unconscious levels, and attached to itself other symbols and motives. The horse associated itself with water. The sinful rider became black, either before or after the stabbing incident determined the sexuality of the whole constellation. If riding is a conventional sexual symbol, waves traditionally horses of the sea, courage a mother's and life's requirement from everyone, none of these were so in ordinary degree with Crane. With baffling and multiplying power they assembled into the supreme experience of his life, when an open boat rode against the snarling of the crests.

But the horse becomes also an instrument of aggression against the rival, the father, and the fantasies of "trampling" begin. Here we are very close to War again, from two sides.

To the earlier analysis of War as a representative of sexual "conflict" must now be added: first, the horse aggressive, a charger, for which the only situation in life is War; and second, courage as a means of gratifying the mother. The obvious situation for the display of courage is War—first he plunged himself as Jimmie into civilian fights (*Maggie*), but for a prolonged display he had to move to *The Red Badge of Courage*. *Therefore* it is a "war-song" that wins the favor, earlier, of the offer of the King's wife, and *The Red Badge* is his war-song. We have seen the making of the mother-image "sorry" in this novel. The "great death" in Chapter IX, a height of Crane's early art, seems to image the death of the father.

This "tall soldier," Henry Fleming's friend, is the second most important character. His name "Jim" is also that of the soldier whose death is most remarkable in Crane's later war-writings ("The Price of the Harness"), but is it that of a father-image? We recall that the painter in *The Third Violet* is not jealous only of Oglethorpe but actually of his father, who takes his girl for a ride: "With their heads close together they became so absorbed in their conversation that they seemed to forget the painter. He sat on a log and watched them." Gossip about this ride makes the girl's eyes flash "wrath and defiance." Well, this father's name is "ol' Jim" Hawker on page six, but "John" on page sixty-two, after Oglethorpe's first name has been revealed: it is "Jem"; so that Hawker's rivals have (but very nervously) the same name, and it is the name of a general Crane-mask in his earliest as his latest work, the boy Jimmie. This brief selection of evidence is intended not to secure conviction about the "tall soldier" but simply to introduce two most surprising circumstances of his death. Marching like a "spectre" along wounded to death, Jim's only fear is lest he be "*run over*" by the artillery wagons (that is: their horses); Henry "hysterically" cries out that he will guard him, but the tall soldier continues to beg in terror. And his only desire is to get to a certain place for his death: "a little clump of bushes . . . the mystic place of his intentions. . . . there was a resemblance in him to a devotee of a mad religion. . . . he had at last found the place for which he had struggled. . . . He was at the rendezvous." I am not going to analyze the sexual and religious elements here except to add that as "Henry Fleming" pursues him to the place "There was a singular race."

Rivalry against the father, and the wish to *be* the father. The more uncertain our analysis, the more singular Crane's identifications appear. We took Henry Johnson's rescue of the boy Jimmie from the fire in *The Monster,* and being punished for his rescue with facelessness and idiocy, though protected absolutely by the father, who is punished for *this* "rescue" by ostracism in the society—we took the Negro's rescue to represent the "rescue" swarming in Crane's mind at the time when he was writing the story, his marriage; and we even saw the name "Cora" displaced and disguised as the one "coral" flame in the father's laboratory during the rescue. Probably this was right. But there must be more present, which is not to be explained so. First, as the Negro rescues the Crane-mask, the boy, he represents not only Crane but Crane's father. The rescue-structure of the story is like a musical development: Jimmie's attempt to rescue the flower, and punishment, Johnson's rescue of him, and punishment, Dr. Trescott's rescue of Johnson, and punishment. But second, a rescue may be a rape, and it is only in this unsatisfactory way that I can understand the extraordinary events in the father's room during the fire. Johnson wails a Negro swamp-wail at the threshold (one recalls what is known of "Vashti in the Dark"). "Then he rushed across the room. An orange-coloured flame leaped like a panther at the lavender trousers. This animal bit deeply into Johnson. There was an explosion at one side, and suddenly before him there reared a delicate, trembling sapphire shape like a fairy lady. With a quiet smile she blocked his path and doomed him and Jimmie." Her talons catch him as he tries to plunge past on her left. He falls on his back. From a jar on the desk a "ruby-red snake-like thing" pours out, coils, swims, and flows at last "directly down into Johnson's upturned face." The father's death, even the father's defiled death, is apparently represented in the story called "The Upturned Face," but what is represented here I am not sure, and it is worth discriminating in this difficult relation between what we do not know and what we do know.

What we can know with some confidence even in *The Monster* is that when the idiot Negro, who formerly cared for the doctor's horse, gibbers about a horse, he does so as if he were the horse: " 'I am taking you to Alek Williams, Henry, and I——' The figure chuckled again. 'No, 'deed! No, seh! Alek Williams don' know a hoss!' . . . 'I didn't say anything about horses. I was saying——' 'Hoss? Hoss?' said the quavering voice from these near shadows. 'Hoss? 'Deed I don' know all erbout a hoss! 'Deed I don't.' . . ." Into Henry Fleming's eyes in *The Red Badge* "came a look that one can see in the orbs of a jaded horse." Even Crane's conversation shows the obsession: "Say, when I planted those hoofs of mine on Greek soil . . ." One wonders with pain, at last, just what form he has—animal or man—in his dying words to Barr: "Robert—when you come to the hedge—that we must all go over——"

Another thing that we can know, and it must be the end, is that the hero of *The Red Badge of Courage* and the victim of "The Blue Hotel" meet—these two characters *meet*, Henry Fleming rescues the Swede and the Swede dooms Henry Fleming—in a passionate story written midway between these masterworks. The aggression against the father, the wish to be the father, and the solution for panic. Is Henry Fleming now both Stephen and the Reverend Mr. Crane? It is long after the Civil War for "The Veteran," he is old now, a hero. When he explains that he was afraid at that time, no one believes him. A hired man, a Swede, drunk, sets the barn afire, and screams, a "maniac." Old Fleming had been telling the men that young Jim Conklin "went into it from the start just as if he was born to it. But with me it was different. I had to get used to it." "I think Steve was born a coward," a friend of Stephen Crane's told me last year, "but he wouldn't stay one." Old Fleming was used to it now: entering the inferno, he "took five horses out, and then came out himself, with his clothes bravely on fire. He had no whiskers, and very little hair on his head. . . . Some one noticed at the time that he ran very lamely, *as if one of the frenzied horses had smashed his hip.*" He saves then the paralyzed Swede. The long flames sing. "And then came this Swede again, crying as one who is the weapon of the sinister fates. 'De colts! De colts! You have forgot de colts!' Old Fleming staggered. It was true. . . . 'I must try to get 'em out.'" The men exclaim: " 'Why, it's suicide for a man to go in there!' Old Fleming stared absent-mindedly at the open doors. 'The poor little things!' he said. He rushed into the barn.

"When the roof fell in, a great funnel of smoke swarmed toward the sky, as if the old man's mighty spirit, released from its body—a little bottle—had swelled like the genie of fable. The smoke was tinted rose-hue from the flames, and perhaps the unutterable midnights of the universe will have no power to daunt the colour of this soul."

A Bibliographical Note

Volumes in print are *The Red Badge of Courage* (various editions), *Twenty Stories by Stephen Crane* (which includes *Maggie, The Monster*, "The Blue Hotel") edited with an introduction by Carl Van Doren (Knopf 1940, World 1945), and *The Collected Poems of Stephen Crane* (Knopf 1930). *The Work of Stephen Crane*, a limited and expensive edition in twelve volumes (1925–1927) for which we are indebted to Wilson Follett and Mr. Knopf, with introductions of biographical value by Charles Michelson, Robert H. Davis, Thomas Beer, to Volumes XII, II, VII, and other introductions by Joseph Hergesheimer, Follett, Carl Van Doren, William Lyon Phelps, Amy Lowell, Willa Cather, H. L. Mencken (X), and Sherwood Anderson, is out of print. It is badly arranged and omits some work of interest, such as *The Blood of the Martyr* (Peter Pauper Press, 1940), *Legends* (*The Bookman*, May 1896), *A Lost Poem* (Harvard Press, New York, 1932, and *The Golden Book*, February 1934), Crane's first printed story "The King's Favor" (Syracuse *University Herald*, May 1891, and *The Argot*, March 1935), and especially most of the *Sullivan County Sketches*, which are now collected with an introduction by Melvin Schoberlin (Syracuse 1949). Out of print also are the pioneer collection of Vincent Starrett, *Men, Women and Boats* (1921 and, later,

Modern Library), and an assembling with *Maggie* of *George's Mother* and *The Blue Hotel* (1931). A new selection of the prose, attentive equally to short and long tales, would be desirable; Carl Van Doren neglects several very important small works. Crane's original collections can sometimes still be picked up cheaply: *The Little Regiment* (1896), *The Open Boat* (London 1898), *Wounds in the Rain* (1900), *Whilomville Stories* (1900), *The Monster* of 1901, *Last Words* (1902).

Ames W. Williams's and Vincent Starrett's admirable *Stephen Crane: A Bibliography* (1948) is now available. Since this will be standard, materials not mentioned there are asterisked.

The main source for the life of course is Thomas Beer's *Stephen Crane: A Study in American Letters*, 1923. To this should be added his article on Mrs. Stephen Crane (*The American Mercury*, March 1934, p. 289, replying to one by Helen R. Crane in January, p. 24); one in *Vanity Fair* (August 1922, p. 63), a reply to Ford Madox Ford in the *New York Evening Post Literary Review*, July 19, 1924 (p. 910); and *The Mauve Decade*, 1926, scattered allusions. Crane's letters are uncollected. Those printed will be found in the *Newark Sunday Call, May 3, 1896, *The Literary Digest*, June 23, 1900, *The Academy*, August 11, 1900 (p. 116), *The Members of the Society. . .* , East Aurora, 1895, *The Colophon*, 1930 (Part 4, No. 6), *The New Colophon*, January 1948 (p. 33), *The Month at Goodspeed's*, September and October 1937, *Two Letters* to Joseph Conrad, 1926; Frederick Lewis Allen, *Paul Revere Reynolds*, 1944, Ch. 6; Herbert Faulkner West, *A Stephen Crane Collection*, Dartmouth, 1948; Williams and Starrett, p. 13; and *apud* Garland, Peaslee, Curtis Brown, Conrad, below. The letters to Hitchcock are in the Berg Collection of the New York Public Library, others are in private hands, and there is a useful Stephen Crane collection in the Newark Public Library.

On Crane at Claverack there is Harvey Wickham (*The*

American Mercury, March 1926, pp. 291–97) and two articles by Lyndon Upson Pratt in *American Literature*, the first (1939, x, 460–67) dealing also with his colleges, the second (1939, xi, 1–10) on General Van Petten and *The Red Badge of Courage*. On Lafayette and Syracuse there are *Colonel Ernest G. Smith (*Lafayette Alumnus*, February 1932), Clarence L. Peaslee (*Monthly Illustrator*, August 1896, pp. 27–30), Frank W. Noxon (*The Step Ladder*, January 1928, pp. 4–9), Thomas E. Martin (*The Argot*, March 1935), Mansfield J. French (*Syracuse University Alumni News*, January 1934), M. Ellwood Smith (*The Syracusan*, December 1, 1917), Lester G. Wells (Syracuse *Alumni News*, October 1946),* Claude Jones (*American Literature*, 1935, vii, 82–84). On Crane in Asbury Park and Port Jervis there are Arthur Oliver (*N.J. Hist. Soc. Proc.*, xvi, 454–63), Willis Fletcher Johnson (*International Book Review Literary Digest*, April 1926, pp. 288–90), a niece Edna Crane Sidbury (ditto, March 1926, pp. 248–50), Victor A. Elconin (*American Literature*, November 1948, xx, 275–90).

The main authorities for the New York years are *Corwin Knapp Linson (*Saturday Evening Post*, April 11, 1903, p. 19), Hamlin Garland (ditto, July 28, 1900, pp. 16–17, *The Yale Review*, April 1914, pp. 494–506, *Roadside Meetings*, 1930, pp. 189–206, 329–30, 333–34, 379, 393), and R. G. Vosburgh (*The Criterion*, February 1901, pp. 26–27). Irving Bacheller has notes in *Coming Up the Road* (1928, p. 276), *From Stores of Memory* (1933, p. 110), *Manuscript*, May 1901, p. 32, and *The Bookman*, November 1900, p. 218. Crane was interviewed in 1896 by *Herbert P. Williams (*Illustrated American*, July 18, p. 126) and E. St. Elmo Lewis (*Book News*, September, pp. 10–11). *The Philistine* is a source *passim*, and there are negligible notes on it by David H. Dickason (*American Literature*, 1943, xv, 279–87) and by Hubbard's biographer Felix Shay. Edward Marshall has reminiscences in *Literary Life*, December 1900, pp. 71–72; *Curtis Brown in *Contacts* (1935, pp. 222–26); *Reginald Wright Kauffman in *Modern Culture*,

October 1900, pp. 143–45; and Ripley Hitchcock a preface in *The Red Badge of Courage,* 1900.

Materials on the later periods overlap. On Florida and Crane's wars there are Ralph D. Paine's *Roads of Adventure,* 1922, pp. 162–254; an unpublished sketch of Mrs. Stephen Crane by Carl Bohnenberger and his account with Norman Mitchell Hill in *The Bookman,* May–June 1929; Branch Cabell and A. J. Hanna, *The St. Johns,* 1943, pp. 275–86; Richard Harding Davis in *Harper's,* May 1899, pp. 941–48, in *In Many Wars . . .* edited by George Lynch and Frederick Palmer (Tokyo, 1904), in *Notes of a War Correspondent* 1911, pp. 125–28, in his *Adventures and Letters,* 1917, pp. 200, 207, 234–35, perhaps 238, and Fairfax Downey's biography, 1933; Burr McIntosh, *The Litle I Saw of Cuba,* 1899, pp. 68, 72, 103, 125–27, 132–33, 165; *Edward Marshall, *The Story of the Rough Riders,* 1899, pp. 76, 85, 143; *Cecil Carnes, *Jimmy Hare,* 1940, pp. 63 ff.; Van Wyck Brooks, *Sketches in Criticism,* 1932, pp. 156–58; Don C. Seitz in *The Bookman,* February 1933, pp. 137–40, and elsewhere, controverted by facts by Ames W. Williams, in *The New Colophon,* April 1948, pp. 113–23; and the newspapers and magazines.

On Crane in England there are Joseph Conrad's introduction to Beer (1923), a few pages in *Notes on Life and Letters,* 1921, pp. 67–72, his letters to the Cranes in *The Bookman,* May–June 1929, pp. 225–35, 367–74, and other letters in *Jean-Aubry's biography; Jessie Conrad's reminiscences are in *The Bookman,* April 1926, pp. 134–37, and *Joseph Conrad and his Circle* so-called, 1935, pp. 56–58, 72–75. Ford Madox Ford was prolific and fantastic: *Memories and Impressions,* 1911, p. 58; *Thus to Revisit,* 1921, especially pp. 75, 106–22; *New York Evening Post Literary Review,* March 26, 1921, p. 6, and July 12, 1924, pp. 881–82; *New York Herald Tribune Books,* January 2, 1927, p. 1; *Scribner's,* October 1931, pp. 379–86; *The American Mercury,* January 1936, pp. 36–45; *Portraits from Life,* 1937, pp. 21–37; and *Mightier Than the Sword,* 1938, etc. Other memories are those of H. G. Wells

(**Experiment in Autobiography*, 1934, pp. 522–25); Karl E. Harriman (*Literary Review*, April 1900, pp. 85–87, *The Critic*, July 1900, p. 14, and *The New Hope*, October 1934); C. Lewis Hind, *Authors and I*, 1921, pp. 70–74, and *Naphtali*, 1926, pp. 121–22; Edwin Pugh, the London *Bookman*, December 1924, pp. 162–64; and there is a letter of Robert Barr's in Vincent Starrett, *Buried Caesars*, 1923, pp. 83–86.

Contemporary criticism was more thoughtful and perceptive at its best than later criticism has been: George Wyndham on *The Red Badge of Courage* in *The New Review*, January 1896, pp. 30–40; Rupert Hughes ("Chelifer") in *Godey's*, September 1896, pp. 316–19; Edward Garnett in *The Academy*, December 17, 1898, pp. 483–84 (expanded in his *Friday Nights*, 1922, Ch. 12); and especially H. G. Wells in *The North American Review*, August 1900, pp. 233–42. This last essay is reprinted now in Edmund Wilson's *The Shock of Recognition*, 1943; it has interest that Wilson could not find a later or an American account so excellent. Worth mention in various degrees are Harriet Monroe in *Poetry*, June 1919, pp. 148–52; Vincent Starrett in *The Sewanee Review*, June 1920, pp. 405–13; Thomas Beer in *The Saturday Review of Literature*, December 19, 1925, pp. 425–27; Mencken's introduction to Volume X of the Knopf edition and a review by Mark Van Doren in *The Nation* (reprinted in **The Private Reader*, 1942, pp. 156–58); Wilson Follett in *The Bookman*, January 1929, pp. 532–37; Gorham B. Munson's *Style and Form in American Prose*, 1929, pp. 159–170; Matthew Josephson's **Portrait of the Artist as American*, 1930, pp. 232–64; Harry Hartwick's **The Foreground of American Fiction*, 1934, pp. 21–44; Arthur H. Quinn's *American Fiction*, 1936, pp. 532–38; Russell B. Nye in *The Modern Quarterly*, Summer 1940, pp. 48–54; Oscar Cargill's *Intellectual America*, 1941, pp. 84–89; Alfred Kazin's **On Native Grounds*, 1942, pp. 67–72; George D. Snell's **Shapers of American Fiction*, 1947, pp. 223–33; *Caroline Gordon in *Accent*, spring 1949 (the indebtedness to Stendhal is imaginary). Ford's essay in *The Southern Review* (1935) is interesting on technique. On *The Red Badge* particularly there are H. T. Webster in *American Literature* (1939) xi, 285–93, *W. L. Werner in *The New York Times Book Review*, September 30, 1945, p. 4, and V. S. Pritchett in *The Living Novel*, 1948; and on the poetry Henry Lüdeke in *Anglia* (1938) lii 410–22.

There are academic theses, of course, on the history of Crane criticism: Benedict Wolf's (at Columbia) is negligible. John C. Bushman's thesis (University of Illinois) and Jean Whitehead's (Cornell) are excellent, these two students having the advantage over professional critics that they had read most of Crane's work. Paul Haines's *Harold Frederic* (New York University) was very helpful. These are all unpublished, as are Crane's notebook (see E. V. Mitchell's *The Art of Authorship*, 1935, pp. 69–70) which was once promised from Huntington; C. K. Linson's long memoir which was finished twenty years ago; and other things.

ADDITIONAL BIBLIOGRAPHY (1962)

The previous note tried to be rather full. This is purely helpful; I have made no attempt to keep up. The main additions to work available are edited by William Gibson (*Selected Prose and Poetry*, 1950), Robert Wooster Stallman (*Stephen Crane: An Omnibus*, 1952, a Modern Library edition of the *Red Badge*, and *Stories and Tales*, 1955), and Daniel G. Hoffman, *The Red Badge of Courage and Other Stories* (1957). There are paperbacks of the war novel (as: The Pocket Library, 1954), and paperback selections of the familiar stories drift in and out of print (one of the latest has a preface by Ralph Ellison). Use is made of unpublished poems in Hoffman's *The Poetry of Stephen Crane* (1957). The *Letters*, edited with prolix commentaries by Stallman and Lillian Gilkes (1960), supersedes earlier collections of the letters to Nellie Crouse and others.

The most substantial contributions to biography are to be found in this *Letters*, Stallman's *Omnibus*, Corwin K. Linson's finally published *My Stephen Crane* (edited by Edwin H. Cady, 1958), and Lillian Gilkes's biography of Cora Crane (1960). A note on page 94, or the end of it, is out of date; manuscripts of the *Red Badge* turned up and are fully handled in Stallman's *Omnibus*. Willa Cather has a piece in *The Prairie Schooner*, 1949, xxiii, 231-7. Many biographies and the collections of the letters of others add glimpses. Perhaps the four most interesting articles in journals are on the Garland-Crane relationship (Donald Pizer in *The Huntington Library Quarterly*, 1960, xxiv, 75-82), the shipwreck experience (Cyrus Day in *Boston University Studies in English*, 1958, iii, 193-213; but see my comments in *The Arts of Reading*, Ralph Ross and others, 1960, pp. 279-80), Crane's relation with Richard Harding Davis (Scott C. Osborn in *American Literature*, 1956, xxviii, 50-61), and the Brede play "The Ghost" (Edith R. Jones in *The Atlantic*, July 1954).

The best critical book on Crane that has appeared is certainly Hoffman's; it is too long, but very thoughtful, and I am pleased in consequence at its hospitality to the suggestion here made about Crane's indebtedness to Olive Schreiner's *Dreams* and its skepticism (pp. 204-6) about the importance of any debt to Emily Dickinson. The *American Quarterly* has articles by Joseph J. Kwiat on Crane's relation to painting (1952, iv, 331-38) and Marcus Cunliffe on *Maggie* (1955, vii, 31-44). Many literary histories, critical studies, and textbooks now contain brief accounts. Stallman's intelligence as a critic may be judged in the light of his thinking, apparently, that the famous "wafer" in the *Red Badge* is sacramental; I blush to report this; but he has good remarks, also. There is a study by Lars Ahnebrink called *The Beginnings of Naturalism in American Fiction* (1950) which I have not seen.

General Index

333

Index of Works

Note: Roman numerals in parentheses refer to volumes of
The Work of Stephen Crane (1925-27); "MWB" to *Men,
Women and Boats* (1921); and "TS" to *Twenty Stories* (1940)

344

**THE COMPLETE
SHORT STORIES OF MARCEL
PROUST**
Translated by Joachim Neugroschel
Introduction by Roger Shattuck
224 pp.
0-8154-1136-7]
$25.95 cloth

**PLAYWRIGHTS ON
PLAYWRITING
From Ibsen to Ionesco**
Toby Cole
Introduction by John Gassner
320 pp., 2 b/w photos
0-8154-1141-3
$18.95

**THE FABULOUS INSECTS
Essays by the Foremost Nature
Writers**
Edited by Charles Neider
288 pp.
0-8154-1100-6
$17.95

**THE GROTTO BERG
Two Novellas**
Charles Neider
Introduction by Clive Sinclair
200 pp.
0-8154-1123-5
$22.95 cloth

**THE LIFE AND DEATH OF
YUKIO MISHMA**
Henry Scott Stokes
318 pp., 39 b/w photos
0-8154-1074-3
$18.95

**PLYMOUTH ROCK AND
THE PILGRIMS
And Other Speeches**
Edited by Charles Neider
368 pp., 1 b/w photo
0-8154-1104-9
$17.95

**MAN AGAINST NATURE
Firsthand Accounts of
Adventure and Exploration**
Edited by Charles Neider
512 pp.
0-8154-1040-9
$18.95

**JOSEPH CONRAD
A Biography**
Jeffrey Meyers
464 pp., 32 b/w photos
0-8154-1112-X
$18.95

**GEORGE ELIOT
The Last Victorian**
Kathryn Hughes
416 pp., 22 b/w photos
0-8154-1121-9
$19.95

**HEMINGWAY
Life into Art**
Jeffrey Meyers
192 pp.
0-8154-1078-6
$27.95 cloth

**SHAKESPEARE
The Man and His Achievement**
Robert Speaight
416 pp., 24 b/w photos
0-8154-1063-8
$19.95

**GRANITE AND RAINBOW
The Hidden Life of
Virginia Woolf**
Mitchell Leaska
536 pp., 23 b/w photos
0-8154-1047-6
$18.95